MW01492127

# The Sages

## Character, Context & Creativity

## Volume IV: From the Mishna to the Talmud

מגיד
MAGGID

Binyamin Lau

# THE SAGES

## Character, Context & Creativity

### Volume IV: From the Mishna to the Talmud

Translated by

Ilana Kurshan

Maggid Books

*The Sages: Character, Context & Creativity*
*Volume IV: From the Mishna to the Talmud*

First Maggid English Edition © 2015
Koren Publishers Jerusalem

*Maggid Books*
*An imprint of Koren Publishers Jerusalem Ltd.*

POB 8531, New Milford, CT 06776-8531, USA
& POB 4044, Jerusalem 9104001, Israel

www.korenpub.com

Original Hebrew Edition © 2012 Binyamin Lau

The publication of this book was made possible through
the generous support of *Torah Education in Israel.*

Cover artwork by Ora Ruven, oraruven@gmail.com

Map of Jewish Settlements in Babylonia is from
*The Reference Guide to the Talmud* by Rabbi Adin Even-Israel
Steinsaltz (Koren, 2014) and reprinted with permission.

The right of Binyamin Lau to be identified as the author
of this work has been asserted by him in accordance
with the Copyright, Designs & Patents Act 1988.

All rights reserved. No part of this publication may be reproduced,
stored in a retrieval system or transmitted in any form or by
any means, electronic, mechanical, photocopying or otherwise,
without the prior permission of the publisher, except in the case
of brief quotations embedded in critical articles or reviews.

ISBN 978-1-59264-374-5, *hardcover*

A CIP catalogue record for this title is
available from the British Library

Printed and bound in the United States

*The English translation of* The Sages
*was made possible by a generous grant from
the Jay and Hadasa Pomrenze Foundation*

To the members of the Ramban Synagogue in Jerusalem

*May they walk in the light of Your presence,*
*May they bend at the knee to You,*
*May they bless Your people,*
*And from Your blessings may they all be blessed.*
(High Holiday liturgy)

# Contents

## PART TWO: BABYLONIAN JEWRY DURING THE SASANIAN REVOLUTION



## PART THREE: THE EARLY TALMUDIC PERIOD IN THE LAND OF ISRAEL

# *Author's Preface*

> When we conclude our reading of this volume we might say to its author: "If you have learned much Torah, your reward will be great, and your Master can be relied upon to reward you for your labor." Would it be too much to ask for a fourth volume, dedicated to the talmudic sages of the Land of Israel during the third century, thereby magnifying and glorifying Torah even further?

With these words, Professor Avigdor Shinan concluded his foreword to *The Sages,* volume III. I thank God with all my heart that I have merited to rise to his challenge and present this fourth volume to my readers.

It has been many years since I frequented the halls of the Talmud department at the Hebrew University in Jerusalem, where I was first exposed to the treasure trove of talmudic manuscripts and to the critical reading of rabbinic sources. My initiation into the secrets of talmudic creativity instilled in me a deep sense of awe as I witnessed my teachers carefully and meticulously attend to each letter in the talmudic text. Yet such cautiousness is bound to staunch creativity, which must be able to flow freely and unchecked. In writing this book, I found myself shifting back and forth between profusion and restraint, allowing for some measure of creative license while still seeking to satisfy critical scrutiny. With the completion of this fourth volume, I can only hope that my portrayal of the sages and their teachings reflects both their impressive stature and their authentic natures.

As *The Sages* series continues to unfold and the books reach a wider audience, I am increasingly convinced that rabbinic literature has the potential to enrich all sectors of Jewish society. Following the publication of each of these volumes, I found myself teaching individuals from all backgrounds, all over the world. In our discussions we considered such vital existential questions as: What is the relationship between Judaism and the outside world? Should we have an open or closed economy? Is disagreement an inherent good or a necessary evil? Is it better to remain faithful to the past or to allow for freedom of cultural expression? In considering these questions, I remain inspired by the teachings of the sages.

I wish to thank all those who assisted in the creation of this volume. Mr. Shlomo Goldberg, head of the circulation department of the National Library of Israel, helped me at every stage of the process with patience and kindness. My friend Dr. Uzi Fox reviewed the original manuscript and saved me from errors both major and minor; my son Moshe read and edited the first draft; and my son Yedidya offered comments and suggestions on subsequent revisions. Chana Amit edited the manuscript with deep understanding and humility.

It is a particular pleasure to introduce the English edition of *The Sages*. There is an unfortunate gulf between English and Hebrew readers. Maggid Books, under the leadership of Matthew Miller, has made it its mission to bridge this gap, bringing readers from across the Jewish world into one conversation. The translation was done by Ilana Kurshan. Her masterful work on the second and third volumes of the series, rendering the text as clear and accessible in English as it is in Hebrew, has earned enthusiastic response from readers. The book was edited by Tali Simon, Nechama Unterman, and Tomi Mager who distilled the text into its present shape. Thanks are also due to the editor in chief of Maggid Books, Gila Fine, who worked hard to bring this book to its finely-tuned finish.

This book, like its predecessors, had its genesis in the Ramban Synagogue in Jerusalem, whose threshold is inscribed with the words,

"We walk together in the house of God" (Ps. 55:15). For the past ten years I have merited to pray, study, and work with this community. Many people feel a disconnect between their places of work and their places of worship. I, along with my wife, parents, and children, have merited to find a community that shines its countenance on everyone and radiates warmth and joy. I am delighted to dedicate this book to the members of the Ramban Synagogue. I join in their prayer that together we may merit to illuminate our surroundings with God's light – through prayer, study, and acts of loving-kindness.

Binyamin Lau
Summer 2015/5775
Jerusalem

# *Introduction*

The third century witnessed a foundational literary event in the Land of Israel: The Mishna became the cornerstone of Jewish law. Haim Nahman Bialik described the frenzy that accompanied this literary revolution: "Here is the school of Rabbi Yehuda HaNasi and his pupils hard at work, busy collecting laws, sifting reports, gathering testimonies, arranging, editing, cataloguing – they are committing the Oral Law to writing. They know that they are carrying out a revolution in Jewish tradition."[1] The present volume of *The Sages* series chronicles this major historical development·

The previous volume of this series concluded with the death of Rabbi Yehuda HaNasi (known as Rebbi) in the second decade of the third century CE. The present volume begins at this historical juncture and concludes with the death of Rabbi Yoḥanan in 279 CE. Throughout this period, the Roman Empire was beset by anarchy and the Sasanians staged a political revolution in Babylonia. On the domestic front, the sages experienced a halakhic revolution with the shift from a pluralist to

1. Haim Nahman Bialik, *Halakha and Aggada*, trans. Leon Simon, in *Revealment and Concealment* (Jerusalem: Ibis Press, 2000), 60–61.

a normative approach to Jewish law. A world with many collections of mishnayot attributed to various study houses gave way to a world with a single foundational text from which all case law was derived.

Following its publication, the Mishna became a quasi-sacred work with a fixed text that was interpreted and invoked to explain all other teachings.[2] Though most contemporary scholars maintain that it remained an oral text for centuries, it was nonetheless regarded as canonical and authoritative. Even when Rebbi himself sought to amend the text before his death, he was met with resistance from his son, who was responsible for transmitting the tradition to the next generation. The revolution that took place when the Mishna assumed its final form is the subject of this volume, which opens with the sages of the transitional generation – the generation in which the Mishna gave way to the Talmud – and concludes with the death of Rabbi Yoḥanan and the rise of the talmudic academies.

In Part One of this volume we will travel to the various centers of learning throughout the Land of Israel, familiarizing ourselves with the members of the transitional generation. We will witness the end of the era of independence in halakhic decision-making, and we will take note of the vast differences among the various *batei midrash* that were active at the time. In Part Two we will follow Rav from the Land of Israel to Babylonia, equipped with the "book of the Mishna." There, too, we will explore the ambivalent relationship between the free use of earlier sources and the growing authority of Rabbi Yehuda HaNasi's Mishna. In Part Three we will return to the Land of Israel and enter the world of Rabbi Yoḥanan, who transformed the Mishna into the primary source of legal ruling.

The transformation of the Mishna into an authoritative and canonical halakhic text ushered in a major new era in the history of Jewish study: the talmudic age. The Mishna served as the basis for thousands of discussions that involved analyzing its finer points, comparing it to parallel sources, and interpreting each sentence and phrase, thereby creating talmudic discourse. Thus we find ourselves shifting from the era of the Mishna to the era of the Talmud, accompanying the sages of the time.

2. S. Lieberman, "The Publication of the Mishna," *Greek and Hellenism in Jewish Palestine* [Hebrew] (Jerusalem: 5723).

Is it possible to reconstruct the biographies of the rabbinic sages based on talmudic sources, even though these sources were written in a different time and place from the figures they depict? Throughout my work on this series I have had to grapple with this controversial question. In writing about rabbinic sources I have tried to remain consistently faithful to the historical kernel of each story, guided by the principle that there is no reason to suspect every event depicted realistically of being legendary or aggadic. If there are no contradicting sources and no clear and compelling reason to refute a historical description, then I take it at face value.[3] When sources clearly contradict one another, I try to privilege texts that seem to reflect historical reality over those that smack of literary embellishment. Often the Jerusalem Talmud sources are more reliable than their Babylonian parallels, as many scholars have noted.[4] But there are exceptions. Sometimes the more embellished literary sources have become so widely accepted that we cannot ignore them, even if they seem to have no historical basis. One classic example is the depiction of Reish Lakish. Rabbi Shimon ben Lakish of the Jerusalem Talmud sources bears no resemblance to his Babylonian counterpart. The former is a scholar in the beit midrash from cradle to grave; the latter is a robber who jumped into the Jordan river and washed ashore in the beit midrash. Any attempt to reconstruct this figure historically must be based on the Jerusalem Talmud sources, but how can we ignore the colorful account of his gladiatorial background and his climactic confrontation with Rabbi Yoḥanan?

With this volume of *The Sages* series we enter the talmudic era, so the question of the accuracy and reliability of source material becomes all the more critical. Talmudic discourse is based on dialogues that were preserved within the walls of the beit midrash but came down to us after hundreds of years of oral transmission. As such, talmudic passages reflect many generations of rabbinic creativity, from the era of the Mishna until the closing of the talmudic era. Our understanding of the world of the

3. S. Friedman, "The Historical Aggada in the Babylonian Talmud," *A Volume in Memory of Rabbi Saul Lieberman* [Hebrew] (New York and Jerusalem: 5753), 122.
4. The first to make this point was Z. Frankel, *Introduction to the Jerusalem Talmud* 49b–51b [Hebrew] (Breslov: 5630). Also see S. Safrai, *Issues in Historiography* [Hebrew] (Jerusalem: 5748), 73, and others.

talmudic sages is based on the talmudic pages containing these passages. The talmudic page appears before the modern-day student as a printed book organized into chapters and pages. But the printed text does not do justice to the hundreds of years of manuscripts transmitted through various historical places and periods by scribes who copied and amended the text both intentionally and inadvertently, such that not a single line is without textual variants.

The first step of academic Talmud study involves determining the most authentic version of the talmudic text by comparing manuscripts from libraries all over the world. This work may seem dull and soulless to traditional yeshiva students, some of whom benefit from the fruits of the academics' labor though they do not engage in it themselves. As the Ḥazon Ish (Avraham Yeshaya Karelitz, 1878–1953) put it, "I am not capable of searching through books for such dry matters, and besides, every soul receives its portion in Torah; it is not my portion to engage in such searches."[5]

The second step of academic Talmud study involves uncovering the compositional history of the talmudic passage. What was the original text with which the first generation of talmudic sages grappled? What did they add and pass to the next generation? Students in the yeshiva world maintain that this kind of talmudic analysis undermines the foundations of the belief in Torah as a monolithic entity. They argue that breaking down a talmudic passage into geological strata which are attributed to various *batei midrash* reduces the solid talmudic edifice to a collection of small pebbles and threatens to destroy the spiritual foundations of the chain of halakhic transmission, which is based on an unwavering faith in the words of the sages.

Just as traditional students of Torah have recoiled from the academic approach, so too have academic scholars recoiled from any connection to the yeshiva world. And so both sides are responsible for the schism between the yeshiva and the academy. When Rabbi Professor Y.N. Epstein was asked to establish a center for Jewish studies at the Hebrew University in Jerusalem, there was an attempt to persuade him to reach out to Rav Kook's yeshiva. Epstein fiercely rejected this suggestion:

5. *The Collected Letters of the Ḥazon Ish* [Hebrew], part II, section 62 (Benei Brak: 5716).

> It does not seem to me that it will be possible to conjoin the yeshiva and the academy. The university will never allow for the imposition of limits on freedom of thought and methods of inquiry, and the yeshiva, if it does not want to lose its identity, will not allow freedom of investigation in the fields of Talmud and Bible. The university already exerts a strong influence on the yeshiva, and that influence will only continue to grow.[6]

Epstein also opposed combining the center for Jewish studies at the university with a rabbinical seminary. It is true that rabbinical seminaries trained their students according to the same German tradition that had given rise to the academic study of Talmud, and thus such a synthesis was not unreasonable. But Epstein, a product of the academy and a champion of intellectual freedom, resisted all efforts to conjoin a religious institution with an academic one. In 1933, he wrote to Professor Judah Leib Magnes, president of Hebrew University:

> Our rabbis have tried for nine years to convert the institute into a rabbinical seminary, and I have always stood in the breach. And now they think the time has come to realize this plan. But in my opinion, there is no place for a rabbinical seminary in Israel. Young rabbis who learned in the yeshivot came here and will continue to come here, and they will remain "rabbis" even though they also are awarded university degrees. I will not train rabbis in the Land of Israel.[7]

6. From a letter from Epstein to Magnes in 1926. I copied the text from letters that were found among Epstein's papers and published by his grandson: M. Epstein, *Professor Y.N. Epstein: A Biography* [Hebrew] (Kibbutz Saad: 5704), 85.
7. See previous note. In light of this letter, it is fascinating to read Rabbi Haim Ozer Grodzinski's letter from early in 1933. He campaigned fiercely to thwart the plan to bring the rabbinical assembly in Berlin to Israel. He, like Epstein, argued that a rabbinical assembly has no place in Israel. For more on this historical episode see M. Breuer, "From Seminary to Yeshiva" [Hebrew], *HaMaayan* 35:4 (Tammuz 5755): 14–26.

The increased contact between the Zionist yeshivot and the sciences and humanities exposes yeshiva students to the academic approach to Talmud study, which in turn instills a sense of both attraction and repulsion. On the one hand, more rabbis and yeshiva students seek out academic training, either for its own sake or with ulterior motives. On the other hand, the yeshivot are much more hostile to the world of academic Jewish studies.[8] The heads of the yeshivot must grapple with the question of whether they can employ academic methods within the yeshiva walls. Certainly Rabbi Abraham Isaac Kook felt that the answer to this question was a resounding yes, as articulated in his vision for a new yeshiva in the Land of Israel:

> We need to establish a great yeshiva in the center of the Jewish settlement in Palestine, one that would be run honorably according to the most modern methods. The study of the Written and Oral Torahs should be the primary focus, and should include also the interpretations of contemporary sages. The spiritual and scientific aspects of Torah need to be held as equal in merit to halakha and Talmud.[9]

Very few members of Rav Kook's beit midrash heeded his rallying cry, but later thinkers developed new approaches to Talmud study.

8. The tension between Talmud study in the yeshivot and in the academy grew fierce in the wake of the founding of the Revadim program by Dr. Pinhas Hyman of Bar-Ilan University. Several major rabbis waged a powerful battle against this program, arguing that it threatened to undermine their students' faith. For a summary of the issue, see "The Revadim Approach" (*Shitat HaRevadim*) on Wikipedia. Certainly it is the case that as the yeshiva world became more familiar with the academic world, it became increasingly hostile to it. When yeshiva students were unaware of the tensions between Torah learning and the academic field of Jewish studies, they felt at liberty to rely on the fruits of academic learning. See my article on this subject: "Four Methodological Issues in the Halakhic Rulings of Rav Ovadia Yosef" [Hebrew], *Netuim* 9 (Elul 5762): 95–117. Also see A. Fox, "'Critical' Notes in the Writings of Rabbi Tzadok HaKohen of Lublin" [Hebrew], in *Me'et LeTzaddik: A Collection of Articles on Rabbi Tzadok HaKohen and His Teachings*, ed. G. Kitzis [Hebrew] (Jerusalem: 5760): 255–257.
9. *Iggrot HaReiya* 1 (Jerusalem: 5722), 118.

Dozens of years after Rav Kook, Rav Shagar (Shimon Gershon Rosenberg) sought to combine yeshiva learning with academic scholarship in a quest for spiritual meaning.[10] "Meaning" is the essence of his approach, and refers to the revelation of God's word through the study of God's Torah. The student must ask how a particular textual passage relates to his or her way of life as a religious individual, a question that gives rise to a new type of Torah scholar. Rav Shagar believed deeply that while it was necessary to import academic techniques to the yeshiva, the academy also had to recognize that dry academic research could benefit from an infusion of meaning. To implement this approach, Rav Shagar was invited by Rabbi Benjamin Ish Shalom to serve as the head of the beit midrash of Beit Morasha in Jerusalem over twenty years ago.

For more than a dozen years I have borne witness to this effort in the beit midrash of Rav Yehuda Brandes, who succeeded Rav Shagar as the head of Beit Morasha. Rav Brandes, who is shaped by his experiences both learning in yeshiva and teaching in an academic Talmud department, has implemented Rav Shagar's approach while adding his own unique stamp. In his classes, it is the talmudic text itself and not the later commentaries that is the focus of study. He is forever challenging his students to ask how God's Torah compels and guides us in our lives. He insists that the tractate being studied must be made relevant to students and must illuminate their spiritual worship. It is not easy to make the transition from acquiring analytical skills to delving into questions of meaning, and there is always the concern that some students will not be able to find their way.[11]

Those who are critical of this approach worry about the secularization of the Talmud. This concern was not lost on Rav Shagar. He told of a student who fled his beit midrash on the grounds that Rav Shagar "secularized" Rabbi Haim of Volozhin by rendering him comprehensible and relevant. Rav Shagar responded as follows:

10. Rav Shagar, *He Shall Study His Torah* [Hebrew] (Efrat: 5769), 193–197.
11. For an overview of Rabbi Brandes's approach, see the introduction to *The Knowledge of Your Torah* [Hebrew], Tractate Ketubot (Jerusalem: 5767), 10.

> This requires a revolution in our underlying assumptions. We need a different understanding of holiness, a holiness whose roots are not in the transcendence espoused by Rabbi Haim of Volozhin and his mitnagdic disciples, but rather in the immanence celebrated by the Hasidim.... What is necessary here is not just a continuation of the hasidic tradition but also a true encounter with Rav Kook's call to reinspire holiness. The way of learning that I am championing is in line with Rav Kook's goal of sanctifying the secular. True, there is a very fine line between sanctifying the secular and secularizing the sacred, between deriving pleasure and causing harm.[12]

It is my prayer that *The Sages,* volume IV, which now joins a wealth of lively creative discourse about the Talmud, will serve as a guide to students of Torah from a variety of backgrounds and *batei midrash* who find themselves drawn and attuned to the voices of the sages.

12. Rav Shagar, *He Shall Study His Torah,* 199–200.

# Part One

# *The Transitional Generation*

| | | |
|---|---|---|
| The Elders of the Generation after Rabbi Yehuda HaNasi | The Early Years of the Babylonian Sages<br>Shmuel in Nehardea and Rav in Sura | The Early Years of the Talmud in the Land of Israel<br>The World and Teachings of Rabbi Yoḥanan |
| 199–235 | 226–254 | 235–279 |
| The Beginning of the Anarchic Period in the Roman Empire | The Sasanian Revolution in the East | Anarchy in the Roman Empire and the Rise of Palmyra |

# Preface

The third volume of this series closed with the death of Rabbi Yehuda HaNasi (Rebbi), who left behind an organized Jewish society which had made its peace with Roman rule. Rebbi's tenure was a period of political stability in which the institutions of religious leadership in the Land of Israel were strengthened and solidified. Following his death, there were no major political changes. It would be at least another ten years before the Roman Empire would enter its period of anarchy and the Jews would have to confront growing economic and security concerns.[1]

At the close of the second century and the beginning of the third, Roman authorities worked to organize the administration of imperial affairs around several major cities. Both the imperial administration and the Jewish people held the patriarchy in considerable esteem. As we saw in the previous volume, Rabbi Yehuda HaNasi was regarded as heir to the Davidic dynasty and was celebrated with the verse, "The breath of our life, the Lord's anointed" (Lam. 4:20).[2] Rebbi's stature may be

1. M.D. Herr, "The Question of Periodization of the Second Temple and the Period of the Mishna and Talmud in Jewish History," in *Exile After Diaspora: Studies in the History of the Jewish People* [Hebrew], eds. A. Mirsky et al. (Jerusalem: 5748), 64–74.
2. See *Sages* III, Part Five.

attributed both to the general economic security at the time and to his close relationship with the imperial authorities. Given the dire situation in which the Jews found themselves after the Hadrianic decrees (138 CE), it is a marvel that less than one hundred years later they enjoyed such prosperity in their land. As the historian and archeologist Michael Avi-Yonah put it, "A nation that had been defeated in battle managed to take hold of its territory, consolidate its forces, create a new organizational system with central and local authorities, safeguard its power, and tailor its laws to the exigencies of the moment."[3]

The sages of the Yavneh generation lived in small settlements like Benei Brak and Peki'in, and their successors, the Usha sages, lived in the Galilean towns of Usha and Beit She'arim. But from the end of the second century onward, the sages of Israel made their homes in major cities throughout the Land of Israel. The centers of Jewish learning and society shifted to Tzippori, Lod, Tiberias, and Caesarea, where permanent *batei midrash* were established.[4] Only in such an environment was it possible to compile the Mishna, a monumental collection of all the legal teachings of the sages of previous generations. Rabbi Yehuda HaNasi, responsible for this achievement, serves as the dividing line between the *Tanna'im* (the sages of the Mishna) and the *Amora'im* (the sages of the Talmud). Those sages who were contemporaneous with Rabbi Yehuda HaNasi and who immediately succeeded him were known as the transitional generation.

When we studied the figure of Rebbi in the previous volume of this series, we also considered his tense confrontations with his colleagues, including Rabbi Ḥiya the Great, Rabbi Pinḥas ben Yair, and Rabbi Elazar HaKappar.[5] In an effort to gain a fuller sense of the relationship between the mishnaic and talmudic periods, the first part of the present volume is dedicated to other, lesser lights who worked alongside Rabbi Yehuda HaNasi.

3. M. Avi-Yonah, *In the Days of Rome and Byzantium* [Hebrew] (Jerusalem: 5741), 43.
4. Y. Gafni, "Yeshiva and Metivta" [Hebrew], *Zion* 43 (5738): 12–37. Gafni tries to demonstrate that the earliest yeshivot in Babylonia did not predate the second generation of talmudic sages. At this historical moment, the *batei midrash* were still organized around the various local rabbinic authorities.
5. See *Sages* III, Part Five.

*Historical Background*

# The Beginning of the Anarchic Period

Its vast reach proved detrimental to the Roman Empire. The central imperial authority lost its power, and the provinces gained increasing control over Rome. As the historian Yisrael Levine put it:

> The third century was primarily a period of crisis. There was an atmosphere of constant warfare, instead of the tranquility that had previously prevailed. Poverty and uncertainty replaced the prosperity and security of the second century, and there were constant rebellions within the imperial ranks as well as threats from abroad. A sense of crisis was also precipitated by rampant inflation, accompanied by a heavy tax burden. The fact that all the Caesars died unnatural deaths and that they reigned for an average of just two years each after the year 235 is symptomatic of this situation and contributed to the instability of the emperor's position. At the same time, the Barbarians gained force along the Rhine and the Danube, and the Sasanians mobilized in the east, resulting in a series of attacks and defeats along the various

> borders. These incursions led to widespread death and destruction, and the land was laid waste.[1]

The event that symbolized the beginning of the anarchic period took place along the shores of the Rhine in the year 238 CE. A violent and brutish officer named Maximinus was responsible for the murder of Emperor Alexander Severus by the Roman army, which in turn led to a wave of terror and violence throughout the empire. Many scholars have studied the fall of the Roman Empire, most famously British historian Edward Gibbon, who exhorts, "Instead of inquiring why the Roman Empire was destroyed, we should rather be surprised that it lasted so long."[2]

1. Y. L. Levine, "The Land of Israel in the Third Century," in *The Land of Israel from the Destruction of the Second Temple Until the Muslim Conquest* [Hebrew], ed. T. Bars et al. (Jerusalem: 1982), 120–121.
2. Quoted in M. Avi-Yonah, *Rome and Byzantium*, 76.

*Chapter One*

# Rebbi's Sons

Upon his death, Rabbi Yehuda HaNasi left behind a detailed will in which he divided his responsibilities among various individuals. His will is quoted in the Babylonian Talmud:

> My son Shimon is a sage and my son Gamliel is patriarch and Ḥanina ben Ḥama shall preside at their head. (Ketubot 103b)

Rabbi Yehuda HaNasi understood that the consolidation of Torah knowledge and political power that he had enjoyed was not sustainable. He served as both a religious leader and an economic and political one, but he recognized that a division of power would be necessary for his successors. And so first he instructed his son Gamliel to succeed him as patriarch, furnishing him with firm instructions: "My son, conduct the patriarchy with men of high standing, and cast bile among the students" (Ketubot 103b).

Rabban Gamliel, son of Rabbi Yehuda, was the third patriarch in a line that could be traced as far back as Hillel the Elder. His grandfather was Rabbi Shimon ben Gamliel of Usha, and his great-grandfather was

Rabban Gamliel of Yavneh. He was awarded the patriarchy by merit of being the firstborn, but his brother Shimon was proclaimed the leader of the sages. The patriarch was responsible for civil matters including taxation, conscription into the army and into the Roman police force, and all public municipal affairs. The sage was responsible for teaching Torah, setting the curriculum in the beit midrash, and continuing the task of compiling the Mishna and organizing the system of Jewish law.

Rebbi's will gives rise to various questions: How were the sages ordained? What was the relative status of the sage and the patriarch? Until the time of Rabbi Yehuda HaNasi, the patriarch and the leader of the sages worked side by side without any overlap in their duties. The authority to ordain the next generation of sages was the province of the sage and not the patriarch; each sage would designate and ordain his best students.[1] Rabbi Yehuda HaNasi, who was both patriarch and sage, went on to re-divide these roles and add a third position as well, that of Rabbi Ḥanina bar Ḥama, who would "preside at their head." Rabbi Ḥanina was responsible for public leadership in matters of justice and religious ethics.[2]

## THE PERIOD OF THE PATRIARCHY OF RABBAN GAMLIEL III

We know very little about Rebbi's son Rabban Gamliel, who was known as Rabban Gamliel III. It is generally agreed that he served as patriarch during the decade following Rebbi's death, 225–235 CE. In the final years of his patriarchy, the Roman Empire began its steep decline, beginning with the collapse of the Severan dynasty.

Rabban Gamliel was primarily responsible for political rather than religious leadership, but even so, he implemented several halakhic

1. The Talmud states, "At first everyone would appoint their students" (Y. Sanhedrin 4:2 [19a]). See G. Alon, "Those Who Are Appointed by Money" [Hebrew], *Studies in Jewish History* 2 (Tel Aviv: 5736), 32–44.
2. E.E. Urbach, "Position and Leadership," *The World of the Sages* [Hebrew] (Jerusalem: 5748), 328. Urbach disagrees with H. Albeck, who explained that Rabbi Ḥanina was the "head of the great yeshiva." See Albeck, *Introduction to the Talmuds* [Hebrew] (Tel Aviv: 5729), 155. I agree with Urbach based on the description of Rabbi Ḥanina's role in sources I will cite below.

rulings during his tenure.[3] Several of the rabbinic decrees attributed to him attest to his commitment to furthering his father's efforts to lighten the economic burden on the farmers. For instance, he instituted new legislation regarding the sabbatical year. Until his time, it was customary to add an additional period before Rosh HaShana of the sabbatical year in which its laws still held force. The Mishna devotes two chapters of Tractate Shevi'it to the laws that apply during this additional period. But in the Tosefta to this tractate, Rabban Gamliel revokes these stringencies in their entirety:

> Rabban Gamliel and his court ordained that the working of the land be permitted until the New Year [of the sabbatical year]. (Tosefta Shevi'it 1:1)

The Tosefta cannot possibly be referring to the second Rabban Gamliel, who was patriarch at Yavneh, because Rebbi makes no mention of any such allowance.[4] Given that Rebbi does not refer to his grandfather's ruling on the matter, it seems that the decree must date to a period after Rebbi's death, presumably to the tenure of Rabban Gamliel III.[5]

Rabban Gamliel III's relaxing of the sabbatical requirements was not embraced by the other sages of his generation, as we learn from the following talmudic passage:

> Rabbi Shimon ben Pazi said in the name of Rabbi Yehoshua ben Levi who reported in the name of Bar Kappara: Rabban Gamliel and his court took a vote concerning these two periods and nullified them [i.e., they ruled that fields may be plowed until the New Year of the sabbatical year]. Rabbi Zeira said to Rabbi Abahu, and some say it was Reish Lakish who said to Rabbi Yoḥanan: How could Rabban Gamliel and his court annul an enactment

3. I am following A. Hyman in *History of the Tanna'im and Amora'im* [Hebrew] (Jerusalem: 5747), 318–320, in contrast to the view espoused by I.H. Weiss, *Each Generation and Its Interpreters* [Hebrew] (New York, Berlin: 1924), 38.
4. This is the understanding of Rabbi Shimon ben Tzemaḥ Duran in his commentary on Tractate Avot, *Magen Avot* (Jerusalem: 5763), 12b.
5. S. Lieberman, *Tosefta Kifshuta* Shevi'it [Hebrew] (New York: 5716), 482–483.

> of Beit Shammai and Beit Hillel? We have learned in a mishna: A later court cannot abolish the edicts of another, earlier court, unless it is greater in wisdom and number. He was confounded for a moment. He then said to him: Say that Beit Shammai and Beit Hillel stipulated the following among themselves at the time they promulgated their enactment: Whoever wishes to nullify it in future years may come and nullify it. (Mo'ed Katan 3b)

This passage captures a particular historical moment in which the sages of the generation after Rebbi test the limits of Rebbi's son's authority in matters of halakha by inquiring whether he is in fact greater than those who enacted the original decree. Rabbi Abahu hesitates before responding. Reluctantly, he concedes that Shammai and Hillel left an opening for a later sage to nullify their decree in the future.[6]

Elsewhere we learn of Rabban Gamliel's efforts to impose the tithing requirement on bread from Syria. Rabbi Oshaya, known as Rabbi Hoshaya in the Jerusalem Talmud, prevented him from doing so, a further indication of the limits placed on patriarchal power.[7]

Another legal innovation attributed to Rabban Gamliel relates to religious rather than economic matters. Up until his time, meat slaughtered by a Samaritan was regarded as kosher. For instance, the Tosefta (Ḥullin 1:1) stipulates that meat slaughtered by a Samaritan is kosher. But in the Talmud (Ḥullin 5b), we are told that Rabban Gamliel and his court ruled that such meat is forbidden. As the Talmud relates, Rabban Gamliel's ruling was not fully accepted by the next generation. Decades after Rabban Gamliel, the rabbinic leadership of Rabbi Yoḥanan and his disciples still refused to accept this enactment.

Rabban Gamliel's ruling was part of a more general trend: During the Temple period and its immediate aftermath, it was customary to

6. See the parallel source in Y. Shevi'it 1:1 [33a], which features Rabbi Yoḥanan.
7. "Rabban Gamliel son of Rebbi wished to impose the tithing requirement in Syria, but Rabbi Hoshaya would not permit him to do so" (Y. Ḥalla 4:4 [60a]). The subject of tithes on produce grown just outside the borders of the Land of Israel requires consideration in its own right. See D. Levine, "Rabbi Yehuda HaNasi and the Boundaries of the Cities of the Land of Israel" [Hebrew], *Cathedra* 138 (Winter 5771): 42–47.

trust the Samaritans when it came to all matters in which they practiced like Jews, and to distrust them when it came to all other matters, such as *eiruv*, *nidda*, Temple ritual, and laws of marital status. Beginning in the Yavneh generation, the sages became increasingly suspicious of the Samaritans, until they were ultimately cut off from the Jewish mainstream.[8]

The Tosefta contains an account of Rabban Gamliel's complex and fascinating relationship with members of the populace:

> There was an incident in which Rabban Gamliel[9] was sitting on a bench belonging to non-Jews in Akko. They said to him: It is not customary to sit on a bench belonging to non-Jews on Shabbat. He did not want to say: One is permitted to do so. So he got up and walked off.
>
> There was an incident in which Yehuda and Hillel, sons of Rabban Gamliel, went to take a bath in Kabul. They said to them: It is not customary to have two brothers take a bath together.
>
> They did not want to say: One is permitted to do so.
>
> So they went in and took a bath one after the other.
>
> There was another incident in which Yehuda and Hillel, sons of Rabban Gamliel, went out in golden slippers on the Sabbath in Biri. They said to them: It is not customary to go out in golden slippers on the Sabbath.
>
> They did not want to say to them: One is permitted to do so.
>
> So they sent them along with their servants. (Tosefta Mo'ed Katan 2:15–16)

8. Y. Elizur, "The Samaritans During Tannaitic Times" [Hebrew], *Israel and the Bible* (Ramat Gan: 5760): 393–414. In this article, written in 1940, Professor Elizur presented his thesis regarding the evolution of the sages' relationship with the Samaritans throughout the tannaitic period. For more recent studies, see *The Book of the Samaritans*, ed. A. Stern and H. Eshel (Jerusalem: 5762).
9. The parallel source in the Babylonian Talmud, Pesaḥim 51a (printed edition), identifies this figure as Rabban Shimon ben Gamliel, but see *Dikdukei Sofrim*, note 20, which states that the accurate version reads "Rabban Gamliel." This is true, too, of the parallel in the Jerusalem Talmud (Pesaḥim 4:1 [30d]).

This source features the third Rabban Gamliel and his sons. The three scenes depicted here offer a sense of the aristocratic airs of the patriarchal family and the reaction of the local Jewish populace. The issue of sitting on a bench belonging to a non-Jew on Shabbat preoccupied commentators for several generations; according to Rashi, it relates to the prohibition on wandering around commercial areas on Shabbat, lest one come to engage in business matters. As this source suggests, the residents of Akko were strict about this prohibition, perhaps because they lived in such a cosmopolitan city. Rabban Gamliel did not observe this stringency himself, but out of respect for the residents of Akko, he simply got up and left when they questioned his behavior. He conceded to them for the sake of peaceful relations, even though they did not treat him with respect. Rabban Gamliel, though he was patriarch, did not have the stature of his predecessors, and so perhaps it is not surprising that he wished to avoid confrontation.

In the second and third scenes, the residents of the Galilee do not hesitate to instruct Rabban Gamliel's sons Hillel and Yehuda in the local customs, even if such customs are stricter than the accepted halakhic norms.[10] The Tosefta and the Jerusalem Talmud do not specify who criticized the sons' behavior, but the Talmud implicates the entire city. This does not mean that the residents of the city did not respect the patriarchal family; elsewhere we learn that the residents of Kabul in fact offered Yehuda and Hillel a royal reception (see Tosefta Shabbat 7:17). But in spite of this display of honor, the sons were not regarded as irreproachable.[11]

Rabban Gamliel is the last of the patriarchs whose teachings were included in *Pirkei Avot*:

> Rabban Gamliel, son of Rabbi Yehuda HaNasi, taught: The study of Torah is commendable when combined with a gainful occupation, for when a person toils in both, sin is driven out of the mind. Study alone without an occupation leads to idleness,

10. See Lieberman's notes in *Tosefta Kifshuta* Mo'ed Katan, 1262–1263.
11. M. Beer, "Honor and Criticism" [Hebrew], *The Sages of the Mishna and the Talmud* (Ramat Gan: 5771), 107–118.

> and ultimately to sin. All who serve on behalf of the community should do so for the sake of Heaven. Their work will prosper because the inherited merit of our ancestors endures forever. God will reward them abundantly as though they had achieved it all through their own efforts. (Avot 2:2)

Rabban Gamliel insists that Torah study be combined with a gainful occupation. He opposes those who idealize total devotion to Torah study (referred to as "eternal life") at the expense of economic pursuits ("temporal life").[12] Rabban Gamliel believed that single-minded devotion to study would ultimately lead to the forsaking of such study. Presumably his teaching was influenced by the economic reality of his day, a time of struggle and scarcity. In light of this state of affairs, Rabban Gamliel directs the sages to step outside the walls of the beit midrash and devote part of their days to pursuing a livelihood.[13]

We have no accounts of the death of Rabban Gamliel. We know only that he was succeeded by his son, Rabbi Yehuda Nesiya, who assumed the mantle of leadership once the Roman anarchic period had already begun.

### MY SON SHIMON IS A SAGE

Shimon, who was designated as "sage," is far better known than his older brother. When he was still a young boy, his father chose him to succeed him as a scholar of Torah. Shimon studied Mishna with his father, read Torah before him, participated in his lectures in the beit midrash, and seems never to have left his father's side.[14]

12. For the origins of the phenomenon of total devotion to Torah study as a religious ideal, see *Sages* II, Part Three. For more on the "Torah and *Derekh Eretz*" movement of Rabbi Samson Raphael Hirsch, see M. Breuer, *Torah with Gainful Occupation: The Movement, Its Leaders, and Its Ideas* [Hebrew] (Ramat Gan: 5747).
13. This type of historical reading of Rabban Gamliel's views on Torah study appears in a book on *Pirkei Avot* written by my uncle, Rabbi Yisrael Meir Lau, entitled *Yaḥel Yisrael* (Jerusalem: 5765), 26.
14. On the special bond between Rebbi and Rabban Shimon ben Gamliel, see Y.N. Epstein, *Introduction to the Text of the Mishna* [Hebrew] (Jerusalem: 5708), 18–24. The two Talmuds often refer to Rebbi and his son Shimon learning Torah together, and to Shimon's important role in finalizing the text of the Mishna.

When we considered the figure of Rabban Shimon ben Gamliel, Rebbi's father, we discussed the two sages who challenged his authority, Rabbi Natan and Rabbi Meir.[15] Decades later, Rabbi Yehuda HaNasi and his son Shimon sat together and learned a mishna that stated Rabbi Meir's opinion anonymously. The child Shimon asked his father about the identity of this anonymously quoted sage, stirring up old grievances:

> His son said to him: Who are these others whose waters we drink, but whose names we do not mention? Rebbi said: These are people who sought to eradicate your honor and the honor of your father's house. Rabban Shimon quoted: "Their love, their hate, their jealousy have already perished" [Eccl. 9:6]. Rebbi quoted back: "The lives of the enemy have ended, but their ruins remain forever" [Ps. 9:7]. Rabban Shimon said to Rebbi: Those words apply only where the enemies' deeds were effective, but the deeds of these rabbis were not effective. He then taught the following version to Rabban Shimon: They said in the name of Rabbi Meir: If it were a substitute offering, it would not be offered. (Horayot 14a)

Rabban Gamliel at first responds harshly, informing his son about the struggles over the patriarchy in the previous generation. The son objects, arguing that this is a thing of the past: "Their love, their hate, their jealousy have already perished." But the father insists that their influence has not entirely dissipated; there are still those who wish to undermine the honor of the patriarchy. Nonetheless, the father softens somewhat, and mentions Rabbi Meir by name when he repeats this teaching: "They said in the name of Rabbi Meir."

### EDITIONS OF THE MISHNA: BETWEEN REBBI AND HIS SON

Rabbi Shimon studied Mishna with his father until the patriarch's dying days. Occasionally, his father would suggest a new version of the text based on some change in the historical reality, or based on the opinion

15. See *Sages* III, Part Three.

of another sage. But Rabbi Shimon was sensitive to any such emendations and insisted on preserving the original text.[16]

To appreciate the significance of these textual changes, we must first understand that the various extant versions of the Mishna can be divided into two major categories depending on their provenance. The first category consists of those mishnayot that originated in the Land of Israel and its environs (including those found in the Jerusalem Talmud and in manuscripts from the Byzantine Empire); the second category consists of those mishnayot that were influenced by the Babylonian Talmud.[17] If we compare the versions of the Mishna that appear in each of the two Talmuds, we can trace the development of its language from the way Rebbi taught it in his youth to the way he taught it in his later years. I will cite two examples:

1. **Mishna Avoda Zara 4:4**

> A non-Jew can nullify his own idol and that of his fellow, but a Jew cannot nullify the idol of a non-Jew. (Mishna Avoda Zara 4:4, as per the printed text)

> A non-Jew can nullify his own idol and that of a Jew, but a Jew cannot nullify the idol of a non-Jew. (Mishna Avoda Zara 4:4, as per the Jerusalem Talmud)

The Mishna deals with the question of how an object used in pagan ritual can be "nullified," that is, cleansed of the stain of its previous use.

16. This section is indebted to the work of one of my earliest teachers in the Talmud department, Professor David Rosenthal. His research on the mishnayot of Avoda Zara first opened my eyes to all that the academic approach has to offer to students of Talmud. The source I discuss in this section is analyzed at length in his doctorate: "Mishna Avoda Zara: A Critical Edition and Introduction" (PhD diss., Hebrew University of Jerusalem, 5741).
17. This is an attempt to simplify the subject of much scholarly discussion and debate. See Y. Zussman, "Manuscripts and Versions of the Mishna" [Hebrew], *Proceedings of the World Congress of Jewish Studies* 5741, 3, 215–250. For a summary of the scholarly debates, see D. Rosenthal, "Mishna Avoda Zara," 179–187.

In order to do so, the believer must treat the object with scorn so as to demonstrate that it no longer has religious significance. According to the version of the Mishna that appears in the printed text of the Babylonian Talmud, a non-Jew can nullify an idol belonging to himself or to another non-Jew, but he cannot nullify an object belonging to a Jew. According to the version in the Jerusalem Talmud, a non-Jew can nullify even an idol that is in the possession of a Jew. This is true of all the various extant versions of the Mishna: Those that originated in the Land of Israel and its environs all read, "A non-Jew can nullify his own idol and that of a Jew," whereas those that originated in Babylonia all read, "A non-Jew can nullify his own idol and that of his fellow."[18]

This distinction is the subject of discussion in the Talmuds as well:

> Rebbi was sitting and teaching Rabbi Shimon his son: A non-Jew can nullify his own idol and that of his fellow, but a Jew cannot nullify the idol of a non-Jew.
>
> He said to him: While you were in the height of your powers, I repeated the tradition to you as follows: A non-Jew can nullify his own idol and that of a Jew.
>
> He said to him: No, my son. An idol that a Jew has worshipped can never be nullified. (Y. Avoda Zara 4:4 [44a])[19]

Rebbi, now an old man, teaches his son that the Mishna states, "his own idol and that of his fellow." The son objects: While you were still in your youth, with the fire still in your belly, you taught it to me differently! The father patiently explains to his son that he cannot hold by the version he taught in his youth, because now he understands that once a Jew takes possession of an idol, it can never be cleansed of the taint of idolatry.

The Jerusalem Talmud teaches that one of Rebbi's leading students, Rabbi Shimon ben Menassia, taught the mishna in the way that Rebbi taught it in his old age, and it is this version that was transmitted to Babylon:

18. This was documented by Epstein, *Text of the Mishna*, 22–25; and Rosenthal, "Mishna Avoda Zara," 175–178.
19. This story appears in Avoda Zara 52b, the parallel source in the Babylonian Talmud.

> And there is a tannaitic teaching along the same lines. Rabbi Shimon ben Menassia says: An idol that a Jew has worshipped can never be nullified. Rav taught this teaching in the name of this *Tanna*[20] who adduced evidence with the following verse: "Cursed be the man who makes a graven or molten image" [Deut. 27:15]. He is cursed forever. (Y. Avoda Zara 4:4 [44a])

Although an aged Rebbi taught his son the authoritative version of the mishna, according to which a non-Jew could never nullify an idol belonging to a Jew, it seems that Rabbi Shimon taught the original version that Rebbi had taught in his youth. Why did Rabbi Shimon refuse to emend the mishna as his father had instructed him?

Saul Lieberman proposes that Rabbi Shimon regarded the Mishna as a closed book, such that even his father could no longer violate its integrity by changing it in any way.[21] David Rosenthal instead suggests that Rabbi Shimon taught the mishna this way not because he felt it reflected an original version, but because it seemed to him more accurate. In any case, this is the version that Rabbi Shimon taught throughout the Land of Israel after Rebbi's death. It became the authoritative version in the Land of Israel, and it appears in all manuscripts that originated there.[22]

### 2. Mishna Bava Metzia 4:1

> Silver acquires gold, but gold does not acquire silver.[23]

20. In the Leiden manuscript, there is a blank space and an erasure at this point, suggesting that the name of the sage who taught Rav this teaching was deleted from the text.
21. S. Lieberman, "The Publication of the Mishna."
22. D. Rosenthal, "Mishna Avoda Zara," 178. Rosenthal cites the extensive work of Rabbi Shlomo Yehuda Rapoport on this subject, as well as Y.N. Epstein, *Introduction to the Literature of the Tanna'im* [Hebrew] (Jerusalem: 5717), 227, note 166.
23. For an explanation of the Mishna based on the Roman economic system, see A. Kleiman, "Two Currencies in Rebbi's Era: Studies in the Mishna, 'Gold Acquires Silver'" [Hebrew], *Zion* 38 (5733): 48–61.

This is the version of the Mishna that appears in the Jerusalem Talmud and in the manuscripts of the Mishna from the Land of Israel. But in the Babylonian Talmud and in the printed texts of the Mishna, we find instead, "Gold acquires silver, but silver does not acquire gold."

A comparison of the discussions of this mishna in the two Talmuds sheds light on the reason for these variants:

> Rebbi taught Rabbi Shimon his son: Gold acquires silver. Rabbi Shimon said to him: My teacher, in your younger years, you taught us the Mishna as follows: Silver acquires gold. Do you now in your old age retract that version and teach us instead: Gold acquires silver?
>
> What did he hold in his youth, and what did he hold in his old age? In his youth, he held that the gold coin, which is more valuable, is considered the currency, whereas the silver coin, which is not as valuable, is considered the commodity, and the silver commodity therefore acquires the gold currency. In his old age, he held that the silver coin, which is more current, is considered the currency, whereas the gold coin, which is not as current, is considered the commodity, and the gold commodity therefore acquires the silver currency. (Bava Metzia 44a)

The parallel source in the Jerusalem Talmud reads as follows:

> His father said to him: Retract, and teach as follows: Gold acquires silver. He said to him: I am not willing to retract. For while you were at the height of your powers, you taught it to me as follows: Silver acquires gold.
>
> Rebbi says that gold is considered the commodity. The Mishna says that silver is considered the commodity. (Y. Bava Metzia 4:1 [9c])

When he was younger, Rebbi held that gold is regarded as currency and thus silver acquires gold; in his old age, he held that gold acquires silver. But the son wishes to hold his father to his original teaching. As a result, we are left with two versions of the Mishna. One is the version Rebbi taught in his old age, holding that gold acquires silver; the other is the version Rabbi Shimon taught, which is that silver acquires gold.[24] The former version was transmitted to Babylonia via Rav while Rebbi was still alive,[25] and it appears in the Babylonian Talmud; the latter version was taught by Rabbi Shimon in the Land of Israel, and it appears in the Jerusalem Talmud.

These two examples, along with many others, attest that Rabbi Shimon took an active role in compiling the words of the sages and editing the text of the Mishna until it assumed its final form.

### RABBI ḤANINA REFUSES HIS APPOINTMENT

Rebbi's third deathbed appointment was conferred on Rabbi Ḥanina bar Ḥama, who was not a member of his family. The Jerusalem Talmud offers an account of this appointment:

> Rebbi would make two appointments. If they proved worthy, they were confirmed. If not, they were removed. When he was dying, he instructed his son Gamliel: Do not do it this way. Rather, appoint them one at a time. And appoint Rabbi Ḥama bar Ḥanina [i.e., Rabbi Ḥanina bar Ḥama] at the head. (Y. Taanit 4:2 [68a])[26]

However, as both Talmuds relate, Rabbi Ḥanina bar Ḥama was not interested in assuming this role:

> After he died, his son Gamliel wanted to appoint him a sage, but Ḥanina did not accept the appointment. (Y. Taanit 4:2 [68a])

The Babylonian Talmud puts it somewhat differently:

> Rabbi Ḥanina did not accept the appointment, because Rabbi Efes was two and a half years older than him. (Ketubot 103b)

24. Epstein, *Text of the Mishna*, 19–22.
25. See my discussion of Rav's descent to Babylonia in Part Two of this book.
26. In *Sages* III, I dealt with this source in the section entitled "Rebbi's Kitchen Cabinet." I am interested now in looking at how Rebbi's instructions were carried out.

This is an interesting political moment. Rebbi's son, presumably Rabban Gamliel, wishes to execute his father's will and appoint Rabbi Ḥanina. But Rabbi Ḥanina opposes the appointment and proposes conferring the title upon Rabbi Efes, a sage about whom very little is known.[27] We do know, however, that Rabbi Ḥanina's suggestion was accepted, and Rabbi Efes assumed the mantle of leadership. He would later be succeeded by Rabbi Ḥanina, as we will see below.

27. Reish Lakish refers to a Rabbi Efes from the south in Eiruvin 65b. And in Genesis Rabba we learn of a Rabbi Efes who served as Rebbi's secretary. Hyman conflates the two in his *Tanna'im and Amora'im,* 241. But Albeck regards them as two distinct individuals in his *Introduction to the Talmuds,* 159.

*Chapter Two*

# Levi ben Sisi

### CHALLENGES TO THE APPOINTMENT OF THE PATRIARCH

The Babylonian Talmud's account of Rebbi's last will and testament includes the disgruntled responses of those sages who did not find their names among those newly promoted. For instance, Rabbi Levi responded to the appointments of Gamliel and Shimon with, "Was it necessary for Rebbi to say this?" That is, is it not obvious that Rebbi would choose his sons as his successors? These words convey the extent of his disappointment and frustration. Shimon, who has just been appointed sage, responds immediately:

> Rabbi Shimon bar Rebbi said: It was necessary, for you and for your lameness. (Ketubot 103b)

This is not the only place in the Talmud where we learn that Rabbi Levi was lame. Later we will explore the reasons for his handicap, but for the time being it suffices to note that Shimon levels a low blow. Presumably he was so offended that he felt he had to strike back where he knew it would hurt.[1]

1. This harsh manner of rebuke is reminiscent of the relationship between Rabbi Ḥiya and Rabbi Yehuda HaNasi. In Tractate Megilla (24b), the Talmud recounts

The Talmud suggests that Levi was objecting not to Shimon's appointment, but to that of Rabban Gamliel, whom he did not think worthy of filling his father's shoes:

> What difficulty did he have? Behold, a verse states, "And the kingship that he [Yehoshaphat] gave to Yehoram, for he was the firstborn" [II Chr. 21:3]. This one [Yehoram] was best-suited to fill the place of his fathers. (Ketubot 103b)

The verse clearly states that positions of leadership are passed to the firstborn, so why did Rabbi Levi take issue with Rabban Gamliel's appointment? As the second half of this source indicates, the firstborn inherits his father's title only if he is the one best-suited for the role. Presumably, then, Rabbi Levi did not think very highly of Rabban Gamliel.

The Talmud considers the question of why Rebbi conferred the role of patriarch on Rabban Gamliel even though he may not have been suitable.

> And Rebbi, for what reason did he do this? Rebbi held that although Rabban Gamliel was not best-suited to fill his fathers' place in wisdom, when it came to fear of sin, he was best-suited among his brothers to fill the place of his fathers. (Ketubot 103b)

a clash between these two sages relating to the subject of those blemishes that render a person unfit to serve in the Temple: "Rabbi Ḥiya said to Rabbi Shimon the son of Rebbi: If you were a Levite, you would be disqualified from standing on the platform [in the Temple to sing] because your voice is gruff. Rabbi Shimon came and told this to his father. He said to him: Go say to Rabbi Ḥiya: When you reach the verse, 'And I will wait for the Lord' [Is. 8:17], will you not be found to be a reviler and a blasphemer?" Rabbi Ḥiya mocks Shimon's gruff voice, and then Rebbi teaches his son to retaliate by commenting on Rabbi Ḥiya's own throaty pronunciation, which is presumably due to his Babylonian accent. It seems, then, that neither of them speaks flawlessly. Y. Ben Shalom suggests that such harsh exchanges appear only in the Babylonian Talmud. See Y. Ben Shalom, "And I Took Two Staffs, One of Which I Named Favor and the Other Unity" [Hebrew] in *Generation to Generation: A Collection of Studies in Honor of Yehoshua Efron*, eds. A. Oppenheimer and A. Kasher (Jerusalem: 5755), 235–250.

Although Rabban Gamliel could not rival his father in wisdom (and hence his brother Shimon was appointed sage), he shared his father's fear of sin, and thus he merited to be appointed patriarch.

### CHALLENGING THE APPOINTMENT OF THE HEAD

According to the Babylonian Talmud, Rabbi Levi objected to the appointment of the new patriarch. But according to the parallel in the Jerusalem Talmud, it was an anonymous elder who objected to Rebbi's will, insisting that he should have a part in the new leadership:

> There was a certain elder there who said: If Ḥanina is appointed before me, then I shall be second, and if Rabbi Efes from the south is appointed before me, then I shall be second. Rabbi Ḥanina agreed to be appointed third. (Y. Taanit 4:2 [68a])

The embittered elder insists that he ought to be second, regardless of who sits at the head. Rabbi Ḥanina does not object. He gladly concedes to Rabbi Efes and to this elder, and assumes for himself the position of third in line.[2] Based on the Babylonian parallel, it seems this elder was Rabbi Levi. Whereas in the Babylonian version his criticism is directed at Rebbi's sons, in the Jerusalem Talmud's version he is concerned about his own position in the hierarchy of leadership. He wants to make sure that he is number two. Perhaps this position afforded special rights from the Roman imperial authorities, or perhaps it was simply a matter of personal honor.

We will now consider the figure of Rabbi Levi in his own right.

### LEVI: STUDYING BEFORE THE SAGES

In the Babylonian Talmud, Levi is described as "studying before the sages" (Sanhedrin 11a), suggesting that he was a student rather than a teacher. In several other sources he is described as a student sitting before Rabbi Yehuda HaNasi. It is difficult to ascertain the nature of his relationship with the patriarch. On one hand, Levi feels comfortable speaking his mind to Rebbi and seems to be quite close to him; on the other hand, he is subjected to the patriarch's scathing criticism.

2. Ofra Meir, *Rabbi Yehuda HaNasi* [Hebrew] (Tel Aviv: 5759), 188.

The Talmud relates that Rabbi Ḥiya once taught a complicated text about sacrifices that become mixed up with non-sacrificial material, such that it is impossible to determine which animal should be consecrated and which should not. The various students each proposed a solution, but Rabbi Ḥiya dismissed each one in turn. The Talmud documents their discussion. At one point, Levi presents his opinion to Rebbi, who responds harshly and hurtfully:

> It seems to me that you have no brain in your skull. (Menaḥot 80b)

At another point in the Talmud, too, Levi challenges Rebbi's teaching and Rebbi invokes the same phrase to put him in his place.[3] These exchanges speak more to the character of Rebbi than to that of Levi. Nonetheless, we often find Levi (who is known in the Jerusalem Talmud as Levi ben Sisi) sitting before Rebbi, interpreting mishnayot, commenting on them, and even recording his own insights: "'I said before my teacher' – And who was this? Our holy teacher [Rebbi]" (Shabbat 156a). We also find him arguing with all the leading sages of his day. On several occasions, the Babylonian sage Shmuel teaches a mishna based on what he reports to have learned from Levi. An important scholar of his generation, Levi was one of Rabbi Yehuda HaNasi's leading disciples, as well as a close associate of the patriarch. No wonder, then, that he was so disappointed upon hearing that he was not included in Rebbi's will.

### THE FAILED APPOINTMENT AT SIMONIA

Rabbi Yehuda HaNasi was responsible for all rabbinical appointments, certainly in the Land of Israel and possibly also in Babylonia. The following midrash describes Rebbi's attempt to appoint Levi as a sage:

> Rebbi was passing Simonia when its inhabitants came out to meet him, saying: Rebbi, give us a man to teach us Torah and Mishna

3. Yevamot 9a; also see the parallel in Y. Yevamot 1:1 (2c). H. Albeck points out that in spite of Rebbi's harsh criticism, Levi included his own claim as part of the Mishna he taught his students! See Albeck, *Introduction to the Talmuds*, 154.

> and be our judge. He gave them Levi ben Sisi. They erected a great platform and set him upon it. (Genesis Rabba 81:2)

This story starts out on a promising note. The people of Simonia, a small town in the Lower Galilee, request a leader who can fulfill all their religious needs: teach them Torah and Mishna, and judge their legal cases. According to the parallel source in the Jerusalem Talmud, they want him to be a jack of all trades, also functioning as cantor, ritual slaughterer, circumciser, and public speaker. Rebbi nominates Rabbi Levi ben Sisi for the role, and the people of Simonia hold an august inauguration ceremony. But this display of honor has the opposite of its intended effect, because Levi ben Sisi gets cold feet. Suddenly tongue-tied, he cannot answer any of the halakhic questions posed to him by the townspeople.[4] The midrash continues:

> When he saw what a sorry plight he was in, he arose early in the morning and repaired to Rebbi. Rebbi asked him: What did the inhabitants of Simonia do to you? He replied: Do not remind me of my plight. They asked me three questions, and I could not answer them. (Genesis Rabba 81:2)

When he is later alone with Rebbi, Levi ben Sisi manages to answer all three questions based on his studies in the beit midrash. When Rebbi asks him why he did not give these same answers to the people of Simonia, Levi responds:

> They erected a great platform for me and set me upon it, and that made me conceited and so I forgot my learning. (Genesis Rabba 81:2)

One of the questions asked by the people of Simona was whether a widow who has no hands can take off her shoe to perform the ritual of

4. They ask him three questions in an attempt to test his knowledge. The first question is about a woman without hands; the second question is about one who spits blood; and the third question is about the mystical secrets of the Book of Daniel.

*ḥalitza,* whereby she frees herself from the obligation to marry her late husband's brother. This is a technical question, but it calls attention to Levi's own handicap. As we have already seen, Levi was lame. The Talmud explains how he came to be this way:

> Rabbi Ḥiya Rabba demonstrated kneeling before Rebbi and became lame, but he was cured. Rabbi Levi bar Sisi demonstrated bending before Rebbi and became lame, but he was not cured. (Y. Berakhot 1:4 [3c])[5]

"Kneeling" and "bending" are two body motions that are part of the prayer service. According to this story, Levi became lame while demonstrating one of these motions to Rebbi. There is something ironic about a sage whose body becomes permanently bent in the position of prayer.[6] Somewhat pathetically, he seeks to serve God and becomes deformed. But another source about Levi's lameness casts this story in a different light:

> They said of Rabban Shimon ben Gamliel that when he rejoiced at the Celebration of the Water-Drawing, he would take eight flaming torches and throw one up and catch another without their touching each other. And when he would prostrate himself in the Temple, he would plant his two thumbs in the ground and bow and kiss the floor and arise. And no one else could do this. This is the form of bowing known as *kida*. Levi demonstrated *kida* by bowing in front of Rebbi, and he became lame. (Sukka 53a)

The Talmud discusses the annual Celebration of the Water-Drawing, contrasting the behavior of Rabban Shimon ben Gamliel with that of

5. A parallel to this story appears in Y. Sukka 5:4 [55c].
6. Elsewhere, the Talmud tells another story about Levi's lameness. In Taanit 25a, we are told that when Levi did not receive a response to his prayer in a time of drought, he spoke to God inappropriately and was therefore punished. The Talmud asks about the contradiction between this account and the story in the Jerusalem Talmud, concluding that it was both his inappropriate response to God and his demonstration of bowing that caused his lameness.

Levi. Unlike Rabban Shimon ben Gamliel, who was concerned with serving God, Levi was preoccupied with impressing Rebbi. Thus, Rabban Shimon ben Gamliel became a model for serving God joyously, whereas Levi became known for his handicap. Clearly the Talmud is criticizing Levi for posturing before Rebbi rather than bowing before God. Levi may have had tremendous respect for Rebbi, but even Rebbi was not God.[7]

The Talmud describes what became of Rabbi Levi:

> Rabbi Efes sat at the head of the academy, and Rabbi Ḥanina sat outside. Levi came and sat with him there. After a while, Rabbi Efes died and Rabbi Ḥanina sat at the head of the academy. Levi did not have someone to sit and study with, so he went down to Babylon. (Ketubot 103b)

When Levi when to Babylon, he was given a very honorable reception. He took it upon himself to disseminate the teachings of the Mishna along with all the commentaries of the sages of the Land of Israel. We will continue with his Babylonian adventures in Part Two, in our discussion of Shmuel and his father.

7. I am grateful to my son Yedidya for this insight.

*Chapter Three*

# Rabbi Ḥiya the Great

## HISTORICAL BACKGROUND: HOW TIBERIAS BECAME JEWISH

Herod Antipas founded the city of Tiberias around the year 20 CE and populated it with non-Jews, including paupers and freed slaves. At first, Jews were reluctant to settle there because the city was built on top of a cemetery.[1] But Herod forced part of the Jewish population to immigrate there as well. After he was ousted in 39 CE, the city was annexed to the kingdom of his nephew, Agrippa I. When Agrippa I died in 44 CE, the city became subject to direct Roman rule as part of Judea, which was annexed by the empire. At that point Rabbi Shimon bar Yoḥai purified the city, and Jews began to settle in it.[2] In the third century, the greatest sage of the period, Rabbi Yoḥanan, made his home in Tiberias. As a result, the Sanhedrin, which was under the leadership of Rabbi Yehuda Nesiya, relocated to Tiberias as well. This was the final destination for the Sanhedrin, as the Talmud relates in the name of Rabbi Yoḥanan (Rosh HaShana 31a).

Rabbi Ḥiya arrived in the Land of Israel just one generation after the purification of Tiberias, when Jews were still reluctant to settle there.

1. Josephus, *Antiquities of the Jews*, 18, 2, 4.
2. Y.L. Levine, "Rabbi Shimon bar Yoḥai, the Bones of the Dead, and the Purification of Tiberias" [Hebrew], *Cathedra* 22 (January 1982).

At the time, Jewish life and learning revolved around the Sanhedrin, with most Jews living in the area between Beit She'arim and Tzippori. Tiberias then began to grow and flourish. For Rabbi Ḥiya – who wanted to be close (but perhaps not too close) to Rabbi Yehuda HaNasi, and who wanted to live in a commercial center where he and his sons could make a living – Tiberias was ideal.[3]

## RABBI ḤIYA THE GREAT'S LINEAGE

Rabbi Ḥiya the Great moved to the Land of Israel from Kafri, located south of the Babylonian city of Sura. According to the medieval Jewish traveler Benjamin of Tudela, the city of Kafri became home to those Jews who were exiled by King Jehoiachin in 597 BCE, as the Bible chronicles: "And I came to the exiles who lived in Tel Aviv by the Kevar river" (Ezek. 3:15).[4] Several historians of Jewish life in Babylonia have argued that Kafri was a site of continuous Torah study from the Babylonian exile until the period of the talmudic sages.[5]

Rabbi Ḥiya the Great came to the Land of Israel with Rabbi Abba, known as Rav, who was the son of both his brother and his sister. This genealogy requires some explanation. Rabbi Ḥiya was the youngest child of Rav Abba bar Aḥa's second marriage. Rabbi Ḥiya's mother had a daughter from a previous marriage who was known as Ima. This daughter, who was Rabbi Ḥiya's stepsister, married Ivo, Rabbi Abba's older son. Ivo and Ima had a son named for his grandfather Rabbi Abba; this son was called Rav. Thus Rav was both Rabbi Ḥiya's brother's son (through his father) and his sister's son (through his mother).[6]

3. On Rabbi Ḥiya's professional life, see Y. Bava Metzia 5:7 [10c] and Ofra Meir, *Yehuda HaNasi*, 74–75.
4. B.Z. Eshel, *Jewish Settlements in Babylonia* [Hebrew] (Jerusalem: 5739), 133.
5. This is what Pirkoi ben Baboi, an eighth-century geonic scholar and a student of Rav Yehudai Gaon, quoted in a letter he wrote, referring to a midrash on the phrase "warrior heroes" (II Kings 24:14): "And what heroism is there in being exiled? The heroism of learning Torah." See B.M. Levine, "From the Geniza Fragments" [Hebrew], *Tarbiz* 2 (5791): 402. On Pirkoi ben Baboi's pro-Babylonian bias, see S. Spiegel, "Pirkoi ben Baboi's Polemic" [Hebrew], in *A Jubilee Volume in Honor of Tzvi Wolfson* (Jerusalem: 5725), 243–274.
6. Several scholars have written about Rav's complicated relationship with Rabbi Ḥiya. See Y.S. Tzuri, *Sefer Rav, Talmudic Biographical Library* [Hebrew] (Jerusalem: 5685), 3–4.

### RABBI ḤIYA'S RECEPTION IN ISRAEL: THE ADVISER FROM A DISTANT LAND

Upon his arrival in the Land of Israel, Rabbi Ḥiya immediately became a force to be reckoned with among the sages of the Galilee. Several stories describe the influence he exerted on Rabbi Yehuda HaNasi, some of which we discussed in the previous volume.[7] In one such story, Rabbi Ḥiya helped Rebbi answer a halakhic question, and Rebbi responded by calling him "My adviser from a distant land," quoting Isaiah 46:11 (Menaḥot 88b). This is a very telling epithet. Rabbi Ḥiya functioned as Rebbi's adviser throughout his entire sojourn in the Land of Israel, and countless sources describe him standing at Rebbi's side. He also frequently criticized the patriarch, particularly regarding his elitism and his detachment. For instance, Rabbi Ḥiya refused to accept Rebbi's belief that Torah should be taught in secret; instead he rebelled by teaching his two sons out in the marketplace.

Over the years, Rabbi Ḥiya became legendary. As Rabbi Ami quotes in the name of Reish Lakish, who lived one generation after Rabbi Ḥiya:

> When those in the Babylonian exile returned to the Land of Israel, their flax did not become worm-infested and their wine did not turn to vinegar, on account of the merit of Rabbi Ḥiya the elder and his sons. (Y. Maaser Sheni 5:5 [56d])

Rabbi Ḥiya became a mythical figure in the Babylonian Talmud as well, where he is described as a crucial link in the transmission of Torah:

> At first, when Torah was forgotten from Israel, Ezra came from Babylonia and reinstated it. When it was forgotten again, Hillel and his sons came and reinstated it. When it was forgotten again, Rabbi Ḥiya and his sons came and reinstated it. (Sukka 20a)

For the Talmud's treatment of the matter, see A.S. Rosenthal, "Rav Was the Son of Rabbi Ḥiya's Brother and Also the Son of His Sister?" [Hebrew], in *The Book of Hanoch Yellin: A Collection of Articles*, eds. S. Lieberman et al. [Hebrew] (Jerusalem: 5723), 281–337.

7. See the section on the relationship between Rabbi Ḥiya and Rebbi in *Sages* III, Part Five.

The continuation of the talmudic story about Rebbi's will underscores Rabbi Ḥiya's senior position in the eyes of the talmudic sages. As we saw above, Rebbi's oldest son Gamliel became patriarch, his second son Shimon became sage, and Rabbi Ḥanina ben Ḥama was appointed head. Rabbi Ḥiya was not mentioned in the will, but his absence did not escape the attention of the sages, who objected, "But Rabbi Ḥiya was there!" (Ketubot 103b). A later talmudic sage proposes that perhaps Rabbi Ḥiya predeceased Rebbi and thus he was not included in Rebbi's will, but this is inconsistent with the story of how Rabbi Ḥiya cried when he saw Rebbi's grave. The Talmud attempts to resolve this contradiction by suggesting that the names of the sages are reversed, that is, it was Rebbi who cried on Rabbi Ḥiya's grave. Then the Talmud challenges the notion that Rabbi Ḥiya died first by citing the story of the eulogy that Rabbi Ḥiya recited about Rabbi Yehuda HaNasi; but here, too, the Talmud suggests that perhaps it was Rebbi who eulogized Rabbi Ḥiya. The Talmud then asserts that there is a description of Rabbi Ḥiya's visit to the patriarchal home just before Rebbi's death, suggesting that Rebbi had to be the one to die first. The editor of this passage then puts the matter to rest by declaring that Rabbi Ḥiya was indeed still alive when Rebbi died, but Rebbi deliberately omitted him from his will for the following reason:

> Rabbi Ḥiya was occupied with the fulfillment of mitzvot, and Rebbi thought: I will not disturb him. (Ketubot 103b)

This explanation reflects an attempt to isolate Rabbi Ḥiya from the political arena and locate him exclusively in the world of Torah study and social service. Any public role that Rabbi Ḥiya might take on would cause him to spend less time teaching Torah, which was his primary occupation. Rebbi therefore exempted Rabbi Ḥiya from a leadership position. Unlike Rabbi Yehuda HaNasi, who edited the Mishna from his ivory tower, Rabbi Ḥiya went out among the people, teaching Torah publicly so that it would not be forgotten. In this capacity, Rabbi Ḥiya maintained close contact with the entire people of Israel, from young students to laypeople.

### RABBI ḤIYA AS MASTER OF *BARAITOT*

Rabbi Ḥiya is known as the master of *baraitot*, a term referring to those teachings from the mishnaic period that were not included in Rabbi Yehuda HaNasi's final text of the Mishna. The Talmud frequently juxtaposes a teaching from the Mishna with a *baraita* in an effort to resolve any contradictions between the sources, to point out their different provenances, or to modify one source so that it better accords with the other. We will cite one example of the Talmud's approach to the difference between the teachings of Rebbi and Rabbi Ḥiya.

The third chapter of Tractate Ḥullin deals with non-kosher animals. The Mishna teaches that if the liver was torn from an animal, that animal is rendered non-kosher. The Talmud elaborates:

> If anything at all remained of the liver, the animal would be kosher, even if the remainder does not even have the volume of an olive. But we learn[8] that so long as an olive's volume remains of it, the animal would be kosher. Rav Yosef said: There is no contradiction. One teaching represents the view of Rabbi Ḥiya, and one teaching represents the view of Rabbi Shimon bar Rebbi. For Rabbi Ḥiya would discard such a piece of meat, whereas Rabbi Shimon bar Rebbi would dip it in relish and eat it. And as a mnemonic, we can say, "The wealthy are thrifty." (Ḥullin 46a)

This is a typical talmudic passage which pits a mishna and *baraita* against one another. According to the mishna, if anything at all remains of the liver, the animal is kosher. But according to the *baraita*, a minimum of

8. The talmudic term used here for "but we learn" is "*t'nan*," which generally refers to a teaching from a mishna. The term "*tanya*" is used to refer to a teaching from a *baraita*. But there are several exceptions to this rule in the talmudic manuscripts. In our case, it is clear that "but we learn" refers to a *baraita* and not to a mishna, and indeed some of the manuscripts read "*vehatanya*." Epstein notes that the term "*t'nan*" sometimes refers to *baraitot* in his *Text of the Mishna*, 814–817. He notes that Nahmanides, too, points out in his teachings on Tractate Shabbat 48b that it is only a general principle and not a hard-and-fast rule that the term "*t'nan*" refers to a mishna and "*tanya*" refers to a *baraita*.

an olive's worth must remain. The *baraita*'s stance is thus more stringent. The Talmud supplies a mnemonic to remember the two positions: "The wealthy are thrifty." Rebbi, the author of the Mishna, was very wealthy, but he was also more likely to rule the piece of meat fit for consumption. Rabbi Ḥiya, the master of *baraitot*, was poor, yet he would more readily discard a suspicious piece of meat.

As this example attests, the Talmud often attributes the editing and compiling of the *baraitot* to Rabbi Ḥiya. This particular *baraita* comes from the Sifra, the halakhic midrash on the Book of Leviticus:

> These are the non-kosher animals.... If the liver was removed and the remainder does not even have the volume of an olive.[9] (Sifra, *Shemini* 2)

It seems that texts from early midrashim such as the Sifra were part of Rabbi Ḥiya's *baraitot*. Rabbi Ḥiya's teachings thus reflect another intellectual tradition, one that belongs to another beit midrash and predates Rebbi.[10]

In the continuation of the passage from the Babylonian Talmud, Rabbi Yoḥanan rules that the halakha is in accordance with the teaching of Rabbi Ḥiya:[11]

> Rabbi Yitzḥak said in the name of Rabbi Yosef who said in the name of Rabbi Yoḥanan: The law is in accordance with those who say that an olive's volume must remain. (Ḥullin 43a)

But the other sages do not accept that Rabbi Yoḥanan ruled in accordance with Rabbi Ḥiya:

9. This is how the text appears in the manuscripts of the Sifra. But the printed version was changed to read "and nothing remains of it," presumably so as to accord with the Mishna. See Epstein, *Text of the Mishna*, 15, note 1.
10. Several commentators and scholars have dealt with the relationship between midrash halakha in the Sifra and the midrashim attributed to Rabbi Ḥiya. See the Malbim's introduction to the Sifra, and Rabbi D.Z. Hoffman's work on midrash halakha. Also see Epstein, *Text of the Mishna*, 15, note 1.
11. We will consider the figure of Rabbi Yoḥanan in Part Two of this volume.

> But did Rabbi Yoḥanan say this? Did not Rabba bar bar Ḥana say that Rabbi Yoḥanan said: The halakha is in accordance with the Mishna? As it is taught: If the liver was removed and nothing at all remained. This implies that if anything at all remained, the animal is kosher, even if it is less that an olive's volume. (Ḥullin 43a)

The sages contend that when there is a contradiction between sources, Rabbi Yoḥanan would rule in accordance with the Mishna. The Talmud explains, "There is a disagreement among the talmudic sages regarding what Rabbi Yoḥanan said" (Ḥullin 43a). For our purposes, suffice it to say that this is just one example of how Rabbi Ḥiya's teachings did not always accord with the Mishna of Rabbi Yehuda HaNasi.

### RABBI ḤIYA'S ADDITIONS TO REBBI'S MISHNA

In addition to being the master of *baraitot,* Rabbi Ḥiya also added commentary and halakhot to Rebbi's Mishna. One example appears in the Jerusalem Talmud in Tractate Bava Metzia, in a passage dealing with the laws of interest:

> Rabbi Ḥiya the Great had some flax. Ass-drivers came to buy it from him. He said to them: I was not thinking of selling it now, but rather on Purim.[12] They said to him: Sell it to us now, for the price which you would get if you sold it later when the crop is abundant. He came and asked Rebbi about this. Rebbi said to him: It is forbidden. He went out and placed Rebbi's ruling in his Mishna collection. And thus it was taught: If one owed money, and another came to take it from him at the threshing floor, and he said: "Go and calculate the amount for me following the prevailing market price, and I will provide it for you over the next twelve months" – this is forbidden. (Y. Bava Metzia 5:6 [10c])

12. The Aramaic word "Puria" refers to Purim, as Professor Leib Moskowitz pointed out to me. The price of the crop depends on the time it is sold. See Sokoloff's dictionary, 462; and see Lieberman, *Tosefta Kifshuta* Bava Metzia, 208, note 42.

Rabbi Ḥiya made his living by growing, weaving, and selling flax. He was famous for the quality of his merchandise, and ass-drivers wished to purchase their supply from him before high season. Rabbi Ḥiya refused their terms because Rebbi taught him that this was tantamount to selling with interest, which is forbidden.[13] He then proceeded to formulate Rebbi's teaching as a legal principle.[14]

As this source demonstrates, some of Rabbi Ḥiya's *baraitot* were based on Rebbi's teachings, which they expanded or interpreted. Other *baraitot* originated in the *batei midrash* in Yavneh, Lod, or even Babylonia, and were never edited by Rebbi.[15] Dozens of talmudic *sugyot*, both in the Babylonian and Jerusalem Talmuds, compare and contrast the Mishna of Rebbi with the *baraitot* of Rabbi Ḥiya and show how both are relevant.[16]

The generation of sages who followed Rabbi Ḥiya insisted that all subsequent Torah teachings could be traced back to Rebbi's Mishna. Ilfa, a colleague of Rabbi Yoḥanan, went so far as to declare, "If Rebbi didn't teach it, then where did Rabbi Ḥiya come up with it?" (Eiruvin 92a).

### RABBI ḤIYA AS LEGAL AUTHORITY: THE LENIENT BABYLONIAN

Several sources depict Rabbi Ḥiya ruling in matters of practical halakha. One example concerns the wearing of sandals whose soles are attached with nails. During the period of the Bar Kokhba revolt, the sages ruled that it was forbidden to wear such sandals on Shabbat on account of

13. Rabbi Ḥiya combined his economic pursuits with a commitment to studying Torah. Ofra Meir depicts these two pursuits as sequential rather than simultaneous. But several sources suggest that Rabbi Ḥiya had a foot in both worlds. See Ḥullin 85b, Genesis Rabba 77, and others.
14. The phrase "*mishnayot gedolot*" is used to refer to the *baraitot* of Rabbi Ḥiya and Rabbi Hoshaya. See Y. Horayot 3:5 (48c). It seems that these *baraitot* were viewed as an extension of Rebbi's Mishna.
15. This is the view expressed by Rabbi Zecharia Frankel in his introduction to the Jerusalem Talmud. See also Epstein, *Text of the Mishna*, 31–32. Epstein agrees with this position and cites several dissenting voices claiming that Rabbi Ḥiya merely expanded upon Rebbi's Mishna.
16. For examples in the Jerusalem Talmud, see Shabbat 1:2 [3a], Mo'ed Katan 2:1 [81a], and Avoda Zara 1:5 [39d].

a particular historical incident involving this kind of footwear.[17] Subsequent generations of sages tried to find ways to relax this prohibition. Rabbi Ḥiya comments:

> Were it not that they call me the lenient Babylonian, I would rule far more leniently. (Shabbat 60b)

Rabbi Ḥiya's statement implies that unlike Rebbi, who permitted the wearing of such sandals only if the majority of the nails had fallen off (leaving fewer than seven), Rabbi Ḥiya would have ruled that it was permissible to wear the sandal even if more nails remained – were it not for the fact that he had developed a reputation for ruling leniently.

### RABBI ḤIYA AND HIS WIFE: IT IS ENOUGH THAT THEY SAVE US FROM SIN

The Mishna in Tractate Yevamot stipulates that "a man is commanded to procreate, but a woman is not." In the context of this law, the Talmud relates the following story about Rabbi Ḥiya's family:

> Yehuda and Ḥizkiya were twins. The formation of one fetus was completed at the end of nine months, and the formation of the other was completed at the beginning of seven months. Yehudit, the wife of Rabbi Ḥiya, had severe labor pains. She changed her clothes and came before Rabbi Ḥiya. She said to him: Is a woman commanded to engage in procreation? He said to her: No. So she went and drank a sterilizing serum. Eventually the matter became known to Rabbi Ḥiya. He told her: If only you would have borne me one more wombful of children. (Yevamot 65b)[18]

17. D. Sperber, "Concerning the Sandal with Nails" [Hebrew], *Sinai* 61 (5727): 69–79; Y. Shahar, "The Prohibition on Wearing Sandals with Nails: The Historical Source of a Law" [Hebrew], in *Caves of Refuge in the Judean Plain* (Tel Aviv: 1987), 395–404.
18. It is not entirely clear how much Rabbi Ḥiya knew when he spoke these words to his wife. Rabbi Shlomo Luria, the Maharshal (1510–1573), in his book *Ḥokhmat Shlomo*, suggests as follows: "'If only you would have borne me one more wombful of children' – Rashi understands this to mean: If only you had not drunk that serum and could give birth again. I have heard that we can understand Rashi as saying: If only that serum would not take effect, and it could be as if you had never drunk it."

This story teaches that Rabbi Ḥiya's wife Yehudit was a learned and strong-willed woman who sought to use her halakhic knowledge to relieve herself of any future pain she might experience in childbirth. Her relationship with her husband is complicated. She feels she must disguise herself before coming to him with her question, presumably because she fears that he would not listen to her otherwise. Only when he mistakes her for an unfamiliar woman and only when he feels no personal stake in her question will he give her the answer she seeks, authorizing her to render herself barren.[19]

We learn about the complicated relationship between Rabbi Ḥiya and his wife from another source in the Babylonian Talmud:

> Yehudit, the wife of Rabbi Ḥiya, experienced unusually painful labor. She said to Rabbi Ḥiya: My mother told me: When you were young, your father accepted *kiddushin* for you [from another man].[20] He said to her: It is not within your mother's power to cause you to become forbidden to me. (Kiddushin 12b)

Yehudit, a mother of twins (and perhaps even a mother of two sets of twins, as Rashi suggests), finds herself deeply distressed. She seeks a way to liberate herself from her duties to her husband. She tries to convince him that she is forbidden to him on the grounds that her mother told her that her father had already betrothed her to another. But this attempt fails. Then she tries another stratagem, taking advantage of her exemption from the commandment to procreate in order to drink a sterilizing serum, as we saw in Tractate Yevamot. Rabbi Ḥiya cannot rebuke her because she did so only after consulting with him. But he laments the fact that his wife will not be able to bear him any more children.

Rabbi Ḥiya's wife remains bitterly bound to her husband, though he seems to treat her quite well:

19. There are several rabbinic sources about women who disguise themselves and come before their husbands. See A. Shinan, "Woman, Mask, and Costume in the Aggadic Literature of the Sages" [Hebrew], in *A Range of Opinions*, ed. D. Kerem (Ministry of Education, 5756).
20. A. Schremmer, *Male and Female He Created Them* [Hebrew] (Jerusalem: 5764), 118.

> Rabbi Ḥiya's wife would aggravate him. When Rabbi Ḥiya would find something in the market, he would wrap it up in his shawl and bring it to her. Rav asked him: But does not she aggravate you? He said to him: It is sufficient that they raise our children and save us from sin. (Yevamot 63a)[21]

Rav, the nephew of Rabbi Ḥiya, is pained to see the tension in his uncle's home. But Rabbi Ḥiya soothes him and teaches him an important lesson about marital harmony. As Rabbi Ḥiya attests, he has given up on having a close personal relationship with his wife, but he nonetheless continues to treat her well. His wife may aggravate him, but he takes consolation in the fact that having her as a sexual outlet serves to guard him against sin. This is clearly a story told from a man's perspective, and the lesson it comes to teach fails to take into account the woman's needs. Nonetheless, the Talmud gives voice to Yehudit's pain.[22]

## RABBI ḤIYA'S SONS BASK IN HIS SHADOW

Rabbi Ḥiya's sons, Yehuda and Ḥizkiya, generally appear together as a pair of scholars.[23] On several occasions they are described as sitting with their father before Rabbi Yehuda HaNasi.[24] Rabbi Ḥiya is often

21. Ibid., 308–309.
22. I discovered a sensitive and enlightening commentary on the passages from Yevamot in the book *Ben Yehoyada* by the Ben Ish Ḥai (Yosef Haim of Baghdad, 1832–1909), who writes, "He would wrap up his gifts for her in his shawl, because the shawl was an item of clothing that was unique to Torah scholars. In so doing, he demonstrated to her that she was a participant in his Torah study. Thus he used the shawl that distinguished him as a scholar to cater to her needs."
23. Yehuda and Ḥizkiya are also referred to as a "pair," as Epstein suggests in his *Text of the Mishna*, 16. But Hyman thinks the term "pair" refers to the name of a particular scholar. This is one example of the plethora of sages that are included in Hyman's *Tanna'im and Amora'im*. Hyman enumerates more than three thousand sages, inspiring Y.L. Levine's critique: "Hyman, who took a maximalist approach, counted about 3,400 sages in the Land of Israel and Babylonia during the period of the Mishna and Talmud." See Levine, *The Status of the Sages in the Land of Israel* [Hebrew] (Jerusalem: 5746), 40.
24. See *Sages* III, Part Five.

depicted as being "bound up" in his sons, as a father figure and teacher who is extremely attentive to everything they do.

Rabbi Ḥiya taught his sons to teach halakha publicly, particularly when traveling. The Talmud relates that once they all went on a business trip to a distant city. Upon their return, Rabbi Ḥiya asked his sons to report on what had transpired there:

> When they returned, their father asked them: Did any case come before you? They answered him: A case of taking an attic ladder to a dovecote came before us, and we permitted it. Rabbi Ḥiya told them: Go and prohibit that which you permitted. (Beitza 9b)

This incident relates to a debate between the houses of Hillel and Shammai regarding the use of a ladder to remove chicks from a nest on a festival. According to Beit Shammai, it is permissible to move the ladder from one place in a dovecote to another, but not from one dovecote to another. According to Beit Hillel, it is also permissible to transfer the ladder to another dovecote.

The sons relate that they permitted moving the ladder from one dovecote to another, as per the ruling of Beit Hillel. Their father instructs them to return to the place where they issued this ruling and revoke it.

The Jerusalem Talmud speaks of an additional journey undertaken by Rabbi Ḥiya's sons, this time down south to Lod. The story appears in a chapter about the miscarriage of deformed fetuses:

> Rabbi Ḥiya the Great went to the south. Rabbi Ḥama, father of Rabbi Hoshaya, and Bar Kappara asked him: If the fetus looks wholly like a man, but its face is that of a beast, what is the law? He came and asked Rebbi. Rebbi said to him: Go and write to them: It is not a viable fetus. Rabbi Yirmiya said: The pair went out. Rabbi Ḥama, the father of Rabbi Hoshaya, and Bar Kappara asked him: If the fetus' two eyes are covered, what is the law? He came and asked Rebbi. Rebbi said to him: Go and write to them: It is not a viable fetus. (Y. Nidda 3:2 [50c])

The encounter between Rabbi Ḥiya and the sages of the south is a tense one. Rabbi Ḥiya is a new arrival among the sages of the Land of Israel, but he has already developed a reputation for himself. Rabbi Ḥama and Bar Kappara, the leaders of the beit midrash in the south, present him with a question: If a baby is born looking like a man but with the face of a beast, is it considered viable?

Rabbi Ḥiya appeals to the patriarch, who responds, "Go and write to them," instructing the sages to release an official ruling from the patriarchal house to the entire Jewish population.[25] Rabbi Ḥiya is followed by the pair, a reference to his twin sons. They too are presented with a question by Rabbi Ḥama and Bar Kappara, and they too relay their question to the patriarch. In both cases, the patriarch rules that the fetus is not thought to be a viable human being, and thus the woman does not contract ritual impurity from having given birth. We learn about the originality of this ruling from another story about the sons of Rabbi Ḥiya:

> Rabbi Ḥiya's sons went out to the villages. They came before their father. He said to them: Did any case come before you? They said to him: A case of a child born with a smooth face came before us, and we ruled the mother impure. He said to them: Go and rule pure what you have ruled impure. What was your reasoning? Presumably you wished to be stringent. But this is a stringency that will lead to a leniency, for you are giving her days of purity. (Nidda 24a)

The sons of Rabbi Ḥiya report to their father about an incident in which a woman gave birth to a baby with a deformed face. They ruled

25. This phrase also appears with reference to Rabban Gamliel the Elder, who lived during the Temple period: "Once Rabban Gamliel and the elders were sitting on the steps of the portico of the Temple Mount and Yoḥanan the Priest, a scribe, was sitting in front of them. They told him: Go and write to them: To my brothers in the Upper Galilee and Lower Galilee: May your peace increase! I hereby inform you that the time of removal of *ḥametz* approaches" (Y. Maaser Sheni 5:4 [56c]). This text seems authentic, suggesting that Rebbi was invoking an established formula for a patriarchal ordinance.

stringently, rendering the woman impure. Their father sends them back to revoke their ruling, because what seemed to them to be a stringency is in fact a leniency.

The Babylonian and Jerusalem Talmuds seem to be describing the same incident. According to the Jerusalem Talmud, the sages of Lod ask Rabbi Ḥiya about a fetus with a deformed face. Rabbi Yirmiya relates that the question is then directed to Rabbi Ḥiya's sons. The patriarch's response, "Go and write to them," is equivalent to the father's response to his sons, "Go and rule pure," suggesting that the two stories are in fact one.

### THE DEATH OF RABBI ḤIYA

The story of the death of Rabbi Ḥiya focuses on his generosity of spirit:

> The Angel of Death could not approach Rabbi Ḥiya. One day he disguised himself as a pauper. He went, knocked on Rabbi Ḥiya's door, and said to him: Bring me some bread. They brought him some bread. He said to Rabbi Ḥiya: Does the master not have mercy on the poor? So why does the master not have mercy on me? He revealed himself to Rabbi Ḥiya, showing him a rod of fire, and Rabbi Ḥiya surrendered to him. (Mo'ed Katan 28a)

Several rabbinic stories describe the Angel of Death's difficulty in causing harm to Torah scholars, who are protected by the Torah they have learned.[26] When the Angel of Death comes to take Rabbi Ḥiya's soul, he encounters an additional complication. Rabbi Ḥiya is not just dedicated to Torah study, but also to the performance of mitzvot. We have already seen that Rebbi exempted Rabbi Ḥiya from any political responsibilities so that he could continue to perform good deeds for others. Rabbi Ḥiya's good deeds, which are described throughout the Talmud as involving education and charity, served as a further obstacle preventing the Angel of Death from approaching him.

Only by dressing up as a pauper can the Angel of Death gain entry to Rabbi Ḥiya's home. Rabbi Ḥiya, who is a truly great man, is prepared

26. The most famous of such stories is about the death of King David. See Shabbat 30b and its parallels.

to sacrifice his own life so as to act graciously toward even the Angel of Death. Ironically, the very act of charity that is supposed to protect him – since charity is supposed to save a person from death – instead turns him over to the Angel of Death's waiting arms.[27]

The Talmud relates that after the death of Rabbi Ḥiya, his two sons set off to make a living, and they subsequently forgot all their learning:

> One of the sons said to the other: Does our father know of this pain we are experiencing? The other one said: How could he know? For it is written, "His sons may attain honor, and he will not know it" [Job 14:21]. The other one replied: But does he then not know? For it is written, "But his flesh will pain him, and his spirit will mourn for him" [Job 14:22]. (Berakhot 18b)

This story, which appears in the context of the Talmud's discussion of what the dead know about the living, provides tragic closure to the series of sad stories about Rabbi Ḥiya's family. Here too we see that the sons feel intimately connected to their father. According to archeological evidence, they are even described as being buried side-by-side with a grave marker that reads, "This is the grave of Rabbi Ḥiya and his sons."

27. Y. Frankel, *Studies in the Intellectual World of the Aggadic Story* [Hebrew] (Tel Aviv: 5741), 58–61. Also see I. Hevroni, "An Arrow in Satan's Eye: Symbols and Significant Spaces in the Stories of Seduction" [Hebrew] (PhD diss., Bar Ilan University, 5765), 154–160.

*Chapter Four*

# Bar Kappara in Lod

## LOD IN THE PERIOD BETWEEN THE BAR KOKHBA REVOLT AND REBBI'S TENURE

Judea in the wake of the Bar Kokhba revolt and the Hadrianic decrees is generally depicted as a wasteland. While settlements in the hills were indeed emptied of Jews, the Judean plain and the city of Lod in particular experienced a revival.[1] There is ample evidence that Lod was rebuilt under Roman rule in the immediate aftermath of the revolt,[2] but the revival of Torah study was a slower process. We find scattered evidence of rabbinic activity in the south during this period, but it was a marked decline from the period before the revolt.[3]

In the year 199 CE the city experienced a turning point. The emperor Severus visited the Land of Israel and conferred on Lod the status of a polis.[4] The character of the city, now known as Diospolis, underwent a major transformation: New institutions were founded

1. M. Avi-Yonah, *Rome and Byzantium*, 21–25.
2. B.Z. Rosenfeld, *Lod and Its Sages* [Hebrew] (Jerusalem: 5757), 71–72.
3. Ibid., 76–79.
4. He gave this designation to other cities in the Land of Israel as well. See D. Golan, *The Severan Emperors* [Hebrew] (Jerusalem: 5770), 59–63.

to deal with matters of administration, education, culture, justice, and government.[5] A new currency was issued, pagan institutions were strengthened, and the formerly Jewish city became increasingly cosmopolitan.[6]

### THE SOUTHERN BORDERS OF THE LAND OF ISRAEL

Lod marked the southern border of Jewish settlement, which raised a series of halakhic questions regarding its status. The Tosefta mentions Lod in a discussion about the borders of the Land of Israel as they are relevant to those commandments which are only incumbent upon residents of the land:

> Rebbi and Rabbi Yishmael the son of Rabbi Yose and Rabbi Eliezer HaKappar spent the Sabbath in the stall of Pazzi in Lod. Rabbi Pinḥas ben Yair was sitting before them.
>
> They said to him: Ashkelon – what do you rule concerning it?
>
> He said to them: They sell wheat in their basilicas, and they bathe and eat their Passovers in the evening.
>
> They said to him: What is the rule about when it is regarded as a land of other nations?
>
> He said to them: When a non-Jew has remained in it forty days, it is unclean.
>
> They said to him: If so, let us vote concerning it to exempt it from tithes.
>
> Rabbi Yishmael the son of Rabbi Yose did not vote with them.
>
> When he went out, Rebbi said: Why did you not vote with us?
>
> He said to him: Concerning uncleanliness which I formerly declared unclean, I have now declared clean. But not tithes. I was afraid of the High Court, lest they remove my head. (Tosefta Ohalot 18:18)[7]

5. M. Amit, *The History of the Roman Empire* [Hebrew] (Jerusalem: 5762), 642.
6. Rosenfeld, *Lod and Its Sages*, 76–79.
7. The language of the Tosefta is difficult to understand. It seems that there was an incident in which Rabbi Yishmael declared something clean, but insisted that he would not be so permissive in the future. He would not go so far as to relax the

This question demonstrates the interrelatedness of Jewish law and economic reality. Any place that is not considered part of the sacred Land of Israel is exempt from the heavy economic burden of tithing, as well as from the requirement to leave the land fallow during the sabbatical year. The sages in Lod inquire about the status of Ashkelon. Rabbi Pinḥas ben Yair's response is puzzling, but it is clear that he regards Ashkelon as a mixed city. As a result, it is exempt from tithing even though it is not considered one of the unclean cities of the other nations.[8]

One of the local sages included in this discussion is Bar Kappara. When we discussed the relationship between Rebbi and Bar Kappara in the previous volume of this series, we asked whether it was possible that Bar Kappara moved as far away as Kfar Devora and built a separate beit midrash there. We also asked whether Bar Kappara and Rabbi Eliezer HaKappar are indeed the same person.[9] We will now turn our attention to Bar Kappara's beit midrash in Lod, which was a mainstay for the sages of the south.

### BAR KAPPARA'S BEIT MIDRASH AND THE SAGES OF THE SOUTH

According to Saul Lieberman:

> Certainly the south was never emptied of its sages, and there was still a beit midrash in the south during the period of the final sages of the Mishna. We frequently find quoted in the Jerusalem Talmud that "Rav Hoshaya, the *Tanna* of Bar Kappara, came from the south," and the sages of the south are mentioned frequently throughout the Jerusalem Talmud.[10]

Although all communities in the Land of Israel were under the supervision of the patriarchy, the sages of the south had their own

tithing requirement because he was afraid of the High Court (of heaven), which would mete out his punishment.

8. A different version of this story appears in Y. Shevi'it 6:1. In his book *Yerushalmi Shevi'it*, vol. 2 (Jerusalem 5747), 50–54, Y. Felix considers various interpretations of this story.
9. He is referred to elsewhere as Rabbi Elazar HaKappar. See *Sages* III, Part Five.
10. S. Lieberman, *Sifrei Zuta* (New York: 5728), 92.

traditions, both with regard to styles of learning and with regard to halakhic ruling. Lieberman demonstrated that Sifrei Zuta, a halakhic midrash on the Book of Numbers, is a product of the beit midrash of the sages of the south, where Bar Kappara presided and Rabbi Yehoshua ben Levi was a leading student. This text makes no mention of Rabbi Yehuda; instead we find the teachings of many sages who are not included in the Mishna. The earliest sources in Sifrei Zuta can be traced to the teachings of Rabbi Shimon bar Yoḥai, a student of Rabbi Akiva, and to Rabbi Eliezer, the leader of the sages in Lod before the Bar Kokhba revolt.[11]

The fact that there was a beit midrash that transmitted sources that were not beholden to the Mishna of the patriarch in Tzippori raises a host of questions regarding the transmission of tannaitic teachings to the *Amora'im*. We will have to consider where Lod fits in to the larger picture when we study the transmission of Torah to centers of learning in Babylonia and Tiberias. For our present purposes, we note that the differences between sources from the north and those from the south may reflect different stages in the editing of the Mishna.

Today we are accustomed to regarding the Mishna as the product of Rabbi Yehuda HaNasi's editorial hand. But the reality is that Rebbi assembled various collections of mishnayot and edited them not once, but in several subsequent editions. As we noted in the previous volume, Rebbi used to study Mishna with his father, Rabban Shimon ben Gamliel, and during their studies, he would edit the Mishna with the assistance of Rabbi Natan the Babylonian.[12] And so we can witness the process by which Rebbi gave the Mishna its final form after revising it in accordance with sources he found or the traditions of the students around him. The sages of the south were not party to this new reorganization. As a result, we can occasionally find scraps from the cutting room floor of the Mishna included in texts from the south. The identification of Sifrei Zuta with the southern beit midrash served to direct scholarly attention to this matter and to the existence of other sources attributed to *Tanna'im* who are not mentioned in the Mishna. These *Tanna'im* may

11. Lieberman, *Sifrei Zuta*, 94–95.
12. See *Sages* III, Part Four.

have offered halakhic rulings that contradict those we find in the Mishna, as the following example attests:

> Bar Kappara found a ring bearing an idolatrous image. An Aramean shepherd boy was running after him, wanting to pick it up. Bar Kappara hit him, cursed him, and commanded the boy: Spit on it! The boy did not agree to do so. He urged him to urinate on it, but he would not agree to do so. They said: A non-Jew may nullify an idol belonging either to himself or his fellow, even under coercion, so long as he knows the character of the idol belonging to him. (Y. Avoda Zara 4:4 [43c])

Bar Kappara searches for halakhic license to appropriate an idolatrous ring. He forces a non-Jewish boy to treat the object with scorn so as to nullify its ritual status and thereby render it permissible. Bar Kappara thus holds that a non-Jew can also nullify his friend's idol, even if it is not his. This indicates that Bar Kappara was relying on the Mishna from Rebbi's youth, according to which a non-Jew may nullify an idol belonging either to himself or to his fellow.[13] Perhaps this reflects a version of the Mishna that was codified in the generation after Rebbi, influenced by earlier mishnayot like those of the sages of Lod, who permitted a non-Jew to nullify the idol of a Jew. This is the suggestion offered by Rabbi Zecharia Frankel:

> Those sages who were contemporaneous with Rebbi and those who immediately survived him added to his Mishna…. And other sages led by Bar Kappara, Levi, and Rabbi Ḥiya departed somewhat from the versions that appear in Rebbi's Mishna and developed new versions of their own…. Not many years after Rebbi's death, the sages of Tiberias, which was the new center of Torah learning from Rabbi Yoḥanan's era and beyond, canonized the Mishna.[14]

13. Epstein, *Text of the Mishna*, 22–23.
14. Rabbi Z. Frankel, *The Methods of the Mishna* [Hebrew] (Leipzig: 5627), 202.

This concludes our discussion of the versions of the Mishna during the transitional generation.

### THE DISPARAGING SAGES OF THE SOUTH

Several sources comment on the disparaging attitudes evinced by the sages from the south. One such source quotes Rabbi Shimon the son of Rebbi, who succeeded his father as sage:

> Rabbi Shimon son of Rebbi would grow angry with those southerners who treated the *maaser sheni* tithe lightly. (Y. Maaser Sheni 4:1 [54d])

*Maaser sheni* was a tax on the full agricultural yield. The produce set aside as *maaser sheni* had to be eaten in Jerusalem. After the destruction of the Temple, when Jerusalem was converted to Aelia Capitolina, many Jews began disregarding this tax, sometimes redeeming the fruit symbolically with a small coin. During the tenure of Rabbi Shimon the son of Rabbi Yehuda HaNasi, an attempt was made to reinstitute the *maaser sheni* tax. When the southerners continued to treat this tax lightly, Rabbi Shimon grew angry.[15] The Jerusalem Talmud describes how Bar Kappara defended the southern custom:

> Bar Kappara took the fruits that were designated for the *maaser sheni* tithe and cut them up in front of Rabbi Shimon. He said: Are these worth anything? Thus far you regarded them as worthless when cut up; but what about now, when they are worth even more once cut up? (Y. Maaser Sheni 4:1 [54d])

In cutting the fruit into negligibly sized pieces, Bar Kappara tried to illustrate to Rabbi Shimon that the stringency that he sought to impose

15. Lieberman demonstrates that during the late tannaitic and early amoraic periods, *maaser sheni* was redeemed for its full worth. See *Tosefta Kifshuta* to *Seder Zera'im*, 767, note 15. Lieberman references B.M. Levin's *Treasury of Customs from Babylonia and the Land of Israel* [Hebrew] (Jerusalem: 5702), 141. Perhaps it was the sages of the south who were responsible for the halakhic development whereby *maaser sheni* became redeemed for a small coin rather than for its full worth.

would only cause more damage. He contends that such stringency would dissuade the people from redeeming their *maaser sheni* fruit at all.[16] In so doing, Bar Kappara sought to bar the newly appointed sage from instituting customs that were contrary to those of the southern sages.[17]

Bar Kappara led an entire generation of sages in Lod. We will encounter his leading colleagues and pupils in the chapters that follow.

16. This explanation is according to the commentary of the Penei Moshe (Rabbi Moshe Margalit, 1710–1780). The Talmud's language is difficult, and I was unable to find a more satisfying interpretation.
17. On his relationship with Rabbi Shimon the son of Rebbi during Rebbi's lifetime, see *Sages* III, Part Five.

*Chapter Five*

# Rabbi Oshaya Rabba

> Rabbi Oshaya Beribbi in his generation is like Rabbi Meir in his generation. Just as Rabbi Meir's colleagues could not fathom the depths of his reasoning, so too Rabbi Oshaya's colleagues could not fathom the depths of his reasoning. (Eiruvin 53a)

Rabbi Oshaya, a member of the transitional generation, has been largely forgotten by history. He was not part of the beit midrash of those who assembled the Mishna in the Galilee, from Usha to Tzippori, and he certainly was not part of Rabbi Yehuda HaNasi's circle. Nonetheless, he became known as the Father of the Mishna (see Y. Bava Kamma 4:1 [4c]), a title conferred upon him by Rabbi Yoḥanan,[1] suggesting that he was held in high regard by the talmudic sages.

## THE THREE-PLY CORD IS NOT EASILY SEVERED: RABBI OSHAYA'S FAMILY IN LOD

Rabbi Oshaya is associated with the beit midrash in Caesarea, but he grew up in Lod and studied in Bar Kappara's beit midrash. In Lod he

1. Y. Kiddushin 1:1 [60a]. Also see Epstein, *Text of the Mishna*, 40.

was born into a well-connected family of sages. The Talmud relates that the following verse was recited about Rabbi Oshaya, his father, and his grandfather: "The three-ply cord is not easily severed" (Eccl. 4:12). His father Rabbi Ḥama bar Bisa, a student of Rabbi Akiva, tried to follow his teacher's example by leaving his home to study Torah. He joined the beit midrash of Rabbi Yehuda HaNasi in the Galilee. His is one of several talmudic stories about sages who traveled far from home to study Torah in distant *batei midrash*:

> Rebbi would praise Rabbi Ḥama bar Bisa to Rabbi Yishmael the son of Rabbi Yose, calling him a great man. Rabbi Yishmael said to Rebbi: When he comes before you, bring him to me. When Rabbi Ḥama bar Bisa came, Rabbi Yishmael said to him: Ask me a question. Rabbi Ḥama bar Bisa asked him: If a woman examined herself with an uninspected examination cloth and placed it in a box, and on the following day she found blood on it, what is the law? Rabbi Yishmael said to him: Should I answer you according to my father's opinion on the matter, or shall I answer you according to Rebbi's opinion? Rabbi Ḥama bar Bisa said to Rabbi Yishmael: Answer me according to Rebbi's opinion. Rabbi Yishmael said: This is the one of whom they say that he is a great person? How could he disregard a teacher's words and instead listen to his disciple's words? But Rabbi Ḥama bar Bisa reasoned: Rebbi is the head of a talmudic academy, and the rabbis frequently study before him, and therefore his teachings are finely honed. (Nidda 14b)

The encounter between Rabbi Yishmael the son of Rabbi Yose and Rabbi Ḥama bar Bisa captures the familiar tension between the Torah one learns at home and the Torah one is taught in school. Both scholars are the children of sages, but Rabbi Yishmael regards himself as his father's disciple, whereas Rabbi Ḥama regards himself as his teacher's disciple. Rabbi Yishmael is always depicted as a devoted son who is committed to transmitting the teachings of his father in Tzippori.[2] But Rabbi Ḥama

2. See *Sages* III, Part Five, where I deal extensively with the figure of Rabbi Yishmael.

is convinced that the real treasure is to be found only far from home, and so he sets out to Rebbi's beit midrash to find it.

**Rabbi Ḥama's Return to Lod**

The Talmud describes Rabbi Ḥama's return home to Lod and his encounter there with his son, Rabbi Oshaya:

> Rabbi Ḥama bar Bisa went and sat twelve years in the academy. When he came back he said: I will not do as the son of Ḥakinai did. He entered and sat down in the local beit midrash. He sent a message to his home that he had returned. His son, Rabbi Oshaya, came and sat before him. Rabbi Oshaya asked him about a talmudic law. Rabbi Ḥama saw that Rabbi Oshaya's studies were sharply honed, and he felt disheartened. He said [to himself]: Had I stayed here, I too would have had offspring like this. Rabbi Ḥama entered his house and his son entered as well. Rabbi Ḥama stood up before him because he thought that he wanted to ask him about talmudic laws. His wife said to him: Does a father stand before his son? Rami bar Ḥama applied the following verse to him: "The three-ply cord is not easily severed." This refers to Rabbi Oshaya, the son of Rabbi Ḥama bar Bisa. (Ketubot 62b)

The story begins with a strong sense of alienation. Rabbi Ḥama has been away from home for so many years that he and his son do not recognize one another.[3] Only when he returns does he discover that the true treasures – both Torah learning and his own son – are to be found back at home, and there was no reason to travel in the first place. The story ends with a sense of awe at the continuity between the generations: "The three-ply cord is not easily severed." In the generation after the Bar Kokhba revolt and the Hadrianic decrees, it was rare to find a

3. H. Safrai, "Women in the Beit Midrash: Challenge and Criticism" [Hebrew], in *A Good Eye: Discussion and Polemic in Jewish Culture: A Festschrift for Tova Ilan*, ed. N. Ilan (Raanana: 1999), 177. For a literary analysis of this story with an up-to-date bibliography, see S. Post, "The Nature of Criticism in Rabbinic Stories in the Babylonian Talmud" (PhD diss., Bar Ilan University, 5770), 183–185.

student who grew up learning from his grandfather and experienced the sense of assuredness that comes of generational continuity. But as we will see in the next section, Rabbi Oshaya entered the world of the sages with a sense of security, confidence, and connection to the generations that preceded him.

**Studying with His Grandfather, Rabbi Bisa**

Among the laws of damages discussed in the Talmud is the question of whether someone may seal his pipe if doing so is likely to cause damage to his downstairs neighbor:

> Rabbi Oshaya said: The courtyard owner can prevent the owner of the pipe from sealing the pipe. Rabbi Ḥama the father of Rabbi Oshaya said: The courtyard owner cannot prevent the owner of the pipe from sealing it. They went and asked Rabbi Bisa. He said to them: The courtyard owner can prevent him from sealing it. Rami bar Ḥama applied the following verse to him: "The three-ply cord is not easily severed" [Eccl. 4:12]. This refers to the son of Rabbi Ḥama the son of Rabbi Bisa. (Bava Batra 59a)

Rabbi Bisa, the grandfather of Rabbi Oshaya, is familiar to us as one of the sages of Lod in the generations after the Bar Kokhba revolt.[4] In this story, he sides with his grandson in a disagreement between father and son, suggesting that the son is the superior scholar. Throughout the Talmud, Rabbi Ḥama is frequently referred to as "the father of Rabbi Oshaya." Very few sages are named for their sons. But of course, the greatest compliment one can pay a father is to identify him with reference to his son, since a father feels only pride, not envy, for his own son.[5]

## RABBI OSHAYA'S MOVE FROM LOD TO TIBERIAS

Rabbi Oshaya, who grew up in Lod alongside his father and studied in the beit midrash of Bar Kappara, left home to study in the new beit

4. Rosenfeld, *Lod and Its Sages*, 111.
5. B.Z. Bacher, *Legends of the Amora'im of the Land of Israel*, 1 (Tel Aviv: 5685), 92, note 5.

midrash founded by Rabbi Ḥiya in Tiberias. The Talmud describes a rancorous exchange between Rabbi Oshaya and Bar Kappara, his former teacher.

The story deals with the halakhic debate between Beit Shammai and Beit Hillel about the law governing a woman who has given birth to a daughter. According to the Torah, a woman must bring a sacrifice once eighty days have passed since the birth. Even if she miscarries, she is still obligated to bring this sacrifice. If during those eighty days she becomes pregnant and miscarries again, she need not bring a second sacrifice. But Beit Shammai and Beit Hillel disagree about the case of a woman who miscarries on the night after the eightieth day. Must she bring another sacrifice for the second miscarriage, or is it still regarded as having taken place within eighty days of the first one? Beit Shammai rules that the woman is exempt from an additional sacrifice; Beit Hillel rules that she is not. The Talmud relates the following story in connection with this legal dispute:

> Rabbi Oshaya was often in attendance before Bar Kappara. He left him and came before Rabbi Ḥiya. One day Rabbi Oshaya met Bar Kappara and asked him: Concerning a man who had three seminal emissions on the eve of the eighth day after his previous emission, what does Beit Hillel say in this case? (Keritot 8a)

The Talmud elaborates at length on the nature of the halakhic question that Rabbi Oshaya asks Bar Kappara. But we will skip ahead to Bar Kappara's response, in which he references Rabbi Ḥiya's Babylonian origins:

> Bar Kappara said to him: What does the Babylonian say in this case?[6] Rabbi Oshaya did not say anything in response.

6. Rabbi Yoḥanan frequently uses the term "Babylonian" to refer to those students who came to the Land of Israel from Babylonia. For a list of sources, see M. Harpaz, "Rabbi Yoḥanan bar Nappaḥa: The Man and his Deeds" [Hebrew] (PhD diss., Tel Aviv University, 5735), 284.

> Bar Kappara then asked again, regarding another topic: What does the Babylonian say in this case? Rabbi Oshaya was silent and did not say anything. Bar Kappara then said to him: We need the teachings of Iya?[7] Let us return to first principles. The verse states "or for a daughter," and this comes to include a case in which a woman miscarries on the eve of the eighty-first day. (Keritot 8a)

Bar Kappara responds confrontationally to the student who abandoned his hometown beit midrash to go study with Rabbi Ḥiya in Tiberias.[8] Bar Kappara's sharp tongue is familiar to us from his interactions with Rabbi Yehuda HaNasi and the members of his circle.[9] We can hear in his words the personal affront of a teacher who watches as his student, a local boy and the grandson of his friend, leaves him to study with the new scholar who has recently arrived from Babylonia and whose Torah is all the rage among the younger generation. In response to the wave of interest in the new beit midrash, he insists, "Let us return to first principles." In Bar Kappara's beit midrash, halakha is derived from its biblical sources, as we saw with the case of Sifrei Zuta. And so Bar Kappara says to the student who has forsaken him, "Teachings that derive from halakhic exegesis are right here. You don't need to go look for new sources; you just need to delve into the sources we already have." Bar Kappara teaches Rabbi Oshaya the ruling by Beit Hillel that when the Bible says, "At the completion of her period of purification for a son or for a daughter" (Lev. 12:6), it includes the night after the eightieth day as well.

This teaching of Hillel appears not in our Mishna but in the Sifra, a halakhic midrash on the Book of Leviticus:

7. Rashi explains that Iya was a derogatory name for Rabbi Ḥiya. See the story about when Rabbi Yehuda HaNasi was insulted by Rabbi Ḥiya, and called him Iya (Mo'ed Katan 16a). For further discussion, see Y. Frankel, *The Aggadic Story: Unity of Form and Content* [Hebrew] (Raanana: 2004), 199.
8. Albeck describes Rabbi Oshaya's early education in neutral terms: "Rabbi Oshaya began studying with Bar Kappara and Rabbi Ḥiya." See Albeck, *Introduction to the Talmuds*, 163.
9. See *Sages* III, Part Five.

> And when it says "Or for a daughter," it comes to include one who miscarries on the eve of the eighty-first day. She is obligated to bring a sacrifice as per Beit Hillel, while Beit Shammai exempts her. (Sifra, *Tazria* 1)

Who is the author of this midrash? The Sifra as a whole is associated with the school of Rabbi Akiva.[10] But not all of Rabbi Akiva's teachings were known to the Galilean sages; some sources were known only to the sages of the south. Rabbi Ḥiya taught Rabbi Oshaya the debate between Beit Shammai and Beit Hillel, but it seems he was not familiar with this particular exegesis. And so Bar Kappara returns his student to first principles, reminding him of the biblical verses that are the source for halakhic exegesis. He shows Rabbi Oshaya that by doing so, he can find the answer to his question.

### THE SOURCES OF RABBI OSHAYA'S LEARNING

Rabbi Oshaya's most famous teachings date to his period of study in Rabbi Ḥiya's beit midrash. He became a leading disciple of Rabbi Ḥiya, working alongside him to canonize Rebbi's mishnayot while also dedicating himself to studying material external to this corpus. Several sources refer to those teachings that were contemporaneous with Rebbi's Mishna but were excluded from it as "*baraitot* of Rabbi Ḥiya and Rabbi Oshaya."

Perhaps the statement that best captures Rabbi Oshaya's role in the development of the Mishna is Rabbi Zeira's categorical assertion:

> Any teaching not taught in the academy of Rabbi Ḥiya or in the academy of Rabbi Oshaya is inaccurate, and you should not raise a challenge from it in the beit midrash. (Ḥullin 141a)

As we can see, the Mishna was studied intensively in the beit midrash of Rabbi Ḥiya and Rabbi Oshaya. Even if all the teachings of the sages were transmitted orally by means of students who memorized and

10. On the differences between the school of Rabbi Akiva and the school of Rabbi Yishmael, see Epstein, "The Midrash of Rabbi Yishmael and Rabbi Akiva" in *Literature of the Tanna'im*, 521–536.

repeated them, it was during this period that the sages began referring to the Mishna as a book and regarding it as the foundation for all their learning.[11] We have already noted that Rabbi Ḥiya and Rabbi Oshaya did not just align themselves closely with Rabbi Yehuda HaNasi's Mishna, but also had access to collections of mishnayot with which Rebbi was not familiar. As a result of their respect for and close study of Rebbi's mishnayot, Rabbi Ḥiya and Rabbi Oshaya's *baraitot* were regarded as authentic, and any source they had not studied was dismissed as inaccurate. The seniority of these sages strengthened the authority of Rebbi's Mishna, but it also conferred authority on *baraitot* that emerged from their own *batei midrash*.

In the following midrash on a verse from Ecclesiastes, Rabbi Levi describes the wealth of sources available to the sages of the period:

> Rabbi Abba bar Kahana went to a certain place. He found Rabbi Levi sitting and interpreting the following verse: "A man to whom God gives wealth, possession, and honor, so that he lacks nothing of all that he desires, yet God does not give him power to enjoy them, but a stranger enjoys them" [Eccl. 6:2]. "Wealth" – this refers to Torah. "Possessions" – these are laws. "Honor" – this is the Tosefta. "So that he lacks nothing of all that he desires" – these are the great collections of the Mishna; for instance, the Mishna of Rav Huna, the Mishna of Rabbi Oshaya, and the Mishna of Bar Kappara. (Y. Horayot 3:5 [48c])[12]

Rabbi Levi describes Rabbi Oshaya as one of those sages in possession of a "great collection" of mishnayot. This is not a reference to the volume of his teachings, but to their significance – they too deserve to be known as Mishna, albeit not as "the Mishna."[13]

11. In the chapter about Rabbi Yoḥanan, we will consider the question of whether Rebbi's Mishna was written down during his era or transmitted orally.
12. Rabbi Oshaya's Mishna was not identical to that of Rebbi. There are several points at which Rabbi Oshaya cites other mishnayot which differ from Rebbi's Mishna and which are based on sources from the school of Bar Kappara or other sages.
13. Albeck, *Introduction to the Talmuds*, 20.

### THE CAESAREAN PERIOD: A COSMOPOLITAN CENTER[14]

Following the death of Rabbi Yehuda HaNasi and the death of Rabbi Ḥiya shortly thereafter, Rabbi Oshaya established himself in Caesarea. There he became the head of a large beit midrash and founded a community of sages who would become famous for compiling the Jerusalem Talmud on Nezikin.[15] Caesarea was the Roman Empire's regional administrative center. It was populated by intellectuals such as the Christian theologian Origen, who compiled the Hexapla, a comparative study of the Hebrew Bible and its Greek translations.[16] Rabbi Oshaya was conversant with Christian and pagan scholars, as sources such as the following attest:

> A philosopher asked Rabbi Oshaya: If circumcision is so precious, why was Adam not created circumcised? He replied: Why do you shave your sideburns but leave your beard? He said: Because it grew with me in my folly. He said: If so, you should blind your eye and cut off your hands because they grew with you in your folly. He said: Is this what our argument has come to? I am astonished. He said: I cannot send you away empty-handed. Whatever was created in the first six days requires further work. Mustard needs sweetening, vetches need sweetening, wheat needs grinding, and man too needs to be perfected. (Genesis Rabba 11)

Rabbi Oshaya tries to outsmart the philosopher by telling him that his acts of grooming are a way of modifying the original created form of the human body. Just as Jews circumcise their flesh, the philosopher shaves his sideburns. The philosopher offers an intelligent response that gains him the upper hand: He shaves his sideburns, which grew in his youth, during his years of folly; but he does not shave his beard, which grew during his years of maturity. He mocks Rabbi Oshaya, saying, "Is this

14. L.I. Levine, *Caesarea Under Roman Rule* (Leiden, Netherlands: 1975).
15. Lieberman, *The Talmud of Caesarea* [Hebrew] (Jerusalem: 5691).
16. Y. Baer, "The People of Israel, the Christian Church, and the Roman Empire" [Hebrew], *Zion* 21 (5716): 15–22. Baer surveyed a long series of rabbinic midrashim and compared them to Origen's teachings.

what our argument has come to?" At this point, Rabbi Oshaya has no choice but to teach the philosopher about humanity's role in perfecting the created world.

This argument is reminiscent of Rabbi Akiva's exchange with Turnus Rufus two generations earlier:[17]

> Turnus Rufus the wicked asked Rabbi Akiva: Which works are more beautiful? Those of the Holy One, or those of flesh and blood?
>
> He said to him: Those of flesh and blood are more beautiful.
>
> Turnus Rufus the wicked said to him: Look at the heavens and the earth. Are you able to make anything like them?
>
> Rabbi Akiva said to him: Do not talk to me about something which is high above mortals, things over which they have no control, but about things which are common among human beings.
>
> He said to him: Why do you circumcise?
>
> He said to him: I also knew that you were going to say this to me. I therefore anticipated your question when I said to you: A work of flesh and blood is more beautiful than that of the Holy One. Bring me wheat stalks and white bread.
>
> He said to him: The former is the work of the Holy One, and the latter is the work of flesh and blood. Is not the latter more beautiful?
>
> Bring me bundles of flax and garments of Beit She'an.
>
> He said to him: The former are the work of the Holy One, and the latter are the work of flesh and blood. Are not the latter more beautiful?
>
> Turnus Rufus said to him: Since God desires circumcision, why does one not emerge from his mother's belly circumcised?
>
> Rabbi Akiva said to him: And why does his umbilical cord come out of him? Does his mother not cut his umbilical cord? So

17. M. Hirshman, *A Rivalry of Genius: Jewish and Christian Biblical Interpretation in Late Antiquity* (New York: SUNY Press, 2012).

> why does he not come out circumcised? Because the Holy One only gave Israel the commandments as a means of refinement. (Tanḥuma, *Tazria* 7)

The midrash speaks to man's responsibility to take action in the world. It is incumbent upon a person not just to take care of the created world, but also to take part in creation: to mill wheat into flour for baking bread, and to spin flax for weaving clothing. Rabbi Akiva's response, as well as that of Rabbi Oshaya, emphasizes man's ability to rise above the natural world in which he lives. But their interlocutors – Turnus Rufus and the philosopher – are unable to accept that man can improve upon God's creation. Their debate became a major bone of contention between Jews and Christians.

### RABBI OSHAYA'S RELATIONSHIP WITH THE PATRIARCHAL HOUSE AFTER REBBI'S DEATH

Following the death of Rabbi Yehuda HaNasi and Rabbi Ḥiya, Rabbi Oshaya became one of the leaders of the generation. The patriarchs who succeeded Rebbi, Rabban Gamliel III and Rabbi Yehuda Nesiya, relied on his advice and approval. For instance, the Jerusalem Talmud relates that when Rabban Gamliel the son of Rebbi wanted to apply the tithing requirement to Syria, it was Rabbi Oshaya who prevented him from doing so (Y. Ḥalla 4:4 [60a]).

Rabban Gamliel III was succeeded by Rabbi Yehuda Nesiya, whom we will consider in his own right. For the time being, we will focus on one story that captures the elderly Rabbi Oshaya's relationship with the young new patriarch:

> A story:[18] Rabbi Oshaya the Elder and Rabbi Yehuda Nesiya were sitting and learning. Rabbi Yoḥanan ran in and whispered into the ear of Rabbi Oshaya the Elder, "A priest with crushed testicles" [Deut. 23:1] – what is the law as to whether he may marry the

18. The Jerusalem Talmud uses the term *dilmah* (spelled with a *heh*) to introduce a story. This term, which is related to the Greek word for "drama," must be distinguished from the Babylonian Talmud's *dilma* (spelled with an *alef*), an expression of doubt.

> daughter of proselytes? Rabbi Yehuda Nesiya said to him: What did he say to you? He said to him: Something to which even the carpenter son of carpenters[19] would not be able to answer. He did not ask me about a proselyte woman…nor did he ask me about a daughter of Israel…. He asked me about the daughter of proselytes. (Y. Yevamot 8:2 [9b])

This story presents Rabbi Oshaya and Rabbi Yehuda Nesiya as equals. When Rabbi Yoḥanan enters the scene with a request to clarify a matter of law, he turns to Rabbi Oshaya the Elder in what seems to be a coded exchange. There is no suggestion that he is insulting the honor of the patriarch. Even the patriarch seems to recognize that he is subservient to Rabbi Oshaya, at least when it comes to halakhic matters.

The following source, too, offers a window into the relationship between Rabbi Yehuda Nesiya and Rabbi Oshaya:

> Rabbi Yehuda Nesiya sent Rabbi Hoshaya a piece of meat and a flask of wine. He replied: Through us you have carried out the obligation to send gifts to the poor [Est. 9:22]. He went and sent him a calf and a barrel of wine. He sent back to him: Through us you have carried out the obligation to send food gifts to one another [Est. 9:22]. (Y. Megilla 1:4 [70d])

This story is humorous and should not be taken too seriously; it would be inaccurate to conclude from this story, as others have suggested, that Rabbi Oshaya was a poor man who could barely support himself.[20] Rabbi Oshaya was not poor, and he was insulted by the patriarch's gift, which did not befit his stature. He therefore responded, "Through us you have carried out the obligation to send gifts to the poor," referring to the penultimate chapter of the scroll of Esther. Presumably he is suggesting that

19. The phrase "carpenter son of carpenters" is a reference to a learned man who is the son of learned men. See Avoda Zara 50b. Presumably Rabbi Oshaya is referring to the continuity of Torah learning through the generations, which his family represents.
20. Hyman in *Tanna'im and Amora'im*, 115.

the patriarch's gift was so modest that it was tantamount to charity. Rabbi Yehuda Nesiya hurries to bring the sage a more suitable gift, and thus he merits his blessing, also a reference to the scroll of Esther: "Through us you have carried out the blessing to send food gifts to one another."[21] By invoking these verses, Rabbi Oshaya teaches Rabbi Yehuda Nesiya that he is deserving of a more respectable gift.

## RABBI YOḤANAN DOES NOT ABANDON HIS ELDERLY TEACHER

Rabbi Oshaya's leading student was Rabbi Yoḥanan, who would travel to Caesarea when he had questions about various mishnayot.[22] As Rabbi Yoḥanan came into his own as a scholar, Rabbi Oshaya felt that he was no longer needed, but Rabbi Yoḥanan continued to consult with him.

The following story illustrates Rabbi Oshaya's towering stature during the final years of his life. The Mishna in Tractate Eiruvin asks, "How do we extend the cities?" That is, how do we widen the perimeter of the city so as to extend the boundary within which one may travel on Shabbat? Since the Mishna was taught orally, there was no orthographic tradition, and so the sages of the Talmud were left to debate whether the word for extend, *me'abrin*, is spelled with the Hebrew letter *ayin* (from the same root as the word for pregnancy) or *alef* (from the same root as the word for limb or wing).[23] The Talmud relates that Rabbi Yoḥanan learned this mishna from Rabbi Oshaya, who spelled it with an *alef*. He brings proof for this position:

> Rabbi Yoḥanan said in the name of Rabbi Oshaya: They add a limb to it. He set his gaze on him and stared at him. He said to

21. This is also how we should interpret the parallel source in Megilla 7a, as is documented in the better manuscripts and as the Ritva states in his commentary. Rashi, who interprets this source differently, was misled by an inaccurate version of the text. For more on this example see D. Rosenthal, "Sources from the Land of Israel and their Transmission to Babylonia" [Hebrew], *Cathedra* 92 (5759): 7–8.
22. Y. Eiruvin 5:1 [19a].
23. A similar debate takes place in Tractate Avoda Zara regarding the spelling of *eideihem*, "their festivals," referring to idolatrous celebrations. See Epstein, *Text of the Mishna*, 8–12.

> him: Why are you staring at me? When I needed your teachings, it was a pleasure for you. Now that I don't need your teachings anymore, should I abandon you? For thirteen years, Rabbi Yoḥanan came before his teacher, even though he did not require his instruction.[24] Rabbi Shmuel said in the name of Rabbi Zeira: It would have been sufficient had he simply greeted his teacher every day, for whoever greets his teacher, it is as if he greets the Divine Presence. (Y. Eiruvin 5:1 [22b])

In a parallel source in the Babylonian Talmud, Rabbi Yoḥanan says:

> Eighteen years I spent with Rabbi Oshaya Beribbi, and I learned only one thing from him about our Mishna: How do we extend the cities? With an *alef*. (Eiruvin 53a)

This source suggests that Rabbi Yoḥanan had to learn the proper spelling of this term in the Mishna. Only when he heard Rabbi Oshaya teach that "they add a limb to it" did he understand that *me'abrin* is spelled with an *alef*. Later, he quoted this teaching in Rabbi Oshaya's name.

Upon hearing himself quoted on one such occasion, Rabbi Oshaya set his gaze on his student. Rabbi Yoḥanan sensed that he was being criticized[25] and said, "Why are you staring at me? When I needed your teachings, it was a pleasure for you. Now that I don't need your teachings anymore, should I abandon you?" Perhaps by this point, Rabbi Oshaya was too frail to maintain close relationships with his students. But Rabbi Yoḥanan never stopped visiting him, even if he had nothing new to learn from his teacher. For thirteen years he continued to make regular pilgrimages to his teacher in Caesarea. The Talmud relates that Shmuel said in the name of Rabbi Zeira, a sage of the next generation,

24. A parallel passage appears in Y. Sanhedrin 11:4 [30b]: "Rabbi Hoshaya's face brightened [to hear Rabbi Yoḥanan quote him]. He said to him: When I needed your teachings, it was a pleasure for you. Now that I don't need your teachings anymore, should I abandon you? Rabbi Yoḥanan continued to study with Rabbi Hoshaya for thirteen years, until he no longer required his instruction."
25. Throughout the Jerusalem Talmud, the phrase *tala einav* (literally, "he cast his eyes") connotes a critical gaze.

that it would have been sufficient for Rabbi Yoḥanan to enter the World to Come by the merit of this action alone, for anyone who greets his teacher is regarded as if he greets the Divine Presence.

For his part, Rabbi Oshaya secured his place as a key link in the transmission of Torah from the generation of the *Tanna'im* to that of the *Amora'im*, that is, from the sages of the Mishna to the sages of the Talmud.

*Chapter Six*

# Rabbi Yehoshua ben Levi

> Rabbi Yehoshua ben Levi said: Every day, a heavenly voice resounds from Mount Horeb proclaiming: Woe to the creatures who insult the Torah. For one who does not occupy himself in Torah is considered an outcast, as is stated, "A golden nose ring in the snout of a swine, a beautiful woman bereft of reason" [Prov. 11:22]. And it says: "And the Tablets are the work of God, and the writing is God's writing, engraved on the Tablets" [Ex. 32:16]. Do not read "engraved" (*ḥarut*) but "liberty" (*ḥerut*) – for there is no free individual, except for one who occupies himself with the study of Torah. And whoever occupies himself with the study of Torah is elevated, as is stated, "And from Matana [gift, understood as a reference to Torah] to Naḥaliel, and from Naḥaliel to Bamot [heights]" [Num. 21:19]. (Avot 6:2)

Rabbi Yehoshua ben Levi was the leader of the transitional generation in Lod. There are no sources about his origins or his upbringing.[1] But we know that he was a student in Bar Kappara's beit midrash in Lod,

1. B.Z. Rosenfeld, "Rabbi Yehoshua ben Levi: The Man and His Public Life" (PhD diss., Bar Ilan University, 5742), 15, 43–52.

where he became the leading sage and local halakhic authority.[2] When we examine the rabbinic corpus, Rabbi Yehoshua ben Levi is one of the most commonly mentioned sages of the transitional generation, both in halakhic and aggadic literature. Several of these accounts seem richly embellished, and often it is difficult to distinguish between literary and historic accounts of his life.[3]

In the mishna from *Pirkei Avot* quoted above, Rabbi Yehoshua ben Levi hears a heavenly voice warning against casting aspersion on the Torah. He wishes to impart his understanding of how to attain freedom by means of direct involvement with Torah study. By studying Torah, he maintains, a person is freed from dependence on others and is elevated above earthly preoccupations.

Rabbi Yehoshua ben Levi himself was a link between heaven and earth. Several midrashim deal with his visions of the heavenly realms, such as the famous story of Moses ascending on high. While some stories describe his earthly work in administering public affairs in Lod, others link his earthly virtues with his otherworldly qualities.

### A SAGE IN A MIXED CITY: THE RELATIONSHIP BETWEEN JEWS AND NON-JEWS

The city of Lod underwent a dramatic transformation in the year 192. It was declared a polis and, as such, it was administered like any Roman city: Coins were minted, administrative and governmental institutions were founded, and the city became populated by numerous clerks.[4] A source from Rabbi Yehoshua ben Levi's beit midrash about those commandments which apply only in the Land of Israel speaks to the pagan presence in the city:

> Rabbi Yehoshua ben Levi would instruct his students:[5] Do not purchase vegetables for me except from the garden of [a non-Jew

2. Rosenfeld, "Rabbi Yehoshua ben Levi," 113.
3. D. Levine, "Is Talmudic Biography Still Possible?" [Hebrew], *Jewish Studies* 46 (5769): 41–64.
4. Rosenfeld, "Rabbi Yehoshua ben Levi," 178–183.
5. I am following the version of the story that appears in Tractate Shevi'it, though a parallel version appears in Tractate Demai.

named] Sisera. [Elijah the prophet,][6] may his memory be for good, came to him [one of the students] and said to him: Go tell your master: This garden does not belong to Sisera. It belonged to a Jew and Sisera killed him and took it from him. If you want to impose a stringent rule, do so upon yourself, but do not impose it on your colleagues. (Y. Shevi'it 9:9 [39a])[7]

The halakhic commentary on this source is mired in controversy.[8] The Talmud is speaking of agricultural produce from both Jewish and non-Jewish farmers that arrives in the marketplace in Lod. Rabbi Yehoshua ben Levi wishes to be stringent and to buy only from the non-Jewish farmers during the sabbatical year. He regards the entire region as part of the Land of Israel, and so he seeks a plot of land that is not beholden to the laws of the sabbatical year. Then Elijah appears to reveal what is hidden from human eyes: The garden of Sisera does not actually belong to this non-Jew, but is rather Jewish land that was appropriated by a non-Jew, perhaps during the Hadrianic persecution. And so this garden, too, is subject to the laws of the sabbatical year.

It is not uncommon for Elijah to appear suddenly in stories that feature Rabbi Yehoshua ben Levi. In this story, he informs the sage that he has no choice but to act like everyone else. He must retract his ruling about the garden of Sisera, and instead teach that all fruit of this region is permissible to eat. Elijah tells him that if he wants to be more stringent, he may do so on his own, but he may not impose his stringencies on the public.

In spite of his willingness to interact with pagan non-Jews, Rabbi Yehoshua ben Levi has no tolerance for the Christians who began making their home in Lod. The Jerusalem Talmud relates the following story about Rabbi Yehoshua ben Levi's grandson, who nearly choked on a bone before a healer arrived on the scene:

6. The commentators filled in the words "Elijah the prophet," because he is most commonly associated with the phrase "may his memory be for good." See the version of Rabbi Shlomo Sirlio in his commentary on Y. Demai.
7. See the parallel source in Y. Demai 2:1 [22c].
8. For a summary of the various positions, see Felix, *Yerushalmi Shev'it*, 430–431.

> Rabbi Yehoshua ben Levi's grandson swallowed something dangerous. Someone came along and whispered to him in the name of Jesus ben Pantera and he recovered.[9] When he went out, Rabbi Yehoshua ben Levi said to him: What did you whisper over him? He said: Such and such a word. He said to him: It would have been better for him if he had died rather than needing your whispering. And it was "as an error that went out from before the ruler" [Eccl. 10:5]. (Y. Shabbat 14:4 [14d])

Even if we do not know the identity of the man who tried to heal Rabbi Yehoshua ben Levi's grandson, it is clear that he was associated with Jesus, who is referred to as "ben Pantera" throughout talmudic literature.[10] Rabbi Yehoshua ben Levi responds harshly and violently, both to this healer and to other Christians. He fights them fiercely, particularly when they initiate polemical arguments in which they quote biblical verses in an effort to convert those Jews who were sitting on the fence.[11] One talmudic source speaks of a neighbor of Rabbi Yehoshua ben Levi who would harass him by engaging in such polemics:

> There was a certain heretic in the neighborhood of Rabbi Yehoshua ben Levi who used to harass him constantly by citing biblical verses [to prove his sectarian doctrines]. One day Rabbi Yehoshua took a rooster and tied it between the feet of a bed and stared at it intently. He thought: When that moment comes [that the rooster's comb pales and it stands on one foot], I will curse the heretic. When that moment came, however, Rabbi Yehoshua

9. On the Christian practice of whispering over a wound, see Rosenfeld, "Rabbi Yehoshua ben Levi," 180, note 30.
10. S. Lieberman, "Notes on the First Chapter of Ecclesiastes Rabba," *Studies in the Torah of the Land of Israel* [Hebrew] (Jerusalem: 5751), 53–69; D. Rokeah, "Ben Satara is Ben Pantera" [Hebrew], *Tarbiz* 39 [5730]: 13–15; D. Schwartz, "What Should He Have Said? 'And Live by Them'" [Hebrew], *Martyrdom and the Sanctity of Life*, eds. Y. Gafni and A. Ravitzky (Jerusalem: 5753), 73–76.
11. R.T. Herford, *Christianity in the Talmud* (London: 1903).

> dozed off. Thereupon Rabbi Yehoshua said: One may deduce from this occurrence that it is not proper to do this. It is written, "His mercy is upon all His creations" [Ps. 145:9]. And it is written, "Also for the righteous to punish is not good" [Prov. 17:26]. (Berakhot 7a)

This story is based on a talmudic tradition according to which God's anger flares only at one moment each day, and at this moment, the attribute of divine justice stands poised to inflict harm. The changing color of the rooster's comb serves as a sign that this moment has arrived. Armed with this knowledge, Rabbi Yehoshua ben Levi plotted to curse the heretic at the moment when he would be most susceptible to harm. However, he fell asleep and missed his opportunity. Based on this experience, Rabbi Yehoshua ben Levi concluded that it does not befit a righteous person to utter an imprecation, even if it is directed at someone who is truly wicked. This story sheds light on Rabbi Yehoshua ben Levi's personality and his interactions with those around him. Elsewhere he speaks about the value of guarding one's tongue and speaking with the utmost caution:

> Rabbi Yehoshua ben Levi said: A person should never emit an indecent expression from his mouth, for the Torah went out of its way by adding eight letters so as not to include an indecent expression, as it is stated, "From the animals that are pure and from the animals that are not pure" [Gen. 7:8]. (Pesaḥim 3a)

The Bible avoids the use of the word "impure" and instead uses the wordier phrase, "the animals that are not pure," as a way of avoiding indecent language. Rabbi Yehoshua ben Levi teaches that we should follow the Bible's example in our own speech as well.

### RABBI YEHOSHUA BEN LEVI'S RELATIONSHIP WITH THE ELDERS OF THE GENERATION

In rabbinic literature, the sages generally rank highest on the social ladder. But Rabbi Yehoshua ben Levi has his own hierarchy:

> Rabbi Yehoshua ben Levi said: If there is a leader and an elder, the leader takes precedence over the elder who is not a leader.[12] What is the reason? "You stand this day all of you before the Lord your God: the leaders of your tribes, your elders, and your officers, all the men of Israel" [Deut. 29:10]. And it is written: "Then Joshua gathered all the tribes of Israel to Shechem, and summoned the elders, the leaders, the judges, and the officers of Israel" [Josh. 24:1]. Thus Moses gave precedence to the leaders over the elders, while Joshua gave precedence to the elders over the leaders. Moses, because all of them were his disciples, gave precedence to the leaders over the elders. Joshua, because all of them were not his disciples, gave precedence to the elders over the leaders. Moses, because he did not yet have need of them for conquering the land, gave precedence to the leaders over the elders. Joshua, because he needed them for conquering the land, gave precedence to the elders over the leaders. Moses, because he was not fatigued by Torah study, gave precedence to the leaders over the elders. Joshua, because he was fatigued by Torah study, gave precedence to the elders over the leaders. (Y. Horayot 3:5 [48b])

In this passage, the term "elders" refers to the sages, and the term "leaders" refers to those officials who dealt with public affairs. The leaders were the government officials who stood at the administrative helm. The sages did not have to bear the burden of civil administration, and so their position in the municipal hierarchy was not clear. In the words of one contemporary scholar, "What is surprising about Rabbi Yehoshua ben Levi's position is that although he was a leading sage, he prioritized the leaders over the elders. This is because he had tremendous respect for

12. This is the version that appears in the fragments of the Jerusalem Talmud, p. 286, line 7. S. Lieberman demonstrates that this is the most accurate version: "The reason, as the Jerusalem Talmud explains, is because the public needs its leaders." See Lieberman, *Yerushalmi Horayot: Studies in the Torah of the Land of Israel* (Jerusalem: 5751), 252–253. G. Alon disagrees and favors the version that appears in the printed text, in which the elders take precedence over the leaders. But he does not succeed in explaining the text. See Alon, *Studies in Jewish History* 2, 52–53 and note 145.

the difficult role of the leaders, particularly during the tough economic period of the Roman anarchy."[13]

### EXTRADITING A CRIMINAL TO THE ROMAN RULERS: THE STORY OF ULLA BAR KUSHAV

Several rabbinic sources deal with the question of whether a Jew may turn someone over to the Roman authorities. These sources were not merely theoretical, but had real-world implications. Criminals who were wanted by the authorities endangered all the residents of any city that harbored them, as the following source attests:

> If a group of men were walking along and non-Jews met them and said: Give us one of your number that we may kill him, and if not, we will kill all of you – then let them kill all of them, but let them not extradite a single Jew. But if they singled one out, such as they singled out Sheva the son of Bikhri [II Sam. 20], let them extradite him, that they not all be killed.
>
> Rabbi Shimon ben Lakish said: Now this applies only if the man is already slated for execution, as was Sheva the son of Bikhri. But Rabbi Yoḥanan says: It applies even if he is not slated for execution, as was Sheva the son of Bikhri.
>
> Ulla bar Kushav was wanted by the government. He fled to Lod, to the vicinity of Rabbi Yehoshua ben Levi. The agents of the king came and surrounded the town. They said: If you do not give him to us, we will destroy the town. Rabbi Yehoshua ben Levi went to him [Ulla] and convinced him to give himself up. Until then, Elijah, may his memory be for good, had been accustomed to reveal himself to him. When this stopped occurring, Yehoshua ben Levi fasted several times. As a result, Elijah revealed himself to him. Elijah said to him: Should I reveal myself to informers? Rabbi Yehoshua ben Levi said to him: Did I not simply carry out a rule of the law? Elijah said to him: Is this indeed the law for pious ones? (Y. Terumot 8:4 [47b])

13. Rosenfeld, "Rabbi Yehoshua ben Levi," 177.

This story is based on a talmudic debate between Reish Lakish and Rabbi Yoḥanan regarding a halakhic source in the Tosefta about extraditing a criminal for the sake of saving the lives of the rest of the community. The Tosefta distinguishes between the case where it is a specific individual who is wanted, and the case where the authorities demand any one person on behalf of the community. In the latter case, it is forbidden to choose an individual to sacrifice so that the others might live, because the value of human lives cannot be quantified. The talmudic sages disagree about the authorities' motivation in demanding a specific individual: Does it indicate that he is a criminal like Sheva the son of Bikhri, or is he just selected at random?

This discussion is followed by the story of Ulla bar Kushav, an unfamiliar figure. He appears to be a criminal who fled to Lod in search of refuge. With the entire population of the city in mortal danger, Rabbi Yehoshua ben Levi decides to take responsibility for extraditing the man. His decision is consistent with the law in the Tosefta, since it is this specific individual who is wanted by the authorities. Notably, he does not just extradite the criminal; he rather convinces him to give himself up, in what was surely a distressing and difficult exchange.

Even though Rabbi Yehoshua ben Levi follows the law, Elijah regards him as unfit to receive his presence. When Elijah stops revealing himself to him, Rabbi Yehoshua ben Levi realizes that he is being punished by God. After he fasts and prays, Elijah returns to him with the following rebuke: "Should I reveal myself to informers?" Elijah's labeling of Rabbi Yehoshua ben Levi as an informer is quite harsh. After all, one shudders to imagine what would have happened if he had not turned over the wanted man; the entire city would have been destroyed. Elijah insists that the law is different for pious ones.[14] But in this case, the law

14. The law of the pious ones is not part of halakha, but it reflects a sense of what constitutes proper conduct. See S. Safrai, "The Law of the Pious in Tannaitic Literature" [Hebrew], *And Behold There Is No Joseph: A Collection of Essays in Memory of Yosef Amoray* (Tel Aviv: 5733), 136–152. This essay also appears in S. Safrai, *In the Period of the Temple and the Mishna: Studies in Jewish History* [Hebrew], 2 (Jerusalem: 5754), 501–517.

of the pious presumably would have led to widespread massacre for the sake of saving the life a lone criminal.[15]

### RABBI YEHOSHUA BEN LEVI: A RIGHTEOUS MAN BEYOND COMPARE

One of the most marvelous accounts that features Rabbi Yehoshua ben Levi is the story of his relationship to lepers. Leprosy has long inspired fear and repulsion, and until recently, lepers were regarded as contagious and incurable.[16] While some recoiled and kept their distance from the afflicted, others took pity on them and sought ways to defend and protect them. The Talmud describes both of these responses:

> Rabbi Yoḥanan pronounced: Beware of the flies of the man afflicted with leprosy. Rabbi Zeira never sat in a place where the wind blew from their direction. Rabbi Elazar never entered their tents. Rabbi Ami and Rabbi Assi never ate any of the eggs coming from the alley in which they lived. Rabbi Yehoshua ben Levi attached himself to them and studied Torah, for he said, "[Torah is like] a loving gazelle and a graceful doe" [Prov. 5:19]. If it bestows grace upon those who study it, would it not also protect them? (Ketubot 77b)

The first few sages listed here, all from the Galilee, treat the lepers as we would expect: They know that such individuals are afflicted with a contagious illness and need to be quarantined. Each sage has a different way of protecting himself. Rabbi Yoḥanan issues a proclamation that sets the tone, and his students follow his example, each keeping a safe

15. Much has been written about this story and its implications for the laws of extraditing criminals to foreign governments. See M. Alon, "Extradition in Jewish Law" [Hebrew], *Teḥumin* 8 (5747): 263–309, with regard to turning over the criminal Nakash to France. Also see the response written during the Holocaust about the question of whether one may sacrifice one life for the sake of saving many. See, for instance, Rabbi S. Efrati, *From the Valley of Murder* [Hebrew] (Jerusalem: 5721), part 1: "Saving from Death by Causing a Child to Die."
16. A. Shoham-Steiner, *Deviants Against Their Will: Lunatics and Lepers in Jewish Society in Europe of the Middle Ages* [Hebrew] (Jerusalem: 5768).

distance between himself and contagion. Only the final sage listed here (who precedes the others chronologically) behaves differently: Rabbi Yehoshua ben Levi attaches himself to the lepers and teaches them Torah. He believes he is immune as a result of his interpretation of a verse from Proverbs which analogizes Torah to a graceful doe. Rabbi Yehoshua ben Levi reasons that if Torah bestows grace on those who study it, then surely it will also protect them from harm.

### RABBI YEHOSHUA BEN LEVI BETWEEN HEAVEN AND EARTH

Biographers of the sages describe Rabbi Yehoshua ben Levi in fantastical terms, as a righteous man, a miracle man, and even a heavenly being.[17] These descriptions reflect a series of *aggadot* in which Rabbi Yehoshua ben Levi straddles this world and the heavenly realm. Each story connects Rabbi Yehoshua ben Levi's mythical persona to the very human individual who lives among his people and is concerned for their welfare. These *aggadot* have given rise to rich literary analysis. Even Yonah Frankel, who generally regards each talmudic story as a self-contained literary unit, linked several stories from various sources to create a more composite profile of this figure.[18] In the next section, we will enter into the mythical world of Rabbi Yehoshua ben Levi, where myth and reality coincide.

### The Confrontation with the Angel of Death

Just after the Talmud depicts Rabbi Yehoshua ben Levi sitting and studying among the lepers, the *Aggada* breaks through the bounds of realism and casts Rabbi Yehoshua ben Levi into the heavenly realm:

17. See M. Margaliot, *Encyclopedia of the Sages of the Talmud and the Geonim* [Hebrew] (Tel Aviv: 5733); Y. Rihlin, *Bar Livai* (Newark, N.J.: 5766); Hyman, *Tanna'im and Amora'im*; Z. Frankel, *Introduction to the Jerusalem Talmud*; Bacher, *Legends of the Amora'im*, 1.
18. Y. Frankel, "The Figure of Rabbi Yehoshua ben Levi in the Stories of the Babylonian Talmud" [Hebrew], *Proceedings of the Sixth World Congress of Jewish Studies*, 3 (5733), 403–417. Frankel acknowledges the problematic nature of this methodology and the risk that it will lead the scholar astray and give rise to errors: "We would not attempt this approach if not for the fact that it leads ultimately to a new interpretation of the story."

> When it came time for him to die, the Angel of Death was instructed: Go and carry out his wish. When he came and showed himself to him, Rabbi Yehoshua ben Levi said: Show me my place [in heaven]. He said: By your life. He said: Give me your knife lest you frighten me on the way. He gave it to him.
>
> On arriving there the angel lifted him up and showed him his place. Rabbi Yehoshua ben Levi jumped and dropped to the other side. The angel seized him by the corner of his cloak. Rabbi Yehoshua ben Levi said: I swear that I will not go back. The Holy One, Blessed Be He, said: If he ever had an oath of his annulled he must return; but if not, he need not return. The Angel of Death said to him: Give me back my knife. He would not return it. A heavenly voice went forth and said to him: Give it back to him, for it is required for mortals.
>
> Elijah heralded him proclaiming: Make room for the son of Levi, make room for the son of Levi. As he proceeded on his way he found Rabbi Shimon bar Yoḥai sitting on thirteen stools of gold. He said to him: Are you the son of Levi? He said: Yes. He said to him: Has a rainbow ever appeared in your lifetime? He said: Yes. He said: If that is so, you are not the son of Levi. The fact, however, is that there was no such thing [in his lifetime], but he thought: I must not take credit for myself. (Ketubot 77b)

This story is often featured in aggadic collections, books of folk legends, and literature about proper moral conduct.[19] It links the sage who has no fear of death and sits among the lepers with a mythical persona who believes he can defeat the Angel of Death and save humanity from mortality. Ironically, while Rabbi Yehoshua ben Levi achieves otherworldly status in this story, the Angel of Death is depicted as weak and pathetic.[20]

19. R. Kushlovsky found over forty versions of this story. She analyzed the religious and societal influences that shaped each version and gave it its particular slant. See R. Kushlovsky, "Rabbi Yehoshua ben Levi and the Angel of Death" [Hebrew], *Story Follows Story: Encyclopedia of the Jewish Story* (Ramat Gan: 2009), 261–277.
20. R. Kushlovsky, "Humor and Its Role in the Versions of the Story of Rabbi Yehoshua ben Levi and the Angel of Death," *Jerusalem Studies in Jewish Folklore*, vol. 19–20 (5758), 329–344.

According to this story, Rabbi Yehoshua ben Levi is not seeking self-aggrandizement when he requests to see his place in heaven. Rather, he is motivated by the desire to dispossess the Angel of Death of his knife for the sake of humanity. At this point, a heavenly voice intervenes and restrains Rabbi Yehoshua ben Levi, telling him that mortality is a necessary condition of being human; humans need to die as much as they need to live.

From Rabbi Yehoshua ben Levi's conversations with Rabbi Shimon bar Yoḥai (Rashbi), it becomes increasingly clear that the former is not acting out of his own self-interest. Rabbi Yehoshua ben Levi in fact lies to Rashbi when he is asked if a rainbow was seen in his lifetime, lest he seem immodest; it was a well-known principle that a rainbow did not appear during the lifetime of anyone who was completely righteous. The Talmud does not clarify whether Rashbi figured out that his interlocutor was indeed Ben Levi, but that is of no consequence. It is Rabbi Yehoshua ben Levi's self-sacrifice and devotion to humanity that gives this story its power.

### Take Two: Rabbi Ḥanina bar Papa Follows Rabbi Yehoshua ben Levi

The following talmudic story also features a sage who seeks to overcome the Angel of Death:

> Rabbi Ḥanina bar Papa was a close friend [of Rabbi Yehoshua ben Levi]. When it came time for him to die, they said to the Angel of Death: Go and do his will. He went and revealed himself to him. He said to him: Leave me alone for thirty days so I can review my learning, for it is said: Happy is he who comes here with his learning under his belt. He left him alone. After thirty days, he came and revealed himself to him. He said: Show me my place [in heaven]. He said to him: By your life. He said to him: Give me your knife lest you frighten me on the way. He said to him: You wish to do what your friend did to me? He said to him: Bring me a Torah scroll and check – is there anything written in it that I have not fulfilled? He said to him: Did you attach yourself to lepers and study Torah? And even so, when he departed from the world,

> the pillar of fire stood between him and the world. And we are taught that the pillar of fire stands only for one or two individuals in each generation.
>
> Rabbi Alexandri approached the pillar of fire and said to Rabbi Ḥanina: Act for the sake of the honor of the sages. But he did not oblige. Act for the sake of your father's honor; but he did not oblige. Act for the sake of your own honor; and the pillar of fire went away. (Ketubot 77b)

Even on the most cursory reading, we cannot help but note the differences between Rabbi Ḥanina bar Papa and Rabbi Yehoshua ben Levi. Rabbi Ḥanina fulfilled the entire Torah, but he did not risk his life to learn among lepers. Unlike Rabbi Yehoshua ben Levi, who does not ask anything for himself and works on behalf of humanity to rid the world of death, Rabbi Ḥanina seeks recognition and is preoccupied with his own honor: He needs thirty days to review his learning in order to secure his place in heaven; he announces that he has fulfilled the entire Torah; and even the pillar of fire defers to his honor.

**The World According to Rabbi Yehoshua ben Levi: The Uppermost Below, and the Lowly Above**

> Rabbi Yosef the son of Rabbi Yehoshua ben Levi took ill and slipped into a comatose state. When he regained his health, his father asked him: What did you see in the next world? He said: I saw an inverted world! The uppermost in this world are below in the World to Come, and the lowly in this world are above in the World to Come. Rabbi Yehoshua ben Levi said to his son: My son, you have seen a clear world. [Rabbi Yehoshua ben Levi asked]: And how are we regarded there? [Rabbi Yosef answered]: Just as we are regarded here. And I heard them saying: Fortunate is he who comes here with his learning in his hand. And I also heard them saying: Those executed by the government – no other person can stand in their midst. Who are those holy martyrs? If we say that he refers to Rabbi Akiva and his colleagues, is it merely because they were executed by the government that they attained

> such a lofty level, and for no other reason? Rather, Rabbi Yosef refers to those executed in Lod. (Pesaḥim 50a)

The world that Rabbi Yehoshua ben Levi's son glimpses appears to him to be inverted, but according to his father, this is how the World to Come actually looks: learned scholars stand beside those executed by the government. The Talmud clarifies that the latter does not refer to martyrs like Rabbi Akiva, whose place in the World to Come was already secured by the merit of his good deeds in this world. Rather, this term refers to those executed in Lod, perhaps to those Jews who were extradited to the Roman government.[21] The bottom line, as Rabbi Yehoshua ben Levi tells his son, is that one's place in the World to Come does not necessarily correlate with one's place in this world. Rabbi Yehoshua ben Levi internalizes this knowledge, and it informs everything he does.

### Rabbi Yehoshua ben Levi Awaits the Messiah with the Lepers

> Rabbi Yeshoshua ben Levi met the prophet Elijah, who was standing at the entrance of the cave of Rabbi Shimon bar Yoḥai. He said to him: Will I enter the World to Come? He answered him: If the Lord wishes it. Rabbi Yehoshua ben Levi said: I saw two people, but I heard the voices of three. He said to Elijah: When will the Messiah come? Elijah answered him: Go and ask the Messiah himself. [Rabbi Yehoshua ben Levi asked:] And where is he sitting? [Elijah responded:] At the gate of the city. And what is his distinguishing feature? He is sitting among paupers afflicted with disease. All of them untie and tie all of their bandages at the same time. But he unties and ties his bandages one by one, for he says: I might be needed at any moment, so I deal with my bandages this way so that I will not be delayed.

21. Elsewhere the Talmud identifies those executed in Lod as Lulianus and Pappus (see *Sages* II, Part Four). They were certainly not among the righteous, but nonetheless, the fact that they died at the hands of the government accorded them special status in the heavenly realm.

> Rabbi Yehoshua ben Levi went to the Messiah. He said to him: Peace be unto you, my master and teacher! The Messiah said to Rabbi Yehoshua ben Levi: Peace be unto you, son of Levi. Rabbi Yehoshua ben Levi asked him: When is the master coming? He answered him: Today.
>
> Rabbi Yehoshua ben Levi went back to Elijah. He asked him: What did he say to you? He said: He said, peace be unto you, son of Levi. Elijah said to him: He has assured you and your father that you are both destined to enter the World to Come. Rabbi Yehoshua ben Levi said: He lied to me, for he said to me, I am coming today, yet he has not come. Elijah said to him: This is what he was saying to you: "Today, if you heed His voice" [Ps. 95:7)]. (Sanhedrin 98a)[22]

This story begins and ends with Rabbi Yehoshua ben Levi's anxiety about whether he will have a place in the World to Come. In order to receive his answer, he must go to the area where the lepers congregate at the entrance to the city.

When the story opens, Rabbi Yehoshua ben Levi meets Elijah at the cave of Rashbi. He thinks he hears a third voice as well, which makes him wonder about the Messiah. At this point, Rabbi Yehoshua ben Levi forsakes his concern for his own fate and preoccupies himself with a question that affects the general welfare: When will the Messiah come and redeem the world from suffering? This is the story's most crucial moment. Rabbi Yehoshua ben Levi encounters the Messiah at the gates of Rome, sitting among the downtrodden. Only he is accustomed to coming so close to such individuals, since he would often study Torah among the lepers.[23] Rabbi Yehoshua ben Levi asks

22. Yonah Frankel draws on the parallel source in the Jerusalem Talmud (Y. Taanit 1:1 [64a]) to uncover the message that underlies this story: It is whether the Jews repent which determines when the Messiah will come from the gates of Rome. See Y. Frankel, "The Figure of Rabbi Yehoshua ben Levi," 411.

23. The talmudic story alludes to a verse from Isaiah: "Surely he took up our pain and bore our suffering, yet we considered him punished by God, stricken by Him, and afflicted" (Is. 53:4). It is impossible to miss the Christian overtones, though Yonah Frankel chooses to overlook them. See ibid., 403–417.

the Messiah, "When is the master coming?" The Messiah's pledge to come "today" awakens hope and then, presumably when the sun sets, disappointment. Ben Levi returns to Elijah, who explains the Messiah's response: He will come today, but only if the Jews heed God's voice. Elijah consoles Rabbi Yehoshua ben Levi and assures him of his place in the World to Come.

### THE DEATH AND BURIAL PLACE OF RABBI YEHOSHUA BEN LEVI

The following inscription was discovered in Beit She'arim:

> This coffin... / The daughter of Rabbi Yehoshua... / May the memory / Of the righteous be for a blessing.

Another inscription was found in an inner chamber of that same room:

> This is the coffin of Rabbi Yehoshua the....

A third inscription was discovered nearby:

> This is the coffin of Kyra Mega / the wife of Rabbi Yehoshua / Ben Levi, peace.

In the 1970s, Nahman Avigad published these archeological findings from Beit She'arim and asserted:

> These three inscriptions seemingly refer to the members of a single family: Yehoshua the father, Mega his wife, and his unnamed daughter.... There are grounds to speculate that Kyra Mega's husband was buried in the adjacent coffin where the name Rabbi Yehoshua appears, and that his full name was Rabbi Yehoshua ben Levi.[24]

24. N. Avigad, *Beit She'arim*, 3 [Hebrew] (Jerusalem: 5732), 79.

In 2005, B.Z. Rosenfeld lent credence to Avigad's claims when he used these inscriptions as the basis for his description of Rabbi Yehoshua ben Levi's family.[25]

Four years later, these speculations once again came to the fore when a burial cave from the talmudic period was discovered on the grounds of the guest house of a moshav in Tzippori. The entrance to the cave bore the inscription: "This is the burial place of Rabbi Yehoshua ben Levi HaKappar." The owner of the guest house, Mitch Pilcer, excitedly called Atra Kadisha, the *haredi* organization that deals with holy sites, to investigate his findings. The heads of the organization heard about the inscription but expressed no interest whatsoever, insisting that Rabbi Yehoshua ben Levi could not possibly be buried there. When Pilcer asked how they could be so sure, they invoked a rabbinic source:

> Seven individuals entered heaven while still alive, and they are: Seraḥ bat Asher, Bitya bat Pharaoh, Ḥiram king of Tzur, Eved king of the Kushites, Eliezer the servant of Abraham, and the grandson of Rabbi Yehuda HaNasi, and Yaavetz, and some say also Rabbi Yehoshua ben Levi. (Kalla Rabbati 3:23).

If you are in search of Rabbi Yehoshua ben Levi, they said, you must look for him in heaven.

25. B.Z. Rosenfeld, "The Sage Yehoshua ben Levi and His Wife Kyra Mega" [Hebrew], *Cathedra* 224 (Winter 5765): 11–36.

*Chapter Seven*

# Rabbi Yannai and His Circle

Rabbi Yannai was one of the most important contemporaries of Rabbi Yehuda HaNasi. He lived in Kfar Akhbara in the Upper Galilee, near Safed.[1]

### WHO WAS RABBI YANNAI'S TEACHER?

We know nothing about Rabbi Yannai's origins and early education. Several statements in the Talmud, most of which are attributed to Rabbi Yehuda HaNasi himself, describe Rabbi Yannai as

1. The location of Akhbara is the subject of considerable debate. According to *Sefer Yuḥasin* by Rabbi Abraham Zacuto (article five), Akhbara is in the Lower Galilee. The midrash in Leviticus Rabba (16:2) tells of a peddler who would hawk his wares near Tzippori and its environs and reached Akhbara. Although the midrash refers explicitly to the environs of Tzippori, M. Margaliot writes in his critical edition (p. 350, note to line 3), "It is in the Upper Galilee, south of Safed." Rabbi Isaac Luria, also known as the Ari, who lived in Safed in the sixteenth century, writes that he visited the grave of Rabbi Yannai with his student Rabbi Haim Vital: "We came to a village called Akhbara, where we entered the cave of Rabbi Yannai inside an orchard" (*The Book of Visions*, 135–136). S. Klein also cites archeological evidence that suggests that Akhbara is east of Kfar Ḥanania, in the Upper Galilee.

being under the patriarch's aegis, presumably before he moved to the Upper Galilee.[2]

In the absence of more solid evidence, we will focus on one source that describes Rabbi Yannai learning from another sage, who served as an intermediary between him and Rabbi Yehuda HaNasi:

> Rabbi Zeira said: I took great pains in bringing this question before Rabbi Assi, and Rabbi Assi brought it before Rabbi Yoḥanan, and Rabbi Yoḥanan brought it before Rabbi Yannai, and Rabbi Yannai brought it before Rabbi Natan ben Amram, and Rabbi Natan ben Amram brought it before Rebbi: From when does an idolater child convey impurity as if he had an emission? And he said to me: From when he is one day old. And when I came to Rabbi Ḥiya, he told me: From when he is nine years and one day old. And when I came and presented the matter to Rebbi, he said to me: Leave aside my view, and adopt the view of Rabbi Ḥiya, who says: When does an idolater child convey impurity as if he had an emission? When he is nine years and one day old. (Avoda Zara 36b)

We will not enter into all the halakhic details. Suffice it to say that Rabbi Zeira is searching for an answer to his halakhic question, which is relayed from student to teacher until it reaches the patriarchal court. Once he receives the authoritative answer of the patriarch, Rabbi Ḥiya, the master of *baraitot*, comes along and gives a different answer entirely. Rabbi Zeira then proceeds to relay Rabbi Ḥiya's answer to Rebbi, who instructs him to accept Rabbi Ḥiya's answer instead of his own.[3]

2. Epstein writes that Rabbi Yannai was a student of Rebbi. But the evidence he cites is Avoda Zara 36b, which suggests that there was another sage who served as a link between them. See Epstein, *Text of the Mishna*, 234.
3. Several scholars have argued that all the sages mentioned in this passage are members of a single generation, but this seems impossible given that Rabbi Yehuda HaNasi precedes Rabbi Yoḥanan, who precedes his disciples. HaRav Malakhi HaKohen concludes from this passage that Rabbi Zeira and Rebbi were contemporaries: "We can prove that [Rabbi Zeira] lived during Rebbi's time, because he said, 'And when I came and presented the matter to Rebbi,' and the Tosafot explain that anytime one person is quoted as having brought a question to another, the text is teaching that

In this story, Rabbi Natan ben Amram serves as the link between Rebbi and Rabbi Yannai. Who is this sage? His name does not appear elsewhere in rabbinic literature, except in some of the manuscripts, where it serves as a variant for Rabbi Yonatan ben Amram. We encountered this sage in the famous story in which he criticized the patriarch for caring only about Torah scholars and not providing for the general populace.[4] As the story relates, Rabbi Yonatan ben Amram dressed up as an ordinary man during a period of drought and entered the storehouse where Rebbi was standing guard. Before agreeing to give him provisions, Rebbi tested him: "Have you studied Mishna and Torah?" When the sage answered in the negative, Rebbi asked, "If so, how can I support you?" The disguised Torah scholar responded, "Support me like a dog and a raven." Rebbi agreed. Rabbi Shimon, the son of Rebbi, recognized Rabbi Yonatan immediately and explained to his father why the sage acted as he did: "He never wanted to benefit from the honor of Torah" (Bava Batra 8a).

Rabbi Shimon the son of Rebbi calls attention to Rabbi Yonatan ben Amram's humility: He refused to derive any benefit or honor from the Torah he had learned, unlike the patriarch. Presumably he was a fitting teacher for Rabbi Yannai.

### THE RELATIONSHIP TO NON-RABBIS: BETWEEN REBBI AND RABBI YANNAI

With that story as background, we now turn to the following story about Rabbi Yannai:

> A story is told of Rabbi Yannai who went walking along the way and saw a man who was exceedingly wealthy. He said to him: Will you accept my hospitality? He said to him: Yes. Rabbi Yannai

they all lived in the same generation, and so they all were contemporaries of Rebbi." See *Yad Malakhi* (Berlin: 5617), Laws of the Talmud, law 588. More convincingly, H. Albeck argues that two different versions of this story were at some point combined; one featured Rabbi Zeira and one featured Rabbi Ze'iri, who was in fact contemporaneous with Rebbi. See Albeck, *Introduction to the Talmuds*, 621. This does not really make a difference for our purposes, because in any case, Rabbi Natan ben Amram served as an intermediary between Rebbi and Rabbi Yannai.

4. For more on this story in its context, see *Sages* III, Part Five. Also see Meir, *Yehuda HaNasi*, 202.

> brought him into his house and gave him food and drink. He tested him in Torah and found that he knew none. He tested him in Mishna and found that he knew none. He tested him in *Aggada* and found that he knew none. He tested him in Talmud and found that he knew none. He said to him: Hold the glass and recite the Grace. He said to him: Yannai should bless in his own home. Rabbi Yannai said to him: Will you be able to understand and repeat what I say? He said: Yes. Rabbi Yannai said: Say, "The dog ate Yannai's bread." The guest stood up, took hold of Rabbi Yannai, and said to him: You have my inheritance, and you are withholding it from me! He said to him: What is this inheritance of yours which I have? The man said: Once I passed by a school, and I heard the voice of the children saying, "Torah is commanded to us by Moses, an inheritance of the congregation of Jacob" [Deut. 33:4]. The Torah does not read, "the inheritance of Yannai," but rather "the inheritance of the congregation of Jacob." Rabbi Yannai said to him: How have you merited to eat at my table? The guest said: Never in my life have I heard gossip and repeated it to the person spoken about, nor have I ever seen two people quarreling without making peace between them. Rabbi Yannai said: You exhibit such proper conduct, and yet I called you a dog?! Rabbi Yannai recited about him: "To him who sets his path" [Ps. 50:23] – this is one who takes care to follow in its path. He will merit a great reward. For Rabbi Shmuel bar Naḥman said: The path of proper conduct preceded Torah by twenty-six generations, as it is written, "To guard the path to the Tree of Life" [Gen. 3:24]. "The path" refers to the path of proper conduct, and only after that does it mention "the Tree of Life," which is Torah. (Leviticus Rabba 9:3)

This story does not cast Rabbi Yannai in a very positive light, to say the least. Rabbi Yannai is walking along the way when he invites a respectable-looking man to his home. This opening scene already raises the question of whether he would have invited this man had he been dressed in rags. As the meal proceeds, it becomes clear that the guest is ignorant of Torah, and Rabbi Yannai has nothing he can discuss with him. He tries to bring the meal to a close by inviting the guest to lead the Grace After Meals, but in so doing, he stoops so low as to call his guest a dog. The guest calls him on the insult. He tells Rabbi Yannai that even though he has never studied Torah, he has heard schoolchildren quoting a verse declaring that Torah is the inheritance of all of Israel. The Torah belongs to Jews of all colors and stripes, and it is not the exclusive province of any elite group, no matter how learned that group may be. And so the Torah of Rabbi Yannai also belongs to an ignorant wayfarer. The man also tells Rabbi Yannai that he never spoke poorly of another person, nor did he ever avoid an opportunity to reconcile two individuals. Here, too, he alludes to his present situation: He wishes to disregard Rabbi Yannai's harsh words and to reconcile with him.

Rabbi Yannai understands that the man before him is deserving of his respect, even if he is not a member of the beit midrash. He honors the guest with a blessing appropriate to his stature, invoking a verse from Psalms: "He who sacrifices a thanksgiving offering honors Me, and to him who sets his path, I will show the salvation of God" (Ps. 50:23). The word for "him who sets," *vesam,* can also be read as *vesham,* which relates to the Hebrew word *shuma,* an evaluation. One who evaluates and checks the path he follows in life merits divine salvation. The word "path," *derekh,* leads Rabbi Yannai to a verse from Genesis about the "path to the Tree of Life." He suggests that there is a path that precedes the path to the Tree of Life, Torah. This is *derekh eretz,* the "path of proper conduct." One's moral intuitions, the path of proper conduct, precedes Torah knowledge by twenty-six generations.

This midrash reflects the tension between those who believe in Torah for the elite, and those who believe in Torah for the masses. It is intended to shock us into an awareness of the risk of assuming that Torah is the exclusive province of a select few, and that everyone else should be denied access.[5]

5. This story offers a critique of a society that equates Torah knowledge with prestige. The fact that the editors of the Talmud chose to include this story reflects their awareness of this social reality. See A. Rivlin, *Equivalent to Them All: The Sages' Pedagogy* [Hebrew] (Raanana: 1995): 29.

There are striking parallels between the story of Rabbi Yannai and his guest and the story of Rabbi Yehuda HaNasi during the drought. Rabbi Yannai calls his guest who is ignorant of Torah a dog; Rabbi Yoḥanan tells Rebbi to sustain him "like a dog or a raven." Rebbi and Rabbi Yannai both have similar orientations. The two of them represent a world in which knowledge of Torah is the only valid entry ticket. Someone who has learned neither Mishna nor Torah may not be among Rabbi Yannai's houseguests and may not eat from Rabbi Yehuda HaNasi's table.

Presumably it was after his encounter with his houseguest that Rabbi Yannai elected to change his ways and began studying Torah with Rabbi Yonatan ben Amram, the man who had sensitized the patriarch to the rest of humanity.

### WHO IS THE MAN WHO DESIRES LIFE: RABBI YANNAI AND GUARDING ONE'S TONGUE

We have seen several stories about Rabbi Yannai's sharp tongue. In light of these sources, it is interesting to consider one of the classic rabbinic stories about Rabbi Yannai and the value of watching one's language. The story appears as a midrash on a famous passage from the Book of Psalms:

> "Who is the man who desires life, who loves days, that he may see goodness? Keep your tongue from evil and your lips from speaking lies. Turn from evil and do good; seek peace and pursue it" [Ps. 34:12–14]. There is a story of a peddler who used to go around the towns in the vicinity of Tzippori crying out: Who wishes to buy the elixir of life? Come and taste! He entered Akhbara and came close to the house of Rabbi Yannai. Rabbi Yannai was sitting and expounding in his room, and he heard him call out: Who wishes to buy the elixir of life? He said to him: Come here and sell it to me. He said to him: Neither you nor people like you require that which I have to sell. Rabbi Yannai pressed him. The peddler went up to him and brought out the Book of Psalms and showed him the verse, "Who is the man who desires life." What is written immediately thereafter? "Keep your tongue from evil and your lips from speaking lies." Rabbi Yannai said: All my life I have been reading this passage, but I did not know

> how to explain it, until this peddler came and taught me "Who is the man who desires life." (Leviticus Rabba 16:2)

We opened with a story about Rabbi Yannai and his guest who was ignorant of Torah. There we saw that Rabbi Yannai was so convinced that Torah was given only to those who study it that he failed to treat his guest properly. His guest taught him that Torah in fact belongs to everyone, and anyone can teach it.

In this story, Rabbi Yannai, sequestered in his home, learns from a peddler carrying a book of Psalms. The peddler teaches him how to understand the juxtaposition of the verses in the passage from Psalms: "Who is the man who desires life…? Keep your tongue from evil." As the peddler teaches him, the man who watches his language is the one who desires life and sees length of days. This is a pearl of wisdom that the great and hoary sage had not yet acquired. He appreciates the peddler's words and admits that he was previously ignorant of their value.

### RABBI YANNAI'S SOCIAL CIRCLE

Several sources depict Rabbi Yannai as the leader of a group of sages who chose a way of life that combined agricultural labor with intellectual study. The sources about these sages date to the third century. The following source, for instance, suggests that the members of Rabbi Yannai's circle were particularly strict about purity matters:

> Rabbi Shimon ben Lakish went to visit the family of Rabbi Yannai. The women saw him and fled from him. He said to them: I can come home with you! I am like a non-rabbi [*am haaretz*] with respect to purity laws. (Y. Demai 2:3 [23a])

Rabbi Shimon ben Lakish, also known as Reish Lakish, belongs to the next generation of sages, and so we will discuss him later in this book. In this story, he comes to visit Rabbi Yannai's circle and encounters a group of women who are afraid to come too close. It seems that the women's concern reflects the extremely strict observance of these laws on the part of Rabbi Yannai and his circle. Reish Lakish assures them that he is an *am haaretz* when it comes to purity laws, and therefore he is permitted to be in their vicinity. That is, he does not adopt the stringencies of other sages when it comes to such matters.[6]

We find evidence that Rabbi Yannai and his circle worked the land in a source that describes Rabbi Yoḥanan's instructions regarding the use of fruit grown during the sabbatical year. Presumably Rabbi Yoḥanan offered these instructions after Rabbi Yannai's death, when Rabbi Yannai could no longer do so himself:

> Rabbi Yoḥanan instructed those of the house of Rabbi Yannai to grind with a millstone, in accordance with the view of Rabbi Shimon, and to prepare olives in an olive crusher, in accordance with the view of the rabbis. Rabbi Yoḥanan instructed those of the house of Rabbi Yannai not to accept oil as payment for their wine, but rather to take payment in cash. (Y. Shevi'it 8:6 [38b])

Rabbi Yoḥanan's instructions indicate that the members of Rabbi Yannai's circle harvested wheat, olives, and grapes, which they then sold commercially. They seem to have been part of a closed agricultural commune, intimately connected to the earth. There are those who even compare them to the sectarian groups of the Second Temple period.[7]

### GO OUT AND PLANT DURING THE SABBATICAL YEAR: RABBI YANNAI'S INVOLVEMENT IN ECONOMIC MATTERS

Several other sources offer a very different picture of Rabbi Yannai, one in which he is not part of a closed and isolated commune. According to these sources, Rabbi Yannai was deeply involved in the life of his community, and associated with individuals who were not part of his circle or were not even Torah scholars.

6. On the strict observance of the purity laws by certain sages at the end of the tannaitic period, see G. Alon, "Areas of Purity Law" [Hebrew], *Studies in Jewish History*, 1 (Tel Aviv: 5738), 148–176. Also see *Sages* III, Part Two, on those sages who were strict about such matters.
7. See A. Oppenheimer, "Those of the House of Rabbi Yannai" [Hebrew], *Studies in the History of the People of Israel and the Land of Israel*, 4 (Haifa: 5738), 137–145.

One important source describes Rabbi Yannai as a charity collector. After quoting a *baraita* stating that it is forbidden for the charity collector to reassign funds that were designated for a specific purpose, the Talmud asks:

> Is this so? But Rabbi Yannai would borrow money [from the charity fund] and later repay! Rabbi Yannai was different, for it was agreeable to the poor that he should do this, because as long as he delayed in repaying, he could force people to donate more and bring in more funds to the poor. (Arakhin 6a)

The Talmud suggests that Rabbi Yannai would borrow money from the charity fund, thereby emptying the coffers. He would then appeal to the public to refill them. This was a win-win situation: The poor were pleased that more money was collected for them; Rabbi Yannai could enjoy the loans; and the public was no worse for what they didn't know.[8]

One of Rabbi Yannai's more extreme halakhic rulings offers an indication of his involvement with the public welfare and his concern for the general economic situation. As we have seen, the years after Rabbi Yehuda HaNasi's death marked the beginning of the Roman anarchic period. The tax burden on the farmers grew heavier. So long as the empire was ruled by a central administration, there was more of a balance between the needs of the army and those of the citizens. But as the Roman government grew weaker, the army became increasingly abusive of the populace.[9]

During the anarchic period, the Romans suspended the exemption from taxes during the sabbatical year, which had been in effect since the period of Alexander the Great and Julius Caesar. As the Jerusalem Talmud put it, the "coercive kingdom" now enslaved the farmers (Y. Shevi'it 4:2 [35a]). The Jews, who observed halakha stringently but could not withstand the economic pressure, sought creative solutions to enable them to

8. The early and late medieval commentators were troubled by the ethical problems posed by this source. See Rabbi Joseph Karo, *Beit Yosef* on *Yoreh De'ah* 259. Also see the Radbaz's commentary on Maimonides, *Mishneh Torah*, Laws of Gifts to the Poor 8:5.
9. See Avi-Yonah, *Rome and Byzantium*, 80–91.

work the land during the sabbatical year.[10] Rabbi Yannai gave the most sweeping authorization: "Go out and plant during the sabbatical year" (Sanhedrin 26a). This dispensation, which appears in a variant form in the Jerusalem Talmud, generated extensive discussion throughout subsequent generations. How could a sage be so bold as to permit working the land during the sabbatical year because of economic strain? Various answers were suggested.[11] But perhaps it should not be surprising given that Rabbi Yannai lived in an agricultural community. He was a learned sage but he was also sensitive to the financial pressures of those he lived among.

Elsewhere in the Talmud, too, Rabbi Yannai is depicted as an independently minded spiritual leader who is no stranger to agricultural concerns. In one source we find him judging the case of a man whose tree extended beyond the boundaries of his house into the public domain:

> Rabbi Yannai had a tree that extended into the public domain. There was a certain man who also had a tree that extended into the public domain. Members of the public came and objected to this man's incursion into the public space. The man appeared before Rabbi Yannai. Rabbi Yannai said to him: Leave for now, and come back tomorrow. At night Rabbi Yannai sent someone to cut down his own tree. The next day the man came again before Rabbi Yannai. Rabbi Yannai said to him: Go and cut down the tree. The man said to him: But you also have a tree extending into the public domain! Rabbi Yannai said to him: Go see. If my tree is cut down, then cut down yours as well; but if my tree is not cut down, then you need not cut down yours. (Bava Batra 60a)

10. S. Safrai, "Early Historiographical Sources on the Land of Israel" [Hebrew], in *Studies in Historiography*, eds. M. Stern et al. (Jerusalem: 5748), 79.
11. Rashi and Tosafot justify this dispensation by contending that the sabbatical year during that time was rabbinically (rather than biblically) mandated, and had lost its sanctity. The Raavad (Rabbi Abraham ben David, France, 1125–1198) wrote that Rabbi Yannai's statement applied only to those lands that the Babylonian exiles had not reclaimed, in which the laws of the sabbatical year were mandated only rabbinically. See Raavad, *Laws of Shemitta and Yovel* 1:11. The Tosafot also suggested that it was a matter of life and death, since the Jews could not survive the tax burden. See Felix, "Go Out and Plant During the Sabbatical Year" [Hebrew], *Yerushalmi Shevi'it*, 2, 339–353.

Rabbi Yannai lives among the people – among quarreling neighbors who often give each other the evil eye. He knows that only if he holds himself to the highest standards, as if he too were subject to the evil eye of the public, can he uphold his own rulings.

Another story depicts Rabbi Yannai picking fruit during the intermediate days of a festival. The following year, he saw that all the farmers had desisted from picking their fruit during this period. And so Rabbi Yannai followed their example, waiting until the festival was over (Mo'ed Katan 12b).

We may conclude from these sources that there are no grounds for the comparison between Rabbi Yannai's circle and the insular sectarian groups of the Second Temple period. Rabbi Yannai belonged to a group of individuals who combined their Torah study with agricultural labor and were strict about matters of purity. But their leaders involved themselves with the general public. As we have seen, Rabbi Yannai was aware of and responsive to the concerns of ordinary merchants and farmers.

### HAVE WE LABORED FOR NAUGHT? RABBI YANNAI AND REBBI'S MISHNA

One of the central questions confronting students of Talmud is how the Mishna of Rabbi Yehuda HaNasi became the canonical book of Jewish law. The question is even more complicated when we consider the status of the Mishna during the transitional generation between the mishnaic and talmudic periods. At that time, Rebbi's Mishna had just been compiled, and had not yet assumed its central place in the rabbinic consciousness. Certainly other collections of mishnayot containing alternative halakhic opinions could be found in other *batei midrash* throughout the Land of Israel. The Mishna of Rebbi, too, had not yet been closed, nor had the principle been established that "the halakha follows the anonymous opinion."[12]

12. Y. Brandes, "The Origins of the Laws of Halakhic Ruling" (PhD diss., Hebrew University of Jerusalem, 5762), 167–186. For a concise summary of his argument, see "Rabbi Yoḥanan's Revolution in Halakhic Ruling" [Hebrew], *In the Ways of Peace: Issues in Jewish Thought for Shalom Rosenberg*, eds. B. Ish Shalom (Jerusalem: 5767), 515–536.

What was Rabbi Yannai's attitude toward the Mishna of Rebbi and the other collections of mishnayot that circulated in his time? We can start with the announcement he made after Rebbi's death:

> When Rabbi Yehuda HaNasi died, Rabbi Yannai declared: There is no priesthood today. (Y. Berakhot 3:1 [6a])[13]

Rabbi Yannai regarded Rebbi with such esteem that he declared that even priests could touch his body. As such, he accorded him the status of royalty, since even priests may become impure when a king dies. He clearly considered Rebbi to be his own rabbi, and as we have seen, he often quoted his teachings. But he was torn when it came to the halakhic authority of Rebbi's Mishna.[14]

In one instance, his student Rabbi Yoḥanan presented him with a *baraita* that contradicted a mishna. Rabbi Yannai responded humbly: "You are asking a question in Kiddushin to little old Yannai?"

13. The source reads "Rabbi Yudan Nesiya" rather than "Rabbi Yehuda HaNasi," but it is clear that the reference is to the latter because the Jerusalem Talmud speaks about the death of his son, Rabbi Yudan son of Rabbi Yudan HaNasi. That said, many later commentators identified this sage as Rabbi Yehuda Nesiya, the grandson of Rebbi. This is the claim of A.Z. Rabbinovitz, who translated B.Z. Bacher, *Legends of the Amora'im*, 1. In his chapter on Rabbi Yannai, Bacher translated this source as, "When Rabbi Yehuda HaNasi died," but Rabbinovitz noted, "That is, Rabbi Yehuda Nesiya, the grandson of Rebbi." In light of Rabbi Yannai's relationship to Rebbi's grandson, which we will consider below, it is unlikely that he would be willing to contract impurity for such a sage.

    Rabbi Louis Ginzberg debates the identity of this sage in his *Interpretations and Insights in the Jerusalem Talmud* [Hebrew] (Newark: 5701–5721), Berakhot 3:1, 95–96. He writes:

    > There are those who thought that this is the meaning of the statement in Ketubot, "When Rebbi died, there was no more holiness" (103b, and see the Tosafot there). According to this source, Rabbi Yudan Nesiya was the holy sage, Rebbi. Certainly this was the view of Rabbi Shlomo Sirlio, who identified him as Rabbi Yehuda HaNasi in his edition of the Jerusalem Talmud. But according to the story that Rabbi Ḥiya bar Abba and Rabbi Zeira participated in the burial of Rabbi Yehuda Nesiya the grandson of Rabbi Yuda Nesiya, one cannot claim that the allusion here is to our holy Rebbi and to his grandson Rabbi Yuda Nesiya.... We need to say that Rabbi Yudan Nesiya was the grandson of Rebbi.

14. Epstein, *Text of the Mishna*, 234–236.

(Y. Kiddushin 3:6 [64b]). He then interpreted the *baraita* so that it accorded with the mishna, suggesting that the mishna need not be overturned for the sake of a *baraita*.

Elsewhere, too, Rabbi Yannai is pleased when his own teachings accord with Rebbi's Mishna. The Talmud in Yevamot recounts a fascinating story of Rabbi Yannai's circle of sages' encounter with Rebbi's authoritative Mishna. The Talmud discusses the question of whether a man may betroth a woman who is designated for levirate marriage to another man. The Babylonian sages debate the matter, and then the Talmud quotes the following dialogue:

> Rabbi Yannai said: They voted and ruled in our circle: Betrothal [to anyone but the levir] does not take effect on a woman designated for levirate marriage. Rabbi Yoḥanan said to him: Rabbi, isn't this in our Mishna? As we learned in the Mishna: One who says to a woman, behold you are betrothed to me... after your levir performs the rite of *ḥalitza* – she is not betrothed! He said to him: If I had not lifted the clay, would you have shown me the pearl that was underneath it? (Yevamot 92b)

Rabbi Yannai relates that they voted and ruled in his circle – that is, in the circle of scholars and farm laborers at Kfar Akhbara[15] – that if a

15. I do not find Epstein convincing when he writes, "Rabbi Yannai sat in the circle, that is, the court of Rebbi." See Epstein, *Text of the Mishna*, 234. He writes in note 6 that the same teaching that emerged from Rabbi Yannai's circle in the Jerusalem Talmud is taught in Rav's name in the Babylonian Talmud. Epstein writes, "Rav was part of this court, as per Gittin 58b and 59a, and the Jerusalem Talmud in chapter 5 [47b])." That is, Epstein identifies the term "circle" as referring to a court in which various sages served as judges and in which their votes were counted. Epstein assumes that this is the case because Rav was part of one such court and his teaching is identical to that of Rabbi Yannai's circle in the Jerusalem Talmud. But this is a very weak argument. Whenever Rabbi Yannai's circle is mentioned, it is clearly referring to a special group of sages. Each time it is mentioned in the Jerusalem Talmud (Maasrot 1:1, Shabbat 19:1, Pesaḥim 5:4, Yevamot 3:3), Rabbi Yoḥanan states, "The circle would question...". This could not have been Rebbi's circle, because Rabbi Yoḥanan could not have heard their questions since he was still just a young boy at the time, as we will see. Y. Felix asserts that "The term refers to a group of exemplary sages who came primarily from Rabbi Yoḥanan's beit midrash." See Y. Felix, "An Interpretation of the First Chapter

woman designated for levirate marriage is betrothed to someone else, that betrothal does not take effect. When Rabbi Yoḥanan tells his teacher that his insight appears in Rebbi's Mishna, Rabbi Yannai responds joyously, comparing Rebbi's Mishna to gold.

A parallel source in the Jerusalem Talmud suggests that Rabbi Yannai and his circle arrived at their ruling by means of biblical exegesis:

> Rabbi Yannai said: Thirty and some odd sages voted: How do we know that the betrothal of a wife to a husband cannot take effect at all in the case of a levirate widow? The Torah says, "The wife of the deceased shall not be married outside of the family to a stranger; her husband's brother will go in to her and take her as his wife" [Deut. 25:5]. The meaning is that she will not be deemed completely wed to another. (Y. Yevamot 1:1 [2c])[16]

Here too Rabbi Yoḥanan alerts his teacher to the fact that his insight already appears in Rebbi's Mishna (Kiddushin 3:5):

> Rabbi Yoḥanan said to him: And has not the Mishna made this matter perfectly clear: "After your levir will perform the rite of *ḥalitza* – she is not betrothed." (Y. Yevamot 1:1 [2c])

Rabbi Yannai delights in his student's comment:

of Maasrot" [Hebrew], in *Jews and Judaism During the Period of the Second Temple, Mishna, and Talmud: Studies in Honor of Shmuel Safrai*, eds. A. Oppenheimer et al. (Jerusalem: 5753), 289. Felix bases his claim on an article by M. Beer, "The Circle of Sages in the Land of Israel During the Amoraic Period" [Hebrew], *The Sages of the Mishna and Talmud* (Ramat Gan: 5771), 51–58. But in spite of arguments to the contrary, it still seems clear to me that the Talmud is referring to the circle of sages led by Rabbi Yannai.

16. This exegesis is cited in the Babylonian Talmud in the name of Rav, which led Epstein to link Rabbi Yannai's circle to that of Rebbi. He assumes that Rav is asserting that he was part of Rebbi's court of voters, since Rebbi founded a court to rule on lands that had been extorted from Jews, as per Gittin 58b. But as I noted above, there is no reason to link these two matters. It is perfectly reasonable to assume that a teaching that originated in Rabbi Yannai's circle might make its way to Babylonia and be quoted in Rav's name.

> And Rabbi Yannai[17] would praise[18] him: "Those who lavish gold from the purse...." [Is. 46:6]. "My son, keep sound wisdom and discretion; let them not escape from your sight" [Prov. 3:21]. "Be wise, my son, and make my heart glad, that I may answer him who reproaches me" [Prov. 27:11]. "Give instruction to a wise man, and he will be wiser still" [Prov. 9:9]. "The wise man also may hear and increase in learning" [Prov. 1:5]. (Y. Yevamot 1:1 [2c])

Rabbi Yannai responds by praising Rabbi Yoḥanan, invoking fragments of verses from the books of Isaiah and Proverbs.

But in stark contrast to the respect that Rabbi Yannai accords to Rebbi's Mishna in the sources quoted above, there is also evidence that he was at times harshly resistant to the Mishna's authority. Rabbi Yoḥanan would frequently juxtapose the sources he studied with Rabbi Yannai with the sources he studied from Rebbi's Mishna, presumably in Tzippori. In one case, the mishna in Tractate Shabbat distinguishes between the soaking of a gum resin known as asafetida in cold water, and the soaking of that same substance in vinegar. Rabbi Yoḥanan asks Rabbi Yannai a question about this mishna:

> Rabbi Yoḥanan asked Rabbi Yannai: What is the law concerning soaking asafetida in cold water? Rabbi Yannai said to Rabbi Yoḥanan: It is prohibited. Rabbi Yoḥanan said: But haven't we learned in our Mishna: We may not soak asafetida in warm water. This implies that soaking it in cold water is permitted. Rabbi Yannai said: If I cannot resolve a difficulty that you have raised from a mishna, what difference is there between me and you? Our Mishna reflects the opinion of a single individual, as it was taught in a *baraita*: We may not soak asafetida neither in hot water nor in cold water. Rabbi Yose says: In hot water it is prohibited, but in cold water it is permitted. (Shabbat 140a)

17. The source says Yoḥanan rather than Yannai, but this is a scribal error. See the parallel source in Y. Sota 2:5 [18b], which is quoted by the Tosafot.
18. The verb *kalas* is used as a term of praise in the Talmud. See Lieberman, "*Kalas Kilusin*," *Alei Ayin: An Offering of Words to Shlomo Zalman Schocken* [Hebrew] (Jerusalem: 1951), 75–81.

Rabbi Yoḥanan asks, "But haven't we learned in our Mishna?" He is referring, of course, to the Mishna of Rebbi. Rabbi Yannai responds somewhat petulantly, asking Rabbi Yoḥanan what he wants from him if he already accepts Rebbi's Mishna as canonical. Rabbi Yannai explains that although there is an opinion that permits soaking the resin in cold water,[19] it is the opinion of only one sage.[20]

In the parallel source in the Jerusalem Talmud, Rabbi Yannai says, "Have we labored for nought?" (Y. Shabbat 20:3 [17c]). Rabbi Yannai is referring to all the Torah learning that had been collected in all of the various *batei midrash*, the product of much labor and toil. Perhaps he was frustrated by Rabbi Yehuda HaNasi's announcement that he had produced the authoritative, canonical Mishna collection that rendered all other collections irrelevant. This may be the earliest known critique of codification, a process that establishes one authoritative text to the exclusion of all others.[21]

## RABBI YANNAI'S RELATIONSHIP WITH RABBI YEHUDA NESIYA, THE GRANDSON OF REBBI

For all that Rabbi Yannai was deeply respectful of his teacher Rabbi Yehuda HaNasi, he was also deeply disappointed in his teacher's successors. The Babylonian Talmud describes an elderly Rabbi Yannai, whose eyes had already grown dim with age, being carried by Rabbi Simlai, one of his students from Lod who had moved to the Galilee. (In a subsequent

19. This opinion appears in Tosefta Shabbat 16:3. See Lieberman, 76.
20. I.H. Weiss argues that Rabbi Yannai disagreed with Rebbi's Mishna "and thought to himself that he would do with his wisdom exactly what Rebbi had done with his. Why should he renounce his own views because of Rebbi's Mishna?" See Weiss, *Each Generation and Its Interpreters*, 3, 45. Hyman responded, "Is it not clear that Rabbi Yannai was disposed to follow the Mishna's ruling, and he knew that the Mishna was unique and that the law did not follow Rabbi Yose since the sages disagreed with him, and that the law instead follows the sages?" See Hyman in *Tanna'im and Amora'im*, 761. The correct answer is probably somewhere in the middle: Rabbi Yannai did not take issue with Rebbi's entire Mishna, and he never dreamed of editing a Mishna of his own, but since Rebbi's Mishna did not have full authority yet, he also relied on other tannaitic collections.
21. On the notion of codification and its use in Jewish law, see M. Alon, *Ha Mishpat HaIvri* [Hebrew] (Jerusalem: 5733), 738ff.

chapter we will consider the uniqueness of Rabbi Simlai and his role in the patriarchal house.) While they were traveling, the two were intercepted by Rabbi Yehuda Nesiya, Rebbi's grandson:

> Rabbi Yannai was walking while leaning on the shoulder of Rabbi Simlai, his attendant, when Rabbi Yehuda Nesiya came toward them. Rabbi Simlai said to Rabbi Yannai: The person who is coming toward us is distinguished, and the cloak he is wearing is distinguished. When Rabbi Yehuda Nesiya reached Rabbi Yannai, Rabbi Yannai felt his cloak and said to him: The minimum size for contracting impurity is identical for this cloak and for sackcloth.
>
> Rabbi Yehuda Nesiya inquired of him: From where do we know that a son precedes a daughter in inheriting the estate of their mother? Rabbi Yannai replied: The verse states, "the tribes." This indicates a comparison between the possessions of the mother's tribe and those of the father's tribe. Just as the son precedes the daughter with respect to the possessions of the father's tribe, so too, the son precedes the daughter with respect to the possessions of the mother's tribe. Rabbi Yehuda Nesiya said to him: Perhaps just as with the possessions inherited from the tribe of the father, the firstborn son takes a double portion, so too should the firstborn son take a double portion of the possessions inherited from the tribe of his mother? Rabbi Yannai said to his attendant: Pull me and let us continue on our way. This one does not truly wish to learn. (Bava Batra 111a)

In this story Rabbi Yehuda Nesiya appears as the new patriarch dressed in a sumptuous cloak; Rabbi Yannai appears as the wise old man who is losing his eyesight. As is so often the case, the blind person reveals what everyone else cannot see.[22] He assesses the patriarch's cloak by means of halakhic criteria. Unlike an ordinary garment which contracts impurity if its size is a minimum of three by three, this special cloak contracts

22. Y. Frankel, *The Aggadic Story*, 302–305. See p. 211, note 50, on the blind man with extraordinary powers of vision as a trope in classical world literature.

impurity only if it is four by four, like sackcloth. (See Mishna Kelim 28:8.) And so rather than being impressed by the garment, Rabbi Yannai ridicules it.

At this point the story turns to a halakhic discussion about a daughter's inheritance.[23] The question of the inheritance rights of daughters, which is discussed in the Bible, preoccupied the sages during the rabbinic period and beyond.[24] The Mishna offers the following general principle:

> The order of inheritance is as follows: "If a man should die and have no son, you shall transfer his inheritance to his daughter" [Num. 27:8]. The son precedes the daughter, and all the progeny of the son precede the daughter. (Mishna Bava Batra 8:2)

The Mishna clearly states that when the deceased has a son, the daughter does not inherit. But the Tosefta suggests that the matter is somewhat more complicated, because there is a difference between those possessions that were inherited from the father's side and those that were inherited from the mother's side:

> And just as the son takes precedence over the daughter in the estate of the father, so the son takes precedence over the daughter in the estate of the mother. Rabbi Elazar ben Rabbi Yose says in the name of Rabbi Zekharya ben HaKatzav, and so too did Rabbi Shimon ben Yehuda of Kfar Ayvos say in the name of Rabbi Shimon: The son and the daughter have equal claim on the estate of the mother. (Tosefta Bava Batra 7:10)

Rabbi Yehuda Nesiya turns to the aging Rabbi Yannai and asks him about the law in the Mishna, which privileges the son over the daughter

23. I learned this next section from Dr. Y. Finetuch, "Rabbinic Stories and the *Sugyot* That Include Them" (PhD diss., Bar Ilan University, 5769).

24. On inheritance laws during the rabbinic period, see E.E. Urbach, "Laws of Inheritance and the Way of the World" [Hebrew], *Proceedings of the Fourth World Congress of Jewish Studies* (5727), 133–141. This article was reprinted in *The Sages: Their Beliefs and Opinions* [Hebrew] (Jerusalem: 5729).

when it comes to the estate of the mother. Rabbi Yannai responds with halakhic exegesis that compares the estate of the father to that of the mother; in both, the son takes priority over the daughter. Rabbi Yehuda Nesiya then asks: Perhaps the word "tribe" should be interpreted differently, in a way that is related not to the inheritance of the daughter but rather to the inheritance of the firstborn. According to this understanding, the estate of the mother may be compared to the estate of the father in that in both cases, the firstborn inherits double, unlike the accepted halakha in the Mishna. Rather than addressing the topic at hand, Rabbi Yannai lashes out angrily: "This one does not truly wish to learn." Rabbi Yannai's anger is difficult to understand. Why did Rabbi Yehuda's question provoke him so? Was he not just drawing a conclusion based on the rules of halakhic reasoning?

This story has a parallel in the Jerusalem Talmud which, when considered in context, sheds light on the reason for Rabbi Yannai's harsh response:

> Rabbi Yannai and Rabbi Yehuda were sitting and learning. Rabbi Yehuda Nesiya entered and asked: "And every daughter who possesses an inheritance in any tribe" – what is the law as to the son's taking precedence over the daughter? He said to him: This indicates a comparison between the possessions of the mother's tribe and those of the father's tribe. Just as the son precedes the daughter with respect to the possessions of the father's tribe, so too, the son precedes the daughter with respect to the possessions of the mother's tribe. Rabbi Yehuda Nesiya said: Or perhaps one may argue the opposite: Just as in the case of the mother's tribe bequeathing property to the daughter when there is a son, so the father's tribe should bequeath property to the daughter even where there is a son to inherit the property. Rabbi Yoḥanan said to him: Let us get out of here. This man does not want to listen to the teachings of Torah. (Y. Bava Batra 8:1 [16a])

The discussion in the Jerusalem Talmud, too, centers on the exegesis of the word "tribes." Rabbi Yannai supports the first view put forth in the Mishna and argues, in contrast to the opinion of Rabbi Zekharya ben

HaKatzav, that the daughter does not inherit the estate of the mother if there is a son. Rabbi Yehuda Nesiya suggests turning this exegesis on its head to arrive at the opposite conclusion, such that not only does the daughter inherit the mother's estate along with her brother, but they also have equal share in the father's estate.

Here, too, we must wonder why Rabbi Yoḥanan grows furious and does not simply reject the patriarch's exegesis, as happens so often in exegetical disputes between the sages. It seems that we can only understand this story by juxtaposing the versions that appear in both Talmuds. In the Jerusalem Talmud, this story appears in the context of the first mishna of the chapter, which opens with various polemical debates regarding the laws governing a daughter's inheritance. The Talmud first presents a view attributed to the "non-Jewish sages," who interpret the biblical verses differently and rule that a daughter inherits equally alongside her brother.[25] This view stands in contrast to the biblical law and to the rabbinic ruling stipulated in the mishna at the beginning of the chapter.

Rabbi Yannai's anger at Rabbi Yehuda Nesiya's proposed exegesis makes sense in light of the rabbinic polemic against the non-Jewish view that the son and daughter inherit in equal measure. Rabbi Yannai is dismayed by the new patriarch who adorns himself in a regal cloak but is so quick to abandon the Mishna's legal traditions. But the Babylonian Talmud makes no reference to this polemical context. And so it seems likely that the Babylonian Talmud simply copied the story from the Jerusalem Talmud and preserved Rabbi Yannai's anger, even though it does not make sense in the context of the Babylonian version.[26]

25. The notion that the daughter and son inherit equally has its origins in Roman law (Gaius Institutiones 3.2). See *Gai Institutiones or Institutes of Roman Law by Gaius*, trans. E. Poste (Oxford: 1904).

26. In addition, the contrast between Jewish and non-Jewish inheritance laws was much starker in Babylonia than in the Land of Israel. According to Sasanian law, which was already in effect in Babylonia, sisters never took priority over their brothers, but in certain situations, they inherited half of their brother's share. See Y. Elman, "Marriage and Marital Property in Rabbinic and Sasanian Law," *Rabbinic Law in Its Roman and Near Eastern Context*, ed. C. Hezser (Tubingen, Germany: 2003), 227, 256, note 79; idem, "Scripture vs. Contemporary Needs: A Sasanian/Zoroastrian Example," *Cardozo Law Review* 28 (2006): 153–169. The absence of

The story's conclusion suggests that Rabbi Yannai lost the idealism of his youth. As a young man he was closely associated with Rabbi Yehuda HaNasi's beit midrash. As an elderly man parting from the new patriarch, he laments the end of an era and expresses disappointment and lack of faith in the new generation of leaders.

## EPILOGUE: RABBI YANNAI IN POPULAR KABBALA

A steep path descends eastward from Safed and leads to the village of Akhbara. About half an hour's walk from the village is a small hill thought to be the burial place of Rabbi Yannai. It is set apart from the other graves of the righteous, which are more concentrated to the west of Safed. Many of these graves were identified by the Ari, Rabbi Isaac Luria, who noticed that Rabbi Yannai's grave was not among those of his colleagues. Rabbi Yannai was regarded as a precursor of the Ari himself in the kabbalistic world, as is explained by Rabbi Haim Vital (1583–1620) in *Shaar HaGilgulim* (Introduction, 38):

> Then on Sunday of Ḥol HaMo'ed Pesaḥ, I went with him to a village that is called Akhbara, where we entered the cave of Rabbi Yannai, which is in an orchard. A spring flows from the narrow opening of the cave. The Ari told me: The only one buried here is Rabbi Yannai; Rabbi Dostai and Rabbi Nehorai, who are said to be buried here, are in fact not. The Ari's soul then attached itself to Rabbi Yannai's soul, and Rabbi Yannai told him: I, Rabbi Yannai, am buried underneath this marker. You should know that the Holy One, Blessed Be He, told me: Tell Haim Vital, the fellow who came along with you, that he should be careful not to engage in gossip or frivolous talk, and that he should be exceedingly humble. If he does that, I will be with him wherever he goes.

the polemical context in the Babylonian *sugya* renders Rabbi Yannai's anger more difficult to understand, as Lieberman already pointed out in *Yerushalmi Nezikin* (Jerusalem: 5744), 213, lines 21–25: "And indeed the Babylonian version of Rabbi Yehuda Nesiya's question is perplexing, and it is difficult to understand why they grew so angry at him."

*Chapter Eight*

# Rabbi Ḥanina bar Ḥama

As we have seen, Rabbi Yehuda HaNasi's will stated that Rabbi Ḥanina bar Ḥama would preside at the head. We will now consider this sage, who came to the Land of Israel from Babylonia and became the leader of the beit midrash in Tzippori.

### RABBI ḤANINA'S ARRIVAL FROM BABYLONIA TO ISRAEL

Rabbi Ḥanina bar Ḥama came to Israel in his prime, during Rabbi Yehuda HaNasi's tenure. At this point there was very little travel between Babylonia and the Land of Israel, and Rabbi Ḥanina was not given a particularly warm welcome by the wealthy Jews of Tzippori. Nonetheless, Rabbi Ḥanina bar Ḥama describes his arrival in the Land of Israel with wide-eyed enthusiasm:

> Rabbi Ḥanina said: When I came here, I took my belt, my son's belt, and my ass driver's belt, and I tied them around the trunk of a carob tree in the Land of Israel, and they didn't reach all the

> way around![1] I cut off one carob, and my hands filled with honey. (Y. Pe'ah 7:3 [20a])

This is a description of a new immigrant who has nothing but praise for his new land and excitement about its bounty. He immigrated during a period of prosperity, before the Roman Empire began to decline. But these years of plenty would soon come to an end, as the Jerusalem Talmud relates in the name of Rabbi Yoḥanan:

> Rabbi Yoḥanan said: The simple fruit that we ate as children was better than the peaches we now eat in our old age, for even in our own lifetimes, the world has changed. (Y. Pe'ah 7:3 [20a])

Rabbi Ḥanina came to Israel in the hope of helping to build the land. Both Talmuds describe how he worked to repair the roads:

> Rabbi Ḥanina attended to the obstacles and the unevenness of the roads of Israel. (Ketubot 112a)

Rashi explains that Rabbi Ḥanina repaired the roads so that no one would speak negatively about the land and its thoroughfares. This is elaborated upon in the Jerusalem Talmud:

> Rabbi Ḥanina weighed the clods of earth in the Land of Israel so as to fulfill the verse, "For your servants hold her stones dear and have pity on her dust" [Ps. 102:14]. (Y. Shevi'it 4:7 [35c])

Moreover, Rabbi Ḥanina was not dependent upon the support of others, but earned his living from the bounty of the land: He was a beekeeper who harvested honey. According to the Jerusalem Talmud, he also prepared fig honey:

1. The word for "ass" appears in a variant form in the parallel in *Midrash Shmuel* 13. See Bacher, *Legends of the Amora'im*, 1, 3, note 1.

> Rabbi Ḥanina sold bees' honey, and also had some honey from dried figs.[2] After a few days, buyers passed by there, and he said to them: Lest I mislead you, let me inform you that the honey I gave you was in fact dried fig honey. They said to him: We want more of that honey, because it is very good for us. Rabbi Ḥanina separated some of the profits he had made from selling honey and built the beit midrash of Tzippori. (Y. Pe'ah 7:3 [20b])

Rabbi Ḥanina did not just harvest honey. He also became famous as a healer and an expert in natural remedies (Yoma 57a).

### RABBI ḤANINA'S CONNECTION TO REBBI

When we considered the figure of Rabbi Ḥiya the Great, we cited a dialogue between him and Rabbi Ḥanina.[3] Unlike Rabbi Ḥiya, who focused on pedagogy and spent much of his time with students, Rabbi Ḥanina was a master of talmudic argumentation who declared that "if Torah should be forgotten from Israel, I will restore it with my powers of reasoning."

According to an aggadic story in Avoda Zara 10b, Rabbi Ḥanina was present during Rabbi Yehuda HaNasi's meetings with the emperor Antoninus. This story relates that a secret tunnel connected Rebbi's home to the emperor's palace. Each day, two servants would accompany the emperor through the tunnel: One would get killed at the gate of the patriarchal house, and the other would get killed at the entrance to the emperor's palace. The emperor would not permit anyone to be present during his secret meeting with Rebbi. But at one of the meetings, the emperor spotted Rabbi Ḥanina in the room. When he voiced an objection, the patriarch reassured him that "he is not a human being," implying that Rabbi Ḥanina was an angelic presence.

2. There have been several alternative suggestions as to the nature of this honey. Lieberman suggests in *Tosefta Kifshuta* (Terumot, 339, note 4) that it is fig honey, based on Rabbi Zecharia Frankel's commentary on Pe'ah. But Rabbi Shlomo Sirlio and the Penei Moshe (Rabbi Moshe Margalit) identify it as wasp honey. Rabbi Elijah of Fulda says that it refers to the honey of various fruits. Also see Rabbi Adin Steinsaltz's commentary on Pe'ah (Jerusalem: 5757), 172.

3. See *Sages* III, Part Five.

## REBBI'S CIRCLE OF STUDENTS

In volume III of this series we focused on the circle of sages who studied with Rebbi, including Bar Kappara, Rabbi Ḥiya, and Rebbi's son, Rabbi Shimon. Rabbi Ḥanina was also part of this circle, but he does not seem to have been particularly influential, so we did not focus on him then. The following talmudic story offers us a sense of the hierarchy of sages in Rebbi's beit midrash:

> Rav was reading the Torah portion in front of Rebbi. Rabbi Ḥiya entered, and Rav started over again. Bar Kappara entered, and Rav started over again. Rabbi Shimon, the son of Rebbi, entered, and Rav started over again. Rabbi Ḥanina bar Ḥama entered, and Rav said [to himself]: Should I keep starting over so many times? He did not start over. Rabbi Ḥanina grew angry at him. For the next thirteen years, Rav went to him on the eve of Yom Kippur to beg forgiveness, but Rabbi Ḥanina was not appeased. (Yoma 87a)

Some scholars have argued that Rabbi Ḥanina was based in Tzippori, whereas Rav and his uncle Rabbi Ḥiya were primarily active in Tiberias.[4] In any case, this story depicts them all sitting together. The patriarch studies with Rabbi Ḥiya, Bar Kappara, and his son Shimon, all leading sages of their generation. At the time, Rav was still young, and so had the task of reading the portion aloud to the other sages. Each time another sage entered, Rav would go back to the beginning so that sage, too, could hear the portion under discussion. Only when Rabbi Ḥanina entered did Rav refrain from going back to the beginning. In failing to do so, he insulted Rabbi Ḥanina's honor. Rabbi Ḥanina was so hurt that he refused to be appeased until Rav finally returned to Babylon.

The Talmud goes on to relate that the reason Rabbi Ḥanina refused to reconcile with Rav was on account of a dream he had:

> And how could Rabbi Ḥanina do as he did? Did not Rava say: Anyone who forgives those who offended him is forgiven for all

4. We will return to this matter when we discuss Rav's descent from the Land of Israel to Babylon. See Y.S. Tzuri, *Sefer Rav*, 65–75.

> of his sins? But Rabbi Ḥanina had a dream in which he saw Rav hanging from a palm tree. And it is known through a tradition that anyone who is seen hanging from a palm tree in a dream will become a leader. Rabbi Ḥanina said: I learn from this dream that Rav wants to become the head of the academy. I will therefore refuse to be appeased by him so that he will be compelled to go teach Torah in Babylonia. (Yoma 87b)

We can date this story to the beginning of the third century, to the year 206 CE. According to the epistle of Rav Sherira Gaon, Rav departed for Babylonia in 219 CE, a few years before Rebbi's death. We subtract thirteen, since Rav tried to appease Rabbi Ḥanina for thirteen successive Yom Kippur holidays.

### RABBI ḤANINA'S POSITION IN TZIPPORI

According to Rebbi's will, Rabbi Ḥanina was supposed to preside at the head. But he refused to accept this position because Rabbi Efes was two and a half years older than him. Rabbi Efes, as we know, was Rebbi's personal secretary. Only after his death did Rabbi Ḥanina rise to greatness and preside as the head, a communal leader responsible for ethical norms and for the administration of justice. Although he was not the patriarch but rather the local leader of the Jews of Tzippori, several sages from the Land of Israel regarded themselves as his disciples and quoted his teachings in his name. Rabbi Ḥanina, for his part, saw himself as responsible for transmitting the Torah of Rabbi Yehuda HaNasi and disseminating his Mishna.[5]

As we have seen, the wealthy people of Tzippori were not pleased with Rabbi Ḥanina's appointment; the Talmud speaks of an outcry that went forth from this city.[6] Perhaps it was difficult for them to accept an incumbent who made his own living and was not dependent on them financially, and who could therefore speak out freely against any ethical and social infractions. Several sources attest to the difficult relationship between Rabbi Ḥanina and his community in Tzippori, including the following story about an epidemic that broke out in the city:

5. Albeck, *Introduction to the Talmuds*, 155–157.
6. See *Sages* III, Part Five, based on Lieberman's research.

> There was a fatal pestilence in Tzippori, but it did not infect the neighborhood in which Rabbi Ḥanina was living. The people of Tzippori said: How is it possible that the elder lives among you, he and his entire neighborhood in peace, while the rest of the town goes to ruin? (Y. Taanit 3:4 [66c])

The entire city is afflicted, except for the neighborhood of Rabbi Ḥanina. The people of the city cry out against Rabbi Ḥanina and his neighbors, accusing them of indifference: How can you sit there calmly when the rest of the city is on the verge of death? The Jerusalem Talmud quotes Rabbi Ḥanina's response:

> Ḥanina went up and said before them: There was only a single Zimri in his generation, but on his account, 24,000 people died. And in our time, how many Zimris are there in our generation? And yet you are raising a clamor? (Y. Taanit 3:4 [66c])

The comparison of the pestilence in Tzippori to the biblical plague that broke out among the Israelites in the desert is more than just a hint.[7] Rabbi Ḥanina is accusing the wealthy and cosmopolitan Jews of Tzippori of lax moral standards.

The Jerusalem Talmud proceeds to cite another story that offers a window into our understanding of Rabbi Ḥanina's unique role in Tzippori:

> One time they had to declare a fast, but it did not rain. Rabbi Yehoshua carried out a fast in the south, and it rained. The people of Tzippori said: Rabbi Yehoshua ben Levi brings down rain for the people in the south, but Rabbi Ḥanina holds back rain from us in Tzippori. (Y. Taanit 3:4 [66c])

As this source suggests, there is a clear expectation that the spiritual leader of the city will intervene in times of drought. We know this, too, from

7. Rabbi Ḥanina and other sages of his time offered similar critiques of the Jewish community in Tzippori. See A. Bikhler, *Studies of the Period of the Mishna and the Talmud* [Hebrew] (Jerusalem: 5728), 54–57.

the Mishna's description of the procedure on public fast days, in which the spiritual leader was responsible for rallying the people to repent (Mishna Taanit 2:1). The Mishna describes this leader as an elder, which Rashi interprets as "a man of significant stature whose words they would listen to and accept, and who would soften their hearts."[8] But in many of the stories of this tractate, it is not the inspiring leader who is sought after in times of drought, but rather the holy man who can open the heavens, such as Ḥoni HaMe'agel.[9] It is only the holy man who succeeds in petitioning God to send down the rain that is locked in the heavens.

The people of Tzippori challenge Rabbi Ḥanina's competence by comparing him to Rabbi Yehoshua ben Levi. They tell him that his colleague from the south managed to bring rain, and surely he, Rabbi Ḥanina, is holier! Rabbi Ḥanina does not respond to their provocation, but simply waits for the next period of drought:

> They found it necessary to declare a second time of fasting and sent and summoned Rabbi Yehoshua ben Levi. Rabbi Ḥanina said to him: Let my lord go forth with us to fast. The two of them went out to fast, but it did not rain. He went in and preached to them as follows: It was not Rabbi Yehoshua ben Levi who brought down rain for the people of the south, nor was it Rabbi Ḥanina who held back rain from the people of Tzippori. Rather, the hearts of the southerners are open, and when they listen to a teaching of Torah, they submit to it and accept it, whereas the hearts of the people of Tzippori are hard, and when they hear a teaching of Torah, they do not accept it. (Y. Taanit 3:4 [66c])

Rabbi Ḥanina offers ethical counsel to the people of Tzippori. He informs them the rain will fall not because of the merit of the city's

8. See the commentary attributed to Rashi on Tractate Taanit. Also see D. Levine, *Public Fasts and Rabbinic Homilies* [Hebrew] (Tel Aviv: 5761), 78–79. Levine discusses the term used for "significant stature" as one that refers both to the physical and the spiritual.
9. P. Brown of Princeton University dedicated several decades of research to the figure of the holy rainmaker in Roman culture. An entire issue (1998) of the *Journal of Early Christian Studies (JECS)* is dedicated to a critical assessment of his work. For an additional, extensive bibliography, see D. Levine, *Public Fasts and Rabbinic Homilies*, 136–137.

leader; rather, it depends on the ethical conduct of the city's population. This story offers a clear window into Rabbi Ḥanina's difficult relationship with the people of Tzippori, as do other stories in which he criticizes the wealthy elite's administration of the city's economic affairs.

## THE DEATH OF HIS SON AND DAUGHTER

We know very little about Rabbi Ḥanina's family life, with the exception of the tragic death of his son and daughter. It is Rabbi Ḥanina himself who offers an explanation for his son's untimely death:

> Rabbi Ḥanina said: My son Shivhat died for no reason other than that he cut down a fig tree prematurely. (Bava Kamma 91b)

Rabbi Ḥanina explains that since his son cut down a fig tree prematurely, God ended his life prematurely, in accordance with the Torah's strict prohibition on cutting down fruit trees: "You may eat the fruit, but do not cut down the trees. Are the trees your enemies, that you should attack them?" (Deut. 20:19). The midrash explains that cutting down a fruit tree is like destroying the essence of life, as we learn from the Midrash: "In the moment when a fruit tree is cut down, a voice goes out from one end of the world to the other, but the voice is inaudible" (*Pirkei DeRabbi Eliezer* 33).

Another source describes the death of Rabbi Ḥanina's daughter and his way of coping with his grief:

> Rabbi Ḥanina's daughter died. However, he did not cry over her. His wife said to him: How can you not cry? Is it nothing more than a chicken that you have taken out of your house? He said to her: Both? Bereavement and blindness? (Shabbat 151b)

Rabbi Ḥanina responds to the death of his daughter with restraint and dry eyes.[10] His wife is disturbed by his seeming indifference:

10. A.A. HaLevi, *Legends of the Amora'im* [Hebrew] (Tel Aviv: 5737), 18–19. HaLevi compares Rabbi Ḥanina's behavior to the instructions of the stoics, as Aristotle wrote: "So long as nobility remains... assuredly pain will lead to virtue."

"Is it nothing more than a chicken that you have taken out of your house?" He responds, "Is it not enough that I lost my daughter? Must I also cry my eyes out?"

### RABBI ḤANINA'S ADVANCED AGE

The Talmud describes Rabbi Ḥanina's youthfulness in spite of his advanced age:

> Until when is someone considered a young man? Rabbi Ila'a said in the name of Rabbi Ḥanina: As long as he can stand on one leg and remove his shoe or put on his shoe. They said about Rabbi Ḥanina that even when he was eighty years old, he would stand on one leg and remove his shoe and put on his shoe. Rabbi Ḥanina said: The hot water and oil that my mother applied to me in my childhood stood me in good stead in my old age. (Ḥullin 24b)

Rabi Ḥanina was surprised at how he merited to live so long. In another source, he assumes it is because he conceded the role of the head to Rabbi Efes following Rebbi's death. Then he offers another possible explanation:

> Rabbi Ḥanina said: I have had the merit of living a long life. I do not know whether it was because of that incident, or because when I would come up from Tiberias to Tzippori, I would take the long way and go and greet Rabbi Shimon ben Ḥalafta in Ein Tina. (Y. Taanit 4:2 [68a])

Rabbi Shimon ben Ḥalafta was one of the elders of the generation who would frequent Rebbi's beit midrash in Tzippori. But in his old age, his body began to collapse, and he was confined to his home in Ein Tina, by the Kinneret.

> Rabbi Shimon ben Ḥalafta went to greet Rebbi every month. When he grew old, he was no longer able to go. One day he did go. Rebbi asked him: What keeps you from coming to visit me as

> you used to do regularly? Rabbi Shimon answered: The distant have become near and the near have become distant, two have turned into three, and that which makes peace in the home has ceased. "The distant have become near" means: The eyes which used to see at a distance do not see even close-up. "The near have become distant" means: The ears which used to hear everything the first time do not hear even on the hundredth repetition. "Two have turned into three" refers to a cane in addition to one's two legs. "That which makes peace has ceased" refers to the carnal desire that makes peace between husband and wife. (Leviticus Rabba 18:1)

Just as Rabbi Shimon ben Ḥalafta would greet Rebbi, so too would Rabbi Ḥanina greet Rabbi Shimon ben Ḥalafta whenever he was en route to Tzippori. In so doing, Rabbi Ḥanina discovered a remedy for loneliness.

The Jerusalem Talmud describes the changing of the guard in Tzippori as Rabbi Ḥanina grew old. Rabbi Yoḥanan, the leading sage in the Land of Israel during the next generation, was Rabbi Ḥanina's protégé:

> Rabbi Ḥanina was walking, leaning on the shoulder of Rabbi Ḥiya bar Ba in Tzippori. He saw all the people running. He asked him: Why are all the people running? He said to him: It is because Rabbi Yoḥanan is in session and expounding Torah in the schoolhouse of Rabbi Benaia, and all the people are running to hear what he has to say. He said to him: Blessed be the All-Merciful, who has shown me the fruits of my labor while I am still alive. For Rabbi Ḥanina had laid forth all of the *Aggada* before Rabbi Yoḥanan except for Proverbs and Ecclesiastes. (Y. Horayot 3:4 [48b])

### THE DEATH OF RABBI ḤANINA

> Rabbi Yoḥanan was going up from Tiberias to Tzippori. He saw someone coming down from there. He said to him: What do you hear in Tzippori? He said to him: A rabbi has died, and everyone

> in town is running about arranging for his burial. Rabbi Yoḥanan knew that it was Rabbi Ḥanina. So he sent for his best Sabbath garments and tore them. (Y. Bava Metzia 2:11 [8d])

Rabbi Yoḥanan was the leading sage of the Jerusalem Talmud, and he was certainly the leading sage of his generation. This story shows the force of his grief upon hearing of the death of Rabbi Ḥanina: He rips his best clothes as a sign of mourning. Rabbi Yoḥanan studied the teachings of Rabbi Yehuda HaNasi from Rabbi Ḥanina. And so by the merit of Rabbi Ḥanina, Torah was transmitted from the sages of the Mishna to the earliest sages of the Talmud.

# Part Two

## *Babylonian Jewry During the Sasanian Revolution*

| | | |
|---|---|---|
| The Elders of the Generation after Rabbi Yehuda HaNasi | The Early Years of the Babylonian Sages<br>Shmuel in Nehardea and Rav in Sura | The Early Years of the Talmud in the Land of Israel<br>The World and Teachings of Rabbi Yoḥanan |
| 199–235 | 226–254 | 235–279 |
| The Beginning of the Anarchic Period in the Roman Empire | The Sasanian Revolution in the East | Anarchy in the Roman Empire and the Rise of Palmyra |

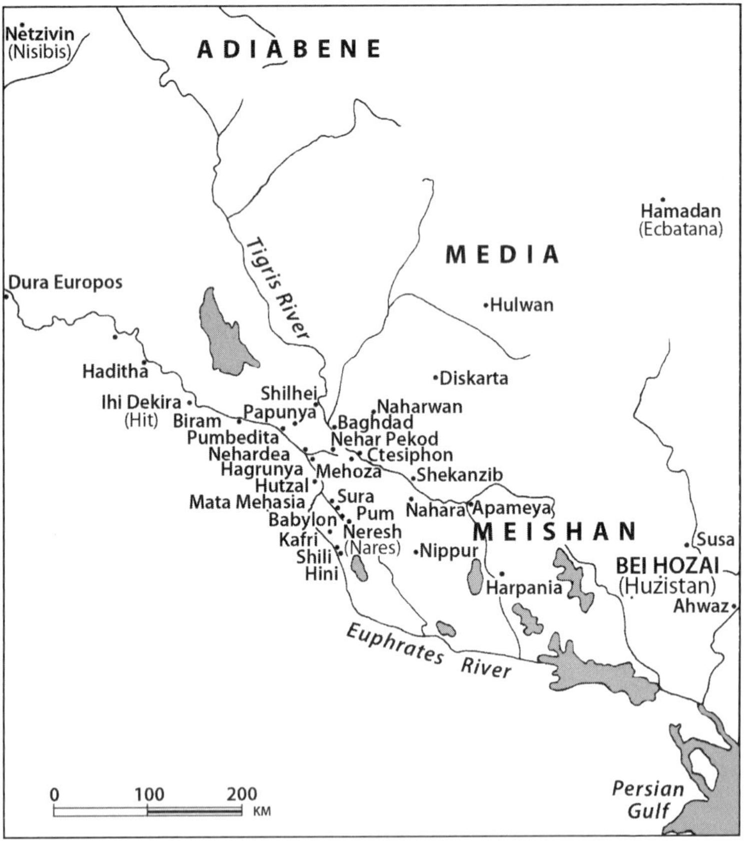


Babylon in the talmudic period

*Historical Background*

# The Sasanian Revolution and Its Significance

The Jews of Babylonia enjoyed religious and political freedom until the end of the first quarter of the third century. The Parthian government, led by King Ardavan, was gracious to the Jews. The king was indifferent to matters of faith, and he allowed the local leadership to manage internal affairs. Then in 226 CE King Ardashir assumed the throne, marking the start of the Sasanian period.[1] The administration of imperial affairs became increasingly centralized and underwent a radical revolution.

The rise of the Sasanians marked not just a political turn of the tide but also a reactionary religious revolution. Zoroastrianism, an ancient Persian faith also known as Mazda, became the official state religion. This old-new religion regarded the empire as the fulfillment of a divine destiny; those who belonged to other faiths were regarded as

1. This section is based on Y. Gafni, *The Jews of Babylonia During the Talmudic Period: Social and Intellectual Life* [Hebrew] (Jerusalem: 5751), 36–43.

an intolerable minority. King Ardashir proclaimed that the Mazda religion and the Sasanian empire were inextricably interdependent: "Religion and state are brothers, and they are eternally inseparable. Religion is the foundation of kingship, and kingship safeguards religion."[2] The Zoroastrian priests, who were known as magi or habari,[3] became increasingly prominent: They were appointed as advisers of the court, heads of the judicial system, and public administrators. Ardashir established spectacular fire temples in accordance with ancient religious dictates, he organized an assembly of priests, and he began compiling religious laws which he sought to make mandatory and binding.[4]

The Sasanian revolution had a direct impact on Jewish life in terms of judicial affairs, responsibilities to the central imperial administration, religious matters, and interaction with non-Jewish neighbors, all of which we will consider in the pages that follow. Ardashir, who died in 241, was succeeded by Shapur I, who led a campaign of conquest and territorial expansion. In the inscription from this period known as Kaba of Zoroaster, which was discovered in Iran in 1936, Shapur I tells of three wars he waged, in Mesopotamia, Syria, and Asia Minor.[5] On his final campaign in 259–260, he succeeded in defeating and capturing the Roman emperor Valerian.

The Sasanian revolution coincided with the first generation of Babylonian sages, led by Rav and Shmuel. Shmuel, who was born in Nehardea, and Rav, who came to Babylonia from the Land of Israel in 219, had to confront the practical implications of the revolution. Rav died in 247, and Shmuel in 254. And so the two of them lived through the reigns of the first two Sasanian rulers.

2. *The Letter of Tansar*, trans. M. Boyce (Rome: 1968), 33–34. Also see M. Beer, "The Political Background and Rav's Affairs in Babylonia" [Hebrew], *The Sages of the Mishna and the Talmud* (Ramat Gan: 5771), 11. I relied heavily on Beer, who drew much of his material from *The Letter of Tansar*.
3. On the Iranian roots of the term *habari* as a reference to the Mazda priests, see A.S. Rosenthal, "The Talmudic Dictionary" [Hebrew], *Irano-Judaica* (Jerusalem: 5742), 38 and 71, note 23.
4. For an extensive bibliography about this assembly of priests, see M. Beer, "The Political Background and Rav's Affairs in Babylonia," 11, note 9.
5. For an extensive bibliography about this inscription, see Y. Gafni, *The Jews of Babylonia*, 38, note 87.

*Chapter Nine*

# The Origins of Babylonian Jewry

Jewish life in Babylonia prior to the talmudic period is shrouded in mystery.

Although students of Talmud generally regard Rav and Shmuel as the first generation of Babylonian Jewish scholars, the Babylonian diaspora long predates these sages. Jews were living in Babylonia even before the destruction of the First Temple, from the exile of King Jeconiah in about 600 BCE. Rav Sherira Gaon writes in his famous epistle about the origins of Babylonian Jewry:

> Know that in the beginning, when Israel was exiled in the exile of King Jeconiah, there were craftsmen and smiths and several prophets among them. They came to Nehardea and Jeconiah and his sons built a synagogue and set it using stones and earth that they had brought with them from the Temple, to fulfill the verse, "Your servants delight in its stones and cherish its dust" [Ps. 102:15]. And they named the synagogue "The Synagogue of

> Shaf VeYatev," that is, "The Temple Journeyed and Settled Here." And the Divine Presence was with them.

Our goal is not to confirm the historicity of Rav Sherira Gaon's account, which was written some 1,500 years after the destruction of the First Temple.[1] For our purposes it suffices to note that the Jews of Babylonia believed that it was exiles from the Land of Israel who built Nehardea's synagogue, Shaf VeYatev, out of stones from the Temple and earth from Jerusalem.[2]

Some scholars have challenged the credibility of the epistle, claiming that Rav Sherira Gaon had his own agenda in seeking to establish a firm foundation for the Babylonian yeshivot.[3] But a more thorough study of testimonies from the Second Temple period until the start of the talmudic period reveals that there was indeed a continuous Jewish presence in Babylonia from Temple times.[4]

### THE JEWS OF MEISHAN AND THE CONVERSION OF THE ADIABENE AND QUEEN HELENA

Josephus writes of a Jewish merchant named Ḥanania who, in the course of his travels, came to Spasini, the major city in Meishan, located south of Babylonia and extending all the way to the Persian Gulf. There he became acquainted with Izates, heir to the throne of Adiabene. Ḥanania

1. Many scholars have noted that this story is a far cry from historical reality and should not be taken at face value. See Y. Gafni, "Synagogues in Talmudic Babylonia" [Hebrew], *Ancient Synagogues: A Collection of Articles*, eds. A. Oppenheimer et al. (Jerusalem: 5748), 147–154. On the more general issue of the credibility of the epistle, see Gafni, *The Jews of Babylonia*, 239–265.
2. Y.N. Epstein understood Shaf VeYatev as meaning "place of residence," which is the name of a village on the outskirts of Nehardea. See Y.N. Epstein, *Studies in Talmudic Literature and Semitic Languages* [Hebrew] (Jerusalem: 5744), 40–41. But the more commonly accepted translation of this name is "journeyed and settled," implying that the Jews of this community journeyed from the Land of Israel and settled in Babylonia. See A.M. Naftal, *The Talmud and Its Creators* [Hebrew] 7 (Tel Aviv: 5751), 3.
3. S.Y. Rapoport, *Biography of Natan ben Yehiel of Rome* [Hebrew] (Warsaw: 5673), 32. Weiss, *Each Generation and Its Interpreters*, 3, 151.
4. Gafni, *The Jews of Babylonia*, 20–24.

introduced Izates to Judaism, and Izates converted along with his mother, Queen Helena, and the entire kingdom of Adiabene.[5]

And so Meishan and the Land of Israel had a longstanding historical connection. But as we shall see from talmudic sources, the Jews of Babylonia referred to the people of Meishan as "dead" because they failed to preserve the purity of their genealogical lines.[6]

## TO OUR BROTHERS IN THE BABYLONIAN DIASPORA: THE EPISTLES OF THE PATRIARCH

At the end of the Second Temple period, the patriarch Rabban Gamliel the Elder sat on the Temple Mount and wrote an epistle to all the Jews of the Diaspora, including the Babylonian exiles:

> To our brothers, residents of the Babylonian diaspora and residents of the Medean diaspora and residents of other diasporas of Israel, may your peace increase! We inform you that the pigeons are still tender, the lambs are thin, and the spring time has not yet come. So it seems fitting in my opinion and in the opinion of my colleagues to add thirty days to this year. (Tosefta Sanhedrin 2:6)[7]

There is no reason to doubt the credibility of this epistle, sent from the seat of the patriarchy to the Babylonian diaspora. The Jerusalem Talmud relates that Mar Ukva the Exilarch,[8] who lived during the early

5. Josephus, *Antiquities of the Jews* 20, 17–96. The story is documented in various rabbinic sources, including Mishna Yoma 3:10 and Bava Batra 11a.
6. Kiddushin 71b. See A. Oppenheimer, "The Relationship Between Meishan and the Land of Israel" [Hebrew], *Zion* 47 (5742): 335–341.
7. This epistle and its parallel sources were studied from various angles. See G. Alon, *The History of the Jews in the Land of Israel*, 1 [Hebrew] (Tel Aviv: 1953), 150.
8. I refer to Mar Ukva as exilarch (*Rosh HaGola*), as was common in traditional rabbinic literature from the period of Rabbi Saadia Gaon and on. G. Herman surveyed all the many sources related to Mar Ukva and refuted the contention that he ever received this title. He argues that the earlier, more reliable sources refer to Mar Ukva as a sage who had the authority to challenge the exilarch. Only in later sources was he promoted to the role of a judge associated with the exilarch, or even to the role

amoraic period, reports that he found two epistles in his archives. One of them reads as follows:

> It seems fitting in my opinion to add thirty days to the year. (Y. Megilla 1:5 [71a])

This source suggests that the archives of the exilarch contained documents that attested to the connection between the patriarchal house and the leader of the Diaspora, even though Rabban Gamliel and Mar Ukva were separated by more than two hundred years.[9]

Other sources, too, indicate that the sages of Jerusalem were aware and considerate of the Babylonian exiles during the Second Temple period. For instance, Rabban Gamliel established that one should begin praying for rain only on the seventh of the month of Ḥeshvan, so that the last of the Babylonian pilgrims could return to the Euphrates (Mishna Taanit 1:2). Based on this source, some scholars date the origin of the exilarchy to the end of the Second Temple period.[10] Other scholars date the establishment of this institution not until the middle of the third century, to the reign of King Shapur I; but even they agree that at the end of the mishnaic period, there were already Babylonian Jews who served as representatives to the Parthian rulers.[11]

of exilarch. See G. Herman, "The Exilarchs in Babylonia During the Sasanian Period" [Hebrew] (PhD diss., Hebrew University of Jerusalem, 5765), 98–111.

9. M. Beer, *The Exilarchs During the Periods of the Mishna and Talmud* [Hebrew] (Ramat Gan: 5736), 16.
10. Scholars debate whether this institution was founded in response to internal Jewish needs, or in service of the Parthian leadership in Babylonia. Jacob Neusner leads the camp of those who argue that the position of the exilarch was primarily political. See Neusner, *A History of the Jews in Babylonia* (Leiden, Netherlands: 1965–68), 92–95. Y. Kaufman proposes that the institution was founded for internal reasons, as a parallel to the institution of the patriarchy in the Land of Israel. See Kaufman, *Exiled and Alienated* 1 [Hebrew] (Tel Aviv: 1929), 519. G. Herman traces the establishment of the institution of the exilarch to the second generation of Babylonian sages. See Herman, "The Exilarchs in Babylonia."
11. Ibid., 136–145.

## ḤANANIA THE NEPHEW OF RABBI YEHOSHUA AND THE ORIGINS OF TALMUDIC BABYLONIA

The next significant development in the history of Jewish life in Babylonia was the arrival of Ḥanania, the nephew of Rabbi Yehoshua. We have already considered his role in spreading talmudic Judaism to Babylonia in the previous volume of this series.[12] As we discussed, Ḥanania came to Babylonia from the Land of Israel before the Bar Kokhba revolt, bringing with him the teachings of the beit midrash at Yavneh. During the crisis of the Hadrianic decrees, he assumed that the Jewish community in the Land of Israel had been destroyed, and so he took upon himself the authority to intercalate the year. In so doing he became the leading authority among the Jews of Babylonia. We know this because the earliest talmudic sages in Babylonia established that the halakha follows his rulings.

We have already encountered several Babylonian sages who came to the Galilee following the Bar Kokhba revolt. The most preeminent among them was Rabbi Natan the Babylonian, who played a key role in shaping the Mishna as a member of the beit midrash of Rabban Shimon ben Gamliel, the father of Rebbi.[13] There was also an exilarch named Rav Huna who was contemporaneous with Rebbi, as Rav Sherira Gaon documents in his epistle:

> And during the time of Rebbi, Rav Huna I was the exilarch in Babylonia. And this is what was said [Horayot 11b]: Rebbi asked Rabbi Ḥiya.... He said to him: Your rival is in Babylonia. And who is he? Rav Huna. (Epistle of Rav Sherira Gaon, Lewin edition, section 84)[14]

12. On Ḥanania and his role in shaping Babylonian Jewry, see *Sages* III, Part Four. Also see *Sages* II, Part Five on Rabbi Yehuda ben Beteira's beit midrash in Netzivin, which dates back to the time of Rabbi Akiva and his colleagues.
13. I offered examples of Babylonian teachings that were brought to the Land of Israel in *Sages* III, Part Four.
14. We have no further details about this exilarch. Rabbinic sources relate that Rav Huna's coffin was delivered to the Land of Israel for burial during the tenure of Rabbi Yehuda HaNasi. See Y. Kilayim 9:3 [32b], Genesis Rabba 33:3. On the messianic aspirations of Rebbi and his relationship with the exilarch, see *Sages* III, Part Five.

Talmudic scholars have already discredited the existence of an exilarch named Rav Huna who was active during Rebbi's tenure, and so we must assume that this account is literary rather than historical.[15] However, these scholars do not question that several sages came to the Land of Israel from Babylonia during this period. We have already studied two such sages, both major figures: Rabbi Ḥiya (and his sons) and Rabbi Ḥanina bar Ḥama. And so we must conclude that Babylonian Jewry was active and flourishing for hundreds of years, even though our earliest records of this community date back only to the beginning of the talmudic period.

### THE CITY OF NEHARDEA BEFORE RAV'S ARRIVAL

According to the epistle of Rav Sherira Gaon, the city of Nehardea regarded itself as the oldest and most important Babylonian city. During the early talmudic period, it had a large and active Jewish community with a variety of religious and educational institutions. Its leaders included Rabbi Sheila and a sage known as "the father of Shmuel."

Josephus describes the city of Nehardea and relates that because of the security there and in Netzivin, these cities were used as treasuries. When the time came, the collected funds were sent to the Temple in Jerusalem.[16]

### BABYLONIAN JEWS' GENEALOGICAL CONSCIOUSNESS

During the third century, the Jews of Babylonia, and certainly those in Nehardea, regarded themselves as possessing an ancient tradition of Torah scholarship based on an unbroken chain of rabbinic leadership, unadulterated by sectarian politics, Christian theology, or other outside influences. Midrash Tanḥuma relates:

> The Holy One, Blessed Be He, acted justly with the Jews in preceding the exile of Tzidkiya by the exile of Jeconiah so that the Oral Torah would not be forgotten. They sat learning Torah in Babylonia from that time until today, and they were not ruled

15. Friedman, "The Historical Aggada," 146–163. Also see Herman, "The Exilarchs in Babylonia," 155–187.
16. Josephus, *Antiquities of the Jews* 18 (310–379).

> by Edom or Greece, and there were no decrees of destruction. (Tanḥuma 58:3)

This midrash seeks to trace the origins of the Babylonian Jewish community to the exile of King Jeconiah, rather than that of King Zechariah. The craftsmen and smiths described in Rav Sherira Gaon's epistle were those leaders of the people who elected to move to Babylonia a decade before the destruction of the First Temple. These exiles established a halcyon and self-assured Jewish society that was not oppressed or driven out by any ruling power. Between the two Babylonian rivers, the Tigris and the Euphrates, the Babylonian diaspora grew into one of the most important centers of world Jewry. This community prided itself in the purity of its lineage, based on a tradition that Ezra the scribe redressed all the problems of impure lineage when he returned from Babylonia to Israel, as the Talmud relates:

> Ezra did not go up from Babylonia until he made it like fine, sifted flour, and only then did he go up. (Kiddushin 69b)

The Babylonian Jews believed that their purity of lineage surpassed that of the Jews of the Land of Israel, a notion that can be traced back at least to Rebbi's time:

> In the days of Rebbi, they sought to treat Babylonia like dough relative to the Land of Israel. Rebbi said to them: You are putting thorns between my eyes! If this is your will, Rabbi Ḥanina bar Ḥama will deal with you. Rabbi Ḥanina bar Ḥama dealt with them. He said to them: I have received the following tradition from Rabbi Yishmael the son of Rabbi Yose, who said it in the name of his father: All lands are like dough relative to the Land of Israel, and the Land of Israel is like dough relative to Babylonia. (Kiddushin 71a)

In this story, the Jews in the Land of Israel counter that Babylonia is like dough relative to the Land of Israel, that is, that it has a mixture of lineages. Rebbi hears this claim and grows upset, since he was descended from Babylonian Jews through his ancestor Hillel. Rebbi refers them to Rabbi Ḥanina bar Ḥama, a Babylonian, who taught in the name of Rabbi Yishmael the son of Rabbi Yose, who in turn taught in the name of his father (a contemporary of Rabban Shimon ben Gamliel), that in fact, "All lands are like dough relative to the Land of Israel, and the Land of Israel is like dough relative to Babylonia."[17] That is, the lineage of the Jews of Babylonia is purer than anywhere else.

A sensitivity to matters of lineage in Babylonia also led to the establishment of precise geographical borders based on family lines. As the Talmud delineates:

> Rav Papa the Elder said in the name of Rav: Babylonia is healthy. Meishan is dead. Media is ill. Eilam is moribund. And what is the difference between the ill and the moribund? Most ill people live, whereas most moribund people die. (Kiddushin 71b)

Rav relates purity of lineage to place of residence. Babylonia, which refers to Nehardea and its environs, is a living, healthy being consisting of Jews of pure lineage, uncontaminated by foreign blood. At the other end of the spectrum is Meishan, which is so completely assimilated that it is considered dead. In between are Media and Eilam.

A study of the borders of Babylonia as determined by genealogical considerations sheds light on the demographics of the Babylonian Jewish community.[18] Most of the Jews were concentrated in fertile Mesopotamia, between the Euphrates and the Tigris. The Talmud relates that the northern border of this region was the subject of a dispute between Rav and Shmuel: "Rav said until Bagda and Avna, and Shmuel said until Mushkanei" (Kiddushin 71b). Both of these places are about fifty-five kilometers north of Baghdad. The southern border was somewhere near the city of Aphamia, known today as Kfar Phamia, on the eastern bank

17. A. Oppenheimer, "Purity of Lineage in Talmudic Babylonia" [Hebrew], *Eros, Engagement, and Prohibitions: Sexuality and Family in History*, eds. Y. Bartel and Y. Gafni (Jerusalem: 5758), 71–82.
18. Ibid. Also see M. Laker, "The Boundaries of Babylonia for Lineage" [Hebrew], *Zion* 50 (5745): 173–183; and Herman, "The Exilarchs in Babylonia," 21–26.

of the Euphrates near Kut Alamara.[19] It is interesting that the southern border actually ran through Aphamia, between the upper and lower cities. One part was within the border when it came to genealogical matters, and one part was outside it. The Jews of the region refused all contact with the residents of the lower city, which was considered part of Meishan, the land of the dead with regard to genealogical matters.

The Jews of Meishan directed all their halakhic questions to the Jews of the Land of Israel. The Talmud relates:

> The people of Meishan took upon themselves not to sail on the Great Sea due to the danger involved. They came and asked Rebbi: Our ancestors were accustomed not to sail on the Great Sea. What shall we do? He said to them: Since your ancestors were accustomed to treat it as a prohibition, do not deviate from the custom of your ancestors, whose souls are at peace. (Y. Pesaḥim 4:1 [30d])

As several scholars claim, this question may have been a response to a shift in the political reality: At a certain point Palmyra lost control over the sea trade between east and west, and the Jews of Meishan, as local residents, stepped in.[20] The most important documentation of Meishan's dependence on the Land of Israel is a talmudic source in which Rav Ukva from Meishan addresses Rav Ashi:

> Rav Ukva from Meishan said to Rav Ashi: You who are close to Rav and Shmuel should follow Rav and Shmuel. We shall follow Rabbi Yoḥanan. (Shabbat 37b)

As this source attests, Rav Ashi the Babylonian, the head of the yeshiva of Mata Meḥasia, is heir to the halakhic legacy of Rav and Shmuel. But the

19. See the maps in Oppenheimer, "Purity of Lineage in Talmudic Babylonia," 71–82, and Laker, "The Boundaries of Babylonia for Lineage," 173–183.

20. Oppenheimer, "The Relationship Between the Land of Israel and Babylonia at the Turning Point Between the Tannaitic and Amoraic Periods" [Hebrew], *Center and Diaspora*, ed. Y. Gafni (Jerusalem: 5764), 130.

people of Meishan view themselves as subject to the halakhic authority of Rabbi Yoḥanan in the Land of Israel.

There were other areas in Babylonia that were home to Jews of impure lineage, among them Naharpania.[21] The Jews of Naharpania are mentioned throughout the Talmud. They were economically well-off because the land was fertile and its crops were of superior quality. Naharpania was also famous for its wine; we learn that Rava, who was a wine merchant, would purchase his wine there. And yet in spite of all that Naharpania had to recommend it, the Talmud relates as follows:

> Rav Hamnuna was sitting before Ulla and was challenging what he had learned. Ulla said: What a man! What a man! If only he were not from Harpania! Rav Hamnuna grew embarrassed. Realizing this, Ulla asked him: To which town do you pay the poll tax? He answered: To Pum Nahara. Ulla said to him: If so, then you are from Pum Nahara.
>
> To what does the name Harpania allude? Rabbi Zeira said: A mountain (*har*) to which all genealogically unfit people turn (*ponin*) when in search of a spouse. A *baraita* taught: Whoever cannot identify his family and his tribe turns there to find a mate. Rava said: And Harpania is deeper than Sheol, for regarding Sheol it is stated, "From the clutches of Sheol I will ransom them, from death I will redeem them" [Hos. 13:14], whereas the disqualification of Harpania's residents has no remedy. The ineligible ones of Harpania stem from the ineligible ones of Meishan, and the ineligible ones of Meishan stem from the ineligible ones of Tarmod, and the ineligible ones of Tarmod stem from Solomon's slaves. And this is reflected by that which people say: Both a large measure and a small measure roll down to Sheol, and from Sheol

21. A. Oppenheimer demonstrates that the Pania River was located southeast of the southwestern border of the region in which the Jews of purest lineage lived. See Oppenheimer, "Purity of Lineage in Talmudic Babylonia," 76–77. Elsewhere he shows that it was customary for Babylonian Jews to bury their dead here, as if en route to the Land of Israel. See Oppenheimer and Laker, "Burial to the West of the Euphrates River and Its Significance" [Hebrew], *Melat* 1 (5743): 157–163.

> to Tarmod, and from Tarmod to Meishan, and from Meishan to Harpania. (Yevamot 17a)

The Babylonian Jewish community had a very well-developed genealogical consciousness. They associated the people of Harpania with those of Meishan and Palmyra, who were descendants of the slaves of King Solomon. And so the Jews of Babylonia intermarried with the residents of Harpania only as a last resort. However, we know from other sources that even in the more central and ancient areas of Jewish settlement, where the residents regarded themselves as genealogically untainted, there were still disputes about lineage. And so the division into areas of pure and impure lineages was not always clear.

As these sources suggest, when we consider the Jewish community in Babylonia during talmudic times, we must keep in mind the significance this population accorded to genealogical purity. It is against this backdrop that we must understand the relationship between the Babylonian Jewish community and the community of Jews in the Land of Israel.

*Chapter Ten*

# Shmuel

We now turn our attention to Rav and Shmuel, the two main pillars of the Babylonian Talmud and the founders of the two major centers of Torah learning in Babylonia for centuries – Sura and Pumbedita.[1] The head of the Babylonian sages was Shmuel, who was born into an illustrious Babylonian family that could trace its lineage back for generations. In the words of the rabbi and scholar Aaron Hyman, "Here is a great man among giants, Shmuel, who was the head of the sages of his generation in Babylonia, and a great sage with regard to intercalation; the halakha follows him with regard to civil matters."[2]

## THE STORY OF THE FATHER OF SHMUEL'S NAME

In sources from the Land of Israel, Shmuel's father is often known by his name, Abba bar Abba (also Abba bar Ba). But in the Babylonian Talmud, he is known as "the father of Shmuel." We might assume that he took

1. On the development of the yeshiva in Babylonia, see Gafni, *The Jews of Babylonia*, 177–185.
2. Hyman, *Tanna'im and Amora'im*, 1120.

on this name after his son became the leading sage in Babylonia, but a geonic source offers the following rather colorful account:

> You asked: Why was the father of Shmuel not called by his own name? They said that Shmuel's father went to do business in a distant place. A non-Jewish woman from Media who was an expert in the language of the birds found him and demanded to sleep with him in exchange for thousands of silver coins. He said to her: Why? She said to him: I heard that tonight you will have a son of unparalleled brilliance. When he heard this, he fled from her and went home that night to his wife and slept with her, and she became pregnant, and he immediately went away again. The matter came before the court, and others attested that she had committed adultery because they did not know that her husband had returned, so they beat her. She gave birth to a son who was called Shmuel. Later Abba, his father, returned and testified in the matter, and Shmuel would say: I knew when they were beating my mother, and I would bend my head toward the strap to absorb the blows, and the scar on my head is still visible. That is why they call him the father of Shmuel – to proclaim to the world that he is indeed his father. (Geonic Responsa, Jacob Musafia, 97)

Against the backdrop of Babylonian Jewry's obsession with purity of lineage, we can understand this story's concern with establishing Shmuel's patrimony indubitably. His mother was suspected of adultery because at the time when Shmuel was conceived, his father was thought to have been traveling for business; only after Shmuel's birth did his father return and testify that he was indeed the father. The source concludes with Shmuel's assertion that the blows that his mother endured during her pregnancy left their mark on his own head as well.

### SHMUEL'S CHILDHOOD UNDER HIS FATHER'S WATCHFUL EYE

Several sources speak of the special bond between Shmuel and his father. The Babylonian Talmud relates that Shmuel once came home to his father in tears:

> The father of Shmuel found Shmuel crying. He said to him: Why are you crying? Shmuel said: Because my teacher hit me. His father said: Why did he hit you? He said: For he said to me: You fed my son and you did not wash your hands. Shmuel's father asked him: And why did you not wash your hands? He said to him: If he is the one eating, why should I wash? Shmuel's father said to him: Not only does this teacher not know the laws of hand-washing, but he also has to hit my son? And the law is that one who is being fed by another requires hand-washing, but the feeder does not require hand-washing. (Ḥullin 107b)

This story captures an intimate exchange between father and son. It is clear from the story that Shmuel is still quite young: He describes sitting before his teacher, in his teacher's home. As was customary in those days, he would also help out with his teacher's children. When he returns home one day, Shmuel laments to his father that his teacher rebuked him for failing to wash his hands ritually before feeding his son. Shmuel's father immediately sides with his son.[3]

Another source teaches how Shmuel's father taught his son to study Torah. In this story, father and son sit learning Tractate Zevaḥim, which deals with the laws of sacrificial worship. The father asks the son a series of questions about the exact location of the animal in the Temple as it is brought to slaughter:

> Shmuel's father inquired of Shmuel: If an offering is inside the courtyard but its legs are outside, what is the law? He said: It is written, "And they shall bring them to God" [Lev. 17:5], which teaches that one who has an offering does not fulfill his requirement to bring it until all of it is inside the courtyard. (Zevaḥim 26a)

3. Shmuel's position on the matter was accepted as halakha. See the responsa of Rav Aḥai, *Parashat Metzora, She'ilta* 90; Maimonides, Laws of Blessings 6:18; *Shulḥan Arukh*, Laws of Hand-Washing 163:2.

The son has no trouble fielding the first question. He cites a verse that teaches that the animal must be entirely within the courtyard of the Temple before it can be slaughtered. The conversation continues:

> If one suspended an offering in the air of the courtyard and slaughtered it, what is the law? Shmuel replied: It is valid. His father said to him: You are mistaken, for we require that the slaughter be performed at the side of the altar, and this requirement is not fulfilled if the animal is suspended in the air. Shmuel's father asked: If the slaughterer was suspended in the air of the courtyard and he slaughtered thus, what is the law? Shmuel said: It is invalid. His father said to him: You are mistaken, for the Torah requires only that the slaughter be performed at the side of the altar, but not that the slaughterer be at the side of the altar. Shmuel's father asked: If he was suspended in the air of the courtyard and he received the blood, what is the law? Shmuel said: It is valid. His father said to him: You are mistaken, for such is not a proper manner of performing the Temple service. Shmuel's father asked: If he suspended the animal in the air of the courtyard and received the blood, what is the law? Shmuel said: It is invalid. His father said to him: You are mistaken, for the Torah requires only that the slaughter be performed at the side of the altar, but not that the blood be received at the side of the altar. (Zevaḥim 26a)

The father asks about a case in which the offering is suspended above the courtyard and then slaughtered. The son responds that it is a valid offering. The father tells him that he is mistaken. Then the father asks about a case in which the slaughterer himself is suspended above the courtyard, and the son, having learned his lesson, responds that it is invalid. But the father tells him that he is mistaken again. The father continues to play with his son as the lesson unfolds, in an effort to teach him to think dialectically and to pay attention not just to the explicit meaning of the sources, but also to their underlying logic.

This is an early stage in Shmuel's education, in which he is learning to hone his critical mind. He is not just repeating sources he has memorized; he is also learning how to evaluate and analyze halakhic material. We can already see the earliest roots of his approach to Torah study, which would fully flower in Nehardea. As Shmuel's student Rabbi Zeira would later put it, "Rabbi Zeira said in the name of Shmuel: We do not learn from laws or from legends or from the Tosefta, but from Talmud" (Y. Pe'ah 2:6 [15d]).

Another story from Shmuel's childhood appears in the Jerusalem Talmud:

> Shmuel fled from his father. He went and stood between two poor shacks. He overheard the poor people saying: On which table service shall we eat today, on our gold service or on our silver service? Shmuel came back and told all of this to his father. His father told him: We must be grateful to those deceivers among the poor people, because on their account, we do not have to believe them all.
>
> Abba bar Ba gave his son Shmuel a few coins to divide up among poor people. The son went out and found a poor person eating meat and drinking wine. He returned home and told his father, who said to him: Give that poor person more, for he is accustomed to this amount. (Y. Pe'ah 8:8 [21b])

This story begins with Shmuel running away from home. Presumably he is not really running away, but just testing the boundaries of his own independence. He arrives at a poor neighborhood where he learns an important life lesson: Not everyone can be trusted.

It seems that Shmuel was raised in an affluent home. His father worked as a merchant and gave charity generously. Shmuel grew up under his father's close watch. He learned about the world from his father – about its beauty, and also about its unsavory underside.

### STUDYING REBBE'S MISHNA IN SHMUEL'S HOME

When Rav moved to Babylonia in the year 219, he brought with him the near-final text of the Mishna, as we will see. But it seems that the Babylonian sages had access to collections of mishnayot even before he arrived. We know, for instance, that Rabbi Natan the Babylonian, who lived one generation earlier, brought a Babylonian mishna collection with him to the Land of Israel. One source that alludes to such a mishna collection dates back to Shmuel's childhood.

A mishna in Tractate Shabbat teaches that girls may go out into the public domain wearing ribbons and some sort of decorative chip in their ears on Shabbat, because these are not regarded as ornaments:

> Girls may go out with ribbons, and even with chips in their ears. (Mishna Shabbat 6:6)

In its discussion of this mishna, the Jerusalem Talmud relates:

> Abba bar Ba instructed Shmuel his son: Do not accept this version of the mishna. Rather: But not with chips in their ears. (Y. Shabbat 6:6 [8c])

Does Shmuel's father willfully change the version of the mishna that he hears from his son, or does he have another version of that same mishna? A *baraita* in the Babylonian Talmud suggests that perhaps there was another version of that mishna that was taught in Babylonia:

> Girls may go out with ribbons in their ears, but not with drawstrings around their necks. (Shabbat 57a)

The language of this source suggests that Shmuel's father may have had a version of the mishna that read, "but not with chips in their ears"; in accordance with this source, he may have corrected the version of the mishna that his son learned.[4] This conversation is also recorded in the Babylonian Talmud, but there Shmuel's father changes the version of the mishna in order to teach his daughters proper conduct:

> Shmuel's father did not let his daughters go out with ribbons, and did not let them sleep next to one another, and he prepared

4. Based on Epstein, *Text of the Mishna*, 211–212.

> ritual baths for them to immerse in during Nisan and mats for immersing during Tishrei. (Shabbat 65a)

Here, too, Shmuel's father disagrees with the Mishna: He does not let his daughters go out wearing ribbons. He also does not let them sleep together, and he prepares ritual baths for them when the rivers overflow their banks, and he sets up mats for them at the end of the dry season when the water is filthy and muddy. According to this source, Shmuel's father did not feel beholden to the Mishna. He acted of his own accord, ruling in halakhic matters for his family and community.

### SHMUEL'S GREATNESS

Shmuel was a true Renaissance man. Several sources describe him as a doctor. Others refer to him as an astronomer; at one point he declares: "The paths of the sky are as clear to me as the paths of Nehardea" (Berakhot 58b).[5] At the same time, he was the leading halakhic authority in Nehardea, responsible for interpreting the Mishna and guiding the local Jewish community. As the Talmud relates, "Nehardea and all of its suburbs followed the rulings of Shmuel" (Ketubot 54a), suggesting that

5. The traditional commentators disagree with regard to Shmuel's secular studies. Some insisted apologetically that his study of science was solely in service of performing calendrical calculations. As Rabbi Yehuda HaLevi wrote in the *Kuzari*, 4:29: "They devoted themselves to this study only in the service of Torah, because the calculation of the revolution of the moon and the variations in its course did not completely tally with the calculation of the time of its conjunction with the sun, the *molad*. The time when the moon is not visible prior to the *molad* and immediately after it can only be calculated with the help of sound astronomical knowledge." In opposition to this view, the Radbaz (Rabbi David ben Solomon ibn Zimra) in Egypt wrote a responsum against those who wished to excommunicate a Jew who was an expert in Aristotelian philosophy. The Radbaz berated them, arguing that the leading sages – Shmuel among them – were knowledgeable about all forms of secular learning (Responsa of the Radbaz, *Oraḥ Ḥayim*, 191). It is interesting, too, to read the responsa of the Rema of Cracow (Rabbi Moses Isserles), who wrote to his relative the Maharshal of Lublin (Rabbi Solomon Luria) after the latter attacked him for invoking secular knowledge in his laws of non-kosher animals. The Rema responded at length about the necessity of mastering these other fields of learning. In his letter, he addresses the Maharshal as one who is "familiar with all the paths of the heavens," invoking Shmuel's description of himself in the Talmud.

he was responsible for all aspects of Jewish life. With time, he became known as "the lion."[6]

### SHMUEL'S RELATIONSHIP WITH LEVI BEN SISI

When we studied Rebbi's will, we discussed the disappointment of Levi ben Sisi, who was Rebbi's leading student. When Rabbi Efes was appointed as head, Levi ben Sisi was still living in the Land of Israel, though he did not participate in the affairs of the study house. Then when Rabbi Ḥanina rose to prominence in Tzippori, Levi ben Sisi moved to Babylonia. He arrived in Nehardea as an adult, already in possession of a reputation as a leading student of Rebbi. He quickly became part of the religious leadership of the city, under Shmuel's father:

The Talmud describes the impression he made when he arrived in Nehardea:

> They said to Rav: A great man who was very tall came to Nehardea, and he was limping, and he taught that wearing a tiara outside on Shabbat is permitted. Rav said: Who is this great man who is tall and limping? It is Levi. From this, we can deduce that Rabbi Efes must have died, and Rabbi Ḥanina was now the head of the academy, and Levi did not have anyone with whom he could sit and study, so he came here to Nehardea. (Shabbat 59b)

We learn from this source that Rav was already in Babylonia, but not in Nehardea. He heard about Levi's arrival from students who were not familiar with this sage and could identify him only by his physical appearance. Rav then proceeds to draw conclusions about the situation of the rabbinic leadership in the Land of Israel.

6. S.Y. Rapoport argues that Shmuel was known by this nickname because of his connections with King Ardashir. See S.Y. Rapoport, *Erekh Milin* (Warsaw: 5674), 194. Rabbi D.Z. Hoffman instead regards his nickname as a reference to the king himself. See Hoffman, *Mar Shmuel* (Leipzig, Germany: 1883), 7.

The Talmud continues to describe Levi's arrival in Nehardea:

> Levi taught in Nehardea that wearing a tiara on Shabbat is permitted, and twenty-four tiaras emerged from all of Nehardea. (Shabbat 59b)

The word for "tiara," *kelila,* refers to a special ornament commonly worn on the heads of bridegrooms until the days of the Hadrianic persecutions. At that point, the sages prohibited it, based on a biblical verse: "Remove the headdress and lift off the crown! This shall not remain as it is; exalt the low and abase the high" (Ezek. 21:31).[7] The sages declared that so long as the high priest was still wearing his headdress, it was permissible to wear the tiara; but once the Temple was destroyed and the high priest no longer wore his headdress, wearing the tiara was prohibited as well. When Rav arrives in Babylonia, he brings with him the ruling that wearing the tiara is permitted. For the Babylonians, this comes as a surprise, and they react by joyously embracing the new policy.

The Talmud relates that Levi would often accompany Shmuel's father in Nehardea. They would set out together in the morning to pray at the Shaf VeYatev synagogue even though it featured a statue of a human being (Rosh HaShana 24b), and from there they would issue halakhic rulings. For instance, together they ruled that one may not eat a non-Jew's *shetita,* that is, a dish made from the flour of kernels that were parched in an oven (Avoda Zara 38b).

The conversations in the Talmud between Levi and Shmuel suggest that there was a significant age gap between them, or at least a gap in stature. Shmuel had not yet received his rabbinic ordination when Levi came down to Babylonia, even though he was already an adult. Levi's nickname for Shmuel, "Ariokh," which means "king" or "lion," was a sign of respect but also a sign of Levi's seniority; this is a name that a teacher would confer upon a student, and not vice versa. Shmuel often quoted halakhot in Levi's name, further suggesting that Levi was the more senior sage. It was he who transmitted Rebbi's Mishna to Shmuel.

7. For background on the tiara, see G. Herman, "The Relationship Between Rav Huna and Rav Ḥisda" [Hebrew], *Zion* 61 (5756): 265, note 18.

Levi died while Shmuel's father was still alive. The Talmud records the eulogy delivered by Shmuel's father:

> When Rabbi Levi ben Sisi died, Shmuel's father came up and eulogized him as follows: "The end of all matter; all has been heard. Fear God" [Eccl. 12:13]. To what may the life of Rabbi Levi ben Sisi be compared? To the story of a king who had a vineyard, and in it were one hundred vines, which produced one hundred barrels of wine each year. With time, he was left with fifty, then forty, then thirty, then twenty, then ten, then just one vine. And still it produced one hundred barrels of wine. And he loved this vine as much as the whole vineyard. In this way, Rabbi Levi ben Sisi was as beloved to God as all other people put together. As it is written, "For this is the whole of man" [Eccl. 12:13]. (Y. Berakhot 2:8 [5c])

In this parable, the king is not just a reference to God, but also to Rabbi Yehuda HaNasi, whose many students left him one by one. The last one standing was Rabbi Levi ben Sisi, who could produce one hundred barrels of wine all on his own. As this parable teaches, all of Rabbi Yehuda HaNasi's Torah learning was preserved thanks to Rabbi Levi ben Sisi, and thus the whole vineyard of Rebbi's disciples was equivalent to this vine alone.

### SHMUEL'S RELATIONSHIP WITH HIS FATHER IN THE NEXT WORLD

The Talmud describes how Shmuel's father remained posthumously involved in his son's life:

> Shmuel's father was entrusted with orphans' money. When he died, Shmuel was not with him, so he did not know about the location of the money. People would call Shmuel "the son of the one who consumed the orphans' money." So Shmuel followed his father to the cemetery and he said to the dead: I seek Abba. They said to him: There are many Abbas here. He said to them: I seek Abba the son of Abba. They said to him: There

> are also many Abba the son of Abbas here. He said to them: I seek Abba the son of Abba and the father of Shmuel; where is he? They said to him: He has ascended to the heavenly academy. Meanwhile, Shmuel noticed his deceased friend Levi [ben Sisi] sitting outside the circle of the dead. Shmuel said to him: Why are you sitting outside the circle of the dead? Why have you not ascended to the heavenly academy? Levi said to him: For they said to me: For as many years as you did not go to the academy of Rabbi Efes and thereby distressed him, we will not admit you to the heavenly academy.
>
> Meanwhile, Shmuel's father arrived. Shmuel saw that he was both crying and laughing, so he said to him: Why are you crying? He said to him: Because you will soon be coming here to join me. Shmuel then said: So why are you laughing? His father said: Because you are highly regarded in this world. Shmuel said to his father: If I am so highly regarded, then let them admit Levi to the heavenly academy on my account. So they admitted Levi. Shmuel then said to his father: Where is the orphans' money? He said: Go take it from inside the bedrock of the mill. The money on the top and bottom is ours, while the money in the middle belongs to the orphans. Shmuel said to him: Why did you place the money this way? He said: So that if robbers should steal any of it, they would steal ours first. And should the ground ravage some of the money, it would ravage ours first. (Berakhot 18b)

Following his father's death, Shmuel is blamed for stealing orphans' money that had been entrusted to his father for safekeeping. For as long as his father was still alive, no one asked any questions; the money was assumed to be secure. But when Shmuel's father dies, the son does not know where the money is kept and his trustworthiness is called into doubt. A distressed Shmuel sets off to find his father in the next world.

When he arrives in the next world, Shmuel encounters Levi ben Sisi. As depicted in this story, the heavenly world is a reflection of the earthly one; here, too, Levi ben Sisi sits outside and no one invites him into the heavenly academy. Just as Shmuel's father restored Levi's honor and stature in the earthly world, now Shmuel takes care to enter him into the World to Come.

Shmuel then meets with his father and receives a lesson no less valuable than the lessons he learned while his father was still alive. His father, who has always guided him in matters of social justice, teaches him the proper way of caring for the money of orphans. This is an other-worldly story with a very down-to-earth message: If there is any chance that money will be lost, it should be our own money, and not the money of others that is entrusted to our care.

### SHMUEL IN THE WAKE OF ḤANANIA

Shmuel became one of the leaders of Babylonian Jewry on account of his seniority and his breadth of interdisciplinary knowledge. One talmudic statement in particular attests to his awareness of his own competence:

> Shmuel said: I am able to establish the proper date of the new moon for the entire Diaspora. (Rosh HaShana 20b)

This is quite a loaded statement. It appears in a passage in Tractate Rosh HaShana that deals with the fixing of the calendar and the secret of intercalating the year, a hallmark of rabbinic authority. With this statement, Shmuel seeks to renounce Babylonian Jewry's dependence on the rabbinic leadership in the Land of Israel. For so long as the calendar was fixed by means of the sanctifying of the new moon, the Land of Israel remained the center and the source for all Diaspora communities – "for out of Zion shall go forth Torah."[8] But as Babylonian Jewry became increasingly established in its own right, the relative stature of the sages of the Land of Israel was called into question, and the Babylonian sages tried to assert their authority when it came to intercalation.

The tension between the two Jewish communities dates back at least to the time of Rebbi's father, Rabbi Shimon ben Gamliel. It was during this period that Ḥanania, the nephew of Rabbi Yehoshua, went

8. S. Safrai, "Sites of the Sanctification of the New Moon and the Intercalation of the Year in the Land of Israel After the Destruction of the Temple" [Hebrew], *Tarbiz* 35 (5726): 27–38.

down to Babylonia and rebelled against the hegemony of the rabbinic authorities in the Land of Israel by attempting to intercalate the year following the Bar Kokhba revolt.[9] As we have seen, Ḥanania was regarded as the founding father of talmudic scholarship in Babylonia. Shmuel, who was born in Nehardea, remarks on several occasions that the halakha follows Ḥanania.[10] It seems that here, too, he follows Ḥanania in his efforts to intercalate the year outside of the Land of Israel.

Shmuel's actions did not go unchallenged by the rabbinical authorities in the Land of Israel:

> Abba, the father of Rabbi Simlai, said to Shmuel: Do you know the explanation of this matter that was taught regarding the secret of intercalation: What is the difference between whether the moon was in conjunction before midday or after midday? Shmuel said: No. Abba said to him: Since the master does not know this, there may also be other things that the master does not know. (Rosh HaShana 20b)

Rabbi Simlai's father was a sage from the Land of Israel who traveled back and forth to Babylonia.[11] He speaks on behalf of the rabbinical leadership in the Land of Israel when he challenges Shmuel with a question about the secret of intercalation. Shmuel falls into his trap, and Rabbi Simlai's father rests his case that Shmuel does not yet know what he is doing.

Rabbi Simlai is clearly criticizing Shmuel and his patriarchal Babylonian stance. His invocation of the details of intercalation suggests that he was connected to those leading sages of the Land of Israel who were experts in such matters. Back in the day, Rabbi Shimon ben Gamliel had sent messengers to Ḥanania in order to stop him from fixing the calendar in Babylonia. The father of Rabbi Simlai, too, seems to be a messenger from the patriarch (either Rabban Gamliel the son of Rebbi, or Rabbi Yehuda Nesiya), sent to put the increasingly dominant Babylonian Jews back in their place.

9. *Sages* III, Part Four.
10. Ibid.
11. B.Z. Rosenfeld, "The Figure and Accomplishments of Rabbi Simlai as a Chapter in the History of Israel-Diaspora Relations in the Third Century" [Hebrew], *Zion* 48 (5743): 229–230 and note 10.

### SHMUEL'S CAPTURED DAUGHTERS AND ḤANANIA

Now that we have discussed Shmuel's father and his very esteemed position in Babylonia, and now that we have taken into account the tension between the Land of Israel and Babylonia regarding genealogical purity, we are in a better position to appreciate the following story about Shmuel's daughters.[12] We begin with the relevant mishna:

> If a woman said: I was taken captive but I am undefiled – she is believed, for the mouth that forbade is the mouth that permitted. But if there are witnesses that she was taken captive, and she says: I am undefiled, then she is not believed. But if after she was wed, witnesses came, then she does not leave [that is, her husband is not obligated to divorce her]. (Mishna Ketubot 2:5)

This law is taught as part of a series of mishnayot that demonstrate the legal principle that "the mouth that forbade is the mouth that permitted." That is, a person who declares that something is forbidden to him when there is no external confirmation of this fact is also believed when he or she announces that the prohibition no longer applies.[13] This applies to the case of a woman who announces that she was taken captive (which would generally mean that she is prohibited from marrying a priest), but then further testifies that she was not raped by her captors (which would mean that she may, in fact, marry a priest). Since it is she who forbade and then permitted herself, she is permitted in marriage to a priest based on her own testimony.

The second half of the mishna teaches that here, as in the other cases listed in the chapter, if external witnesses attest that the woman is in fact prohibited to marry, then she herself is not believed and she may not marry a priest. This stringency is qualified at the end of the mishna: If she has already married a priest, and then the external witnesses come and testify that she was taken captive, we believe her if she

12. This entire section is based on Vered Noam, "The Case of a Story Taken Captive" [Hebrew], *Jerusalem Studies in Hebrew Literature* 19 (5763), 9–21.
13. See Rashi on the mishna that appears in Ketubot 18b, "Behold they are believed."

says she is undefiled, and the priest need not divorce her. However, the Tosefta and a *baraita* quoted in the talmudic *sugya* add that if the witnesses explicitly attest that she was not just captured but also defiled by her captors, then her husband the priest may divorce her, even if she has already borne him children:

> If…witnesses came and said…she was taken captive and she is defiled, then even though she has sons, she leaves. (Tosefta Ketubot 2:2)[14]

The tannaitic sources seem to suggest that so long as the woman is unmarried, the witnesses' testimony that she was captured invalidates her from marrying a priest; once the woman is married, the witnesses can no longer invalidate her. But as far back as the beginning of the amoraic period in Babylonia, during the generation of Shmuel's father, the law was further qualified as follows:

> The father of Shmuel said: The term "married" in our mishna does not literally mean married. Rather, it means that the court has permitted her to marry, even though she did not yet marry. (Ketubot 23a)

That is, from the moment that the captured woman is permitted by the court to marry, no further witnesses may come and deprive her of this right. Following this dispensation, which is taught in the name of Shmuel's father, the Talmud cites this story about Shmuel's daughters:

> There were captured women who were brought to Nehardea to be ransomed. The father of Shmuel placed guards over them so that they would not be violated by their captors. Shmuel asked his father: And until now, who was guarding them? He said: If they were your daughters, would you treat them so lightly? It was "like an error proceeding from a ruler" [Eccl. 10:5], and the

14. See the Tosefta and the *baraita* quoted in Ketubot 23b: "If witnesses came and attested that she was defiled, then even if she has children, she leaves."

> daughters of the master Shmuel were captured. The daughters were taken up from Babylonia to the Land of Israel. They left their captors standing outside and entered the study hall of Rabbi Ḥanina. This one said: I was captured but I am undefiled. This one said: I was captured but I am undefiled. Rabbi Ḥanina permitted them to marry priests. Afterward, their captors entered the study hall. Rabbi Ḥanina said: These women are evidently children of a halakhic master. It became known that they were the daughters of the master Shmuel. Rabbi Ḥanina said to Rav Shemen bar Abba: Go out, take care of your relatives. Rav Shemen bar Abba said to Rav Ḥanina: But there are witnesses abroad [who might come and testify that they are prohibited to marry a priest]! Rabbi Ḥanina said: For the time being, no such witnesses are before us. If witnesses are all the way up north, should she be prohibited now on account of them?[15] (Ketubot 23a)

The crux of this story is Shmuel's father's statement to his son: "If they were your daughters, would you treat them so lightly?" He challenges his son to view his legal rulings as applying universally, including to his own family.[16] Shmuel is punished for his lack of empathy toward the captives when his father's cautionary words prove tragically prescient and his own daughters are taken captive. When they arrive in the Land of Israel they encounter humanity at its best. Rabbi Ḥanina takes care not just to free them but also to help marry them off. The women rely on a law that they probably learned in their father's home: "If a woman said: I was taken captive but I am undefiled – she is believed." They also rely on their grandfather's corollary that once they were permitted to marry, no further witnesses may come along and invalidate them. Rabbi Ḥanina comes and instructs his student, Rav Shemen bar Abba the priest,

15. For the term used in the Talmud to describe the location of the witnesses, see *Arukh HaShalem* by Rabbeinu Natan ben Rabbeinu Yehiel, ed. C.Y. Kohut (Vilna: 5686), 1, 205–206, under "Astana." Various dictionaries offer conflicting definitions of this term, which seems to have its origins in Assyrian. See Kohut, ibid.; S. Krauss, *Tosafot HaArukh HaShalem* (Vilna: 5687), 52; L. Ginzberg, *Notes on the Arukh HaShalem* [Hebrew], ibid. 430.
16. See my article on "The Challenges of Halakhic Innovation" [Hebrew], *Akdamut* 23 (5769), 49–62.

to "take care of your relatives," that is, to marry one of them, in order that no one will be able to question their suitability.

This is a rather extreme case. The halakhic interpretation is somewhat forced because in this incident, the girls return with their captors, leave the men outside, and circumvent the law. As Vered Noam attests, "This part of the incident reinforces the moral of the story, that is, that the human dimension of a situation may demand not just the sensitivity of the halakhic authority, but also a renunciation, by means of a creative manipulation of the law."[17] In any case, the moral of the story is clear: a halakhic authority has to rule as if the fate of a member of his own family were at stake.[18]

The concern that is mentioned at the end of the story – that there might be witnesses at the end of the earth who could come and attest that the women were defiled – seems far-fetched, as many early and late medieval commentators have noted.[19] But a comparison with the version that appears in the Jerusalem Talmud suggests another way of understanding the story's conclusion:

> When he found out who they were, they told Shimon bar Ba: Take care of your relatives. He married the first, who died. Then he married the second, who died. Why was that so? Was it because they had lied? Heaven forbid, they had not lied. But it was because of the sin of Ḥanania, nephew of Rabbi Yehoshua, who had intercalated the year abroad. (Y. Ketubot 2:6 [26c])

17. Vered Noam, "The Case of a Story Taken Captive," 9–2. On the obligation to manipulate Jewish law, see M. Zilburg, *This is the Way of the Talmud* [Hebrew] (Jerusalem: 5722), 26–44.
18. It is instructive to consider the influence of this principle on contemporary halakhic rulings. See Y. Tamar, *Sefer Alei Tamar with Notes on the Jerusalem Talmud*, Seder Nashim (Givatayim: 5742). Tamar relates that Rabbi Sholom Mordechai Schwadron of Berezhany, known as the Maharsham (1835–1911), used to moan as if in pain when the case of a "chained" woman would come before him. When he would find a way to release her, his eyes would light up, calling to mind Shmuel's father's statement, "If they were your daughters, would you treat them so lightly?" And so, as Tamar relates, his heart and his mind were equally involved in issuing halakhic rulings.
19. Noam, "The Case of a Story Taken Captive," 9–21.

This is a rather surprising conclusion to the story. The two women die, and the Talmud tries to account for their deaths by linking them to the "original sin" of Babylonian Jewry, Ḥanania's intercalation of the year. The connection between the death of Shmuel's daughters and Ḥanania's rebellion against the hegemony of the rabbis of the Land of Israel seems rather tenuous, as others have noted.[20] But we can better understand the story's conclusion in light of the special connection between Shmuel and Ḥanania, and in light of Shmuel's boast that he could "establish the proper date of the new moon for the entire Diaspora." The Jerusalem Talmud is cautioning that anyone who seeks to challenge the hegemony of the Land of Israel is risking his or her life. It would have been impossible to kill off Shmuel because he was the head of the Babylonian sages. So instead the Talmud transfers the sin of the father to his daughters, who die on account of their father's challenge to the preeminence of the Land of Israel.[21]

We will now turn our attention from Shmuel to Rav, who arrives from the Land of Israel and alters the entire rabbinic hierarchy in Babylonia.

20. See Rabbi S.Y. Ashkenazi, *Yefeh Mareh: Commentaries and Interpretations on the Stories of the Jerusalem Talmud* (Berlin: 5605–5606), 162a.

21. Tamar, *Sefer Alei Tamar*, Seder Nashim, 94.

## *Chapter Eleven*

# Rav

Rav, who was known as Rabbi Abba, was born in Babylonia and came to the Land of Israel with his uncle Rabbi Ḥiya, who gave him private instruction. While he was in the Land of Israel, Rav studied in the patriarch's beit midrash and learned the official Mishna. Several sources seem to suggest that Rav traveled back and forth several times between Babylonia and the Land of Israel, but we cannot know for sure.[1] We do know that Rav is credited with bringing the official Mishna of Rabbi Yehuda HaNasi to Babylonia; until that point, Babylonian scholars used to study collections of mishnayot issued by various *batei midrash*.

We know about Rav's years of study in the Land of Israel from various sources that describe Rav as a close disciple of Rabbi Yehuda HaNasi. Rabbi Yonatan relates his childhood memories of Rav, then an older student in Rebbi's beit midrash:

1. M.A. Tannenblat, "Rav Founds a Religious Center in the Diaspora" [Hebrew], *A Jubilee Book in Honor of N.M. Gelber* (Tel Aviv: 5723), 58. Also see Albeck, *Introduction to the Talmuds*, 171.

> After Issi bar Hini ascended from Babylonia to the Land of Israel, Rabbi Yoḥanan encountered him teaching his son as follows:[2] *reḥelim*. Rabbi Yoḥanan said to him: Teach him that the word is *reḥelot*. Rabbi Issi said: I pronounce the word as it is written in the Torah, "*reḥelim* two hundred" [Gen. 32:15]. Rabbi Yoḥanan said to him: The language of the Torah is distinct, and the language of the sages is distinct.
>
> Rabbi Yoḥanan said to Issi bar Hini: Who is the head of the academy in Babylonia? Issi said to him: Abba the Tall. Rabbi Yoḥanan said to him: You call him Abba the Tall? I remember when I used to sit seventeen rows behind Rav, who sat in front of Rebbi, and when they would debate, sparks would fly out of Rav's mouth to Rebbi's mouth, and from Rebbi's mouth to Rav's mouth, and I could not comprehend what they were saying – and yet you call him Abba the Tall? (Ḥullin 137b)

In the first part of the story, Rabbi Yoḥanan corrects Issi's pronunciation of the word for "sheep," arguing that the rabbis pluralize this word differently than the Bible. The next part of the story contains two forms of testimony. Rabbi Yoḥanan recollects Rav's early years as a student of Rabbi Yehuda HaNasi. He speaks of Rav admiringly, relating how he would sit in the front row of students exchanging fiery words with the patriarch. But the new arrival from Babylonia, Issi bar Hini, regards himself as Rav's superior, and therefore refers to him using the nickname "Abba the Tall." The conversation between Rabbi Yoḥanan and Issi goes downhill from there, and in the continuation of the story Rabbi Yoḥanan dismisses Issi, convinced that he has little to learn from him.

Rav studied the Mishna along with his uncle Rabbi Ḥiya's *baraitot*, and thus he served as a link between all the tannaitic collections that preceded Rebbi's Mishna and the start of the talmudic era. The

2. The version in the printed text implies that Rabbi Yoḥanan was studying with his son and Issi corrected him. But in the Roman manuscript and in older printings, the language of the text implies that it was Rabbi Yoḥanan who corrected Issi. See also the parallel in Avoda Zara 58b, and Albeck, *Introduction to the Talmuds*, 174, note 68.

Talmud frequently states that Rav was considered to have the authority of a *Tanna* and could therefore dispute tannaitic sources.[3] Certainly he was regarded as the leading talmudic sage on account of his extensive knowledge of Mishna and his ability to compare sources and determine the halakha. Perhaps this is also the reason that he was known simply as Rav, without the need for any other epithet.

### OBTAINING PERMISSION FROM REBBI TO RELOCATE TO BABYLONIA

Rav prepared to return to Babylonia during Rabbi Ḥiya's lifetime. We know this because the Talmud relates that Rabbi Ḥiya attempted to obtain authorization from Rebbi for Rav to rule on halakhic matters:

> When Rabba bar Ḥana was going down to Babylonia, Rabbi Ḥiya said to Rebbi: My brother's son is going down to Babylonia. May he render decisions with regard to prohibited or permitted matters? Rebbi answered: He may render decisions. Rabbi Ḥiya asked: May he adjudicate monetary cases? Rebbi answered: He may adjudicate monetary cases. Rabbi Ḥiya asked: May he permit firstborn animals? Rebbi said: He may permit them.
>
> When Rav was going down to Babylonia, Rabbi Ḥiya said to Rebbi: My sister's son is going down to Babylonia. May he render decisions with regard to prohibited or permitted matters? Rebbi answered: He may render decisions. Rabbi Ḥiya asked: May he adjudicate monetary cases? Rebbi answered: He may adjudicate monetary cases. Rabbi Ḥiya asked: May he permit firstborn animals? Rebbi said: He may not permit them. (Sanhedrin 5a)

Rebbi distinguishes between the two cousins. He authorizes Rabba bar Ḥana to render decisions, adjudicate monetary cases, and permit firstborn animals. But Rav receives only the first two authorizations. He may not permit firstborns, an activity which involves identifying

3. This statement appears five times in the Babylonian Talmud: Eiruvin 50b, Ketubot 8a, Gittin 38b, Bava Batra 42a, and Sanhedrin 83b.

any blemishes on animals that would render them unfit for sacrifice, thereby exempting them from the status of Temple property. If a firstborn is blemished but a sage has not declared it permitted, that animal becomes an albatross around the owner's neck, since the owner cannot do anything with it. Permitting firstborns, a very lucrative field, required the professional expertise of a cattle herder.

The Talmud seeks to understand why Rav was not granted dispensation to permit firstborns:

> What is the reason that Rebbi denied Rav authorization to permit firstborns? If you say it was because Rav was not wise enough, we have already stated that he was exceedingly wise! And if you say that it was because Rav was not an expert in the nature of blemishes, Rav said: For eighteen months I trained among cattle herders in order to know which blemish is permanent and which blemish is temporary. Rather, Rebbi withheld this authorization from him in order to confer honor upon Rabba bar Ḥana. And if you prefer, say that Rebbi did not grant Rav this authorization precisely because of Rav's extraordinary knowledge in this matter, for Rav was exceptionally expert in the nature of blemishes, and if granted authorization, he would permit firstborns on the basis of blemishes with which people are not familiar, and as a result they would rule erroneously, saying: Rav permitted a firstborn with this type of blemish, and they would come to permit a firstborn with a temporary blemish. (Sanhedrin 5b)

As the Talmud explains, Rav was an expert at permitting firstborns: He had both the theoretical knowledge (he was "exceedingly wise") and also the practical training (he was an "expert in the nature of blemishes" after his eighteen-month training with herdsmen). Moreover, he knew how to distinguish between temporary and permanent blemishes. But these qualifications were not sufficient to earn him the dispensation to permit firstborns when he went to Babylonia. The Talmud offers two reasons for this, one of which is political and one of which is practical. According to the first reason, Rebbi does not want him to pose a threat to Rabba bar Ḥana, who has already received this dispensation. And according to the second, Rebbi is concerned that Rav's superior knowledge would lead others to make their own – perhaps faulty – determinations after observing his rulings.

### THE FIRST ENCOUNTER OF SHMUEL AND KARNA

Rav goes down to Babylonia. According to the epistle of Rav Sherira Gaon, he arrives "in the five hundred and thirtieth year of the Greek kingdom," which corresponds to 219 CE.

The Talmud records the first encounter between Shmuel and Rav as a tense confrontation that unfolds like a drama in three acts:[4]

> Shmuel and Karna were sitting on the bank of the royal river. They saw that the river water was rising and turbid. Shmuel said to Karna: A great man is coming from the west who is suffering from a stomach ailment, and the water is rising to greet him. Go and sniff his keg. (Shabbat 108a)

In the opening scene, Shmuel and Karna are presented as sitting together on the riverbank of the Euphrates, the "royal river" where Nehardea is located. As locals, they recognize immediately when something is amiss. They watch as the waters of the river rise turbidly. Shmuel concludes based on the appearance of the river that a great man is arriving from the Land of Israel to the west, and that he is suffering from a stomach ailment that has contaminated the waters. Shmuel sends Karna to "sniff his keg," that is, to find out whether the stranger is a Torah scholar or not. Perhaps there has already been a rumor that a great Torah scholar is due to arrive from the Land of Israel, and they want to investigate him.

> Karna went and met Rav. He asked him: From where is it derived that *tefillin* are not written except on the skin of a kosher animal? Rav answered: For it is written: "So that the Torah of God will be

4. This story is structured like a drama, and ought to be more thoroughly analyzed as such to reveal its deeper message. There are three heroes and three scenes, and each scene features a confrontation between two of the heroes: First Karna and Shmuel, then Karna and Rav, and finally Rav and Shmuel in the closing scene. For a literary analysis of this text, see Gila Fine, "When Rav Met Shmuel: A Bakhtinian Reading of Shabbat 108a" (forthcoming).

> in your mouth" [Ex. 13:9], meaning from that which is permissible in your mouth. Karna asked: From where is it derived that blood is red? Rav said: For it is stated, "The Moabites saw the water from afar and it appeared red like blood" [II Kings 3:22]. Karna asked: From where is it derived that circumcision is performed in that place? Rav said: It is stated here, "his blockage" [Gen. 17:14], and it is stated later, "its blockage" [Lev. 19:23]. Just as the later verse speaks of something that produces fruit, so too the verse here speaks of something that produces fruit. Karna asked: But then one could say that circumcision is performed in one's heart, for it is written, "You shall cut away the blockage of your heart" [Deut. 10:16], or one could say that it is performed on one's ear, for it is written, "Behold their ear is blocked" [Jer. 6:10]. Rav said: We derive the legal significance of "his blockage," which is a complete expression, from the word "its blockage," which is also a complete expression. And we do not derive the legal significance of "his blockage," which is a complete expression, from "the blockage of," which is not a complete expression. Rav said to him: What is your name? Karna said: Karna. Rav said to him: Let it be the will of heaven that a horn emerge from his eye! (Shabbat 108a)

Karna sniffs out Rav, the "great man" newly arrived from the Land of Israel, by testing him with three questions. The answer to the first question can be derived by biblical exegesis: *Tefillin* may be written only on the skin of a kosher animal. The second question is strange: From where it is it derived that blood is red? Rav's answer is based on a verse from the Book of Kings, in which the Moabites see that the water is red as blood. In the third question, Rav asks about circumcision: From where is it derived that the circumcision takes place where it does, and not on another organ of the body? This time Karna pushes Rav further, annoying him until Rav grows exasperated. Ultimately Rav curses his interlocutor by invoking his name, Karna, which comes from the same root as the word for "horn" (*keren*). "Let it be the will of heaven that a horn emerge from his eye!" This bizarre examination thus moves from skin to blood to the sexual organ as Karna prods the new arrival deeper and deeper until he explodes.

The third and final scene takes place in Shmuel's house:

> Eventually Shmuel took Rav into his house. He fed him barley bread and fish hash and gave him beer to drink, but he did not show him to the bathroom, so that he would become diarrhetic. Rav cursed him, saying: Whoever is causing me to suffer will not be survived by sons! And so it was. (Shabbat 108a)

In the first scene of the story, Karna and Shmuel discuss the turbid waters that rise ever higher. In the second scene, Karna digs into the skin and blood of the new arrival. And in the closing scene, Rav and Shmuel meet for the first time on an extremely unequal footing, and here the drama reaches its climax. Rav, who is suffering from a stomach ailment, is brought to the home of Shmuel, a doctor. He is welcomed with barley bread, fish hash, and beer, but he is not shown the way to the bathroom. This form of torture utterly debases the sick man, who loses all self-control and curses Shmuel, telling him that he will have no sons who survive him. The Talmud concludes that so it came to pass.

Some scholars have sought to derive practical halakha from this story. For example, there are those who concluded that a doctor may treat a patient aggressively, ignoring the patient's curses and protestations.[5] But it seems that the story is presenting a different lesson altogether. The talmudic sages did not hesitate to depict themselves in moments of weakness and in embarrassing situations. Here we encounter a sage who has difficulty welcoming a new rabbi who poses a threat to his status as the intellectual giant of his generation. It is a case of "two kings cannot share the same crown," and indeed the tension is palpable even before they first meet.

5. Rav Y. Zilberstein, *The Society for Healing and Halakha,* printout 48. His words are quoted in an article by Y.M. Bar Ilan, "On the Commandment of Nursing" [Hebrew], *Asia* 79–80 (5767), by note 5. The author of the article points out that this is not a good example, because Shmuel does not force treatment on Rav, and Rav does not object. Moreover, at the end of the story, Rav curses Shmuel and the curse seems to receive divine endorsement.

### THE ENCOUNTER WITH RABBI SHEILA[6]

One of the key figures from the early years in Nehardea was Rabbi Sheila, who is mentioned at various points throughout the Talmud as the "head of the *sidra*" in Babylonia. The *sidra* was a place of Torah study; in subsequent generations it would become known as the yeshiva.[7] Rav, who arrives at Nehardea, naturally sets his steps toward the beit midrash. There he sits among the students and listens to a class taught by Rabbi Sheila:

> Rav visited the place of Rabbi Sheila. There was no speaker to stand before Rabbi Sheila and broadcast his words. Rav stood up before him to act as the speaker, and in the course of his speech, he interpreted "the call of the *gever*" as "the call of the man." Rabbi Sheila said to him: Master should say: The call of the rooster. Rav said: A flute that was played for nobles is not acceptable to weavers? When I stood before Rabbi Ḥiya as his speaker, I interpreted "the call of the *gever*" as "the call of the man," and he did not object. But you tell me: Say, "the call of the rooster." Rabbi Sheila said to him: Master is Rav! Let master sit down. Rav said: People say: If you hired yourself out to him, comb his wool. And some say this is what Rav said to Rabbi Sheila: We ascend in matters of sanctity, but do not descend. (Yoma 20b)

The job of the "speaker" is to repeat the words of the sage in a much louder voice so that everyone can hear. A speaker is not supposed to add his own opinions; he merely amplifies the voice of the sage. In this story, Rav finds himself in Rabbi Sheila's beit midrash at a time when there is no speaker present, so he volunteers himself for the task. But on account of his own extensive knowledge, he finds himself unable to

6. According to some of the early medieval commentators including the Rif (Rabbi Isaac Alfasi, 1013–1103) and the Rosh (Rabbi Asher ben Yehiel, 1250–1327), and according to the manuscript versions, the sage referred to here is not Rabbi Sheila but Rava, from the fourth generation of talmudic sages.
7. Gafni, *The Jews of Babylonia*, 183. Gafni quotes Rabbi Saadia Gaon, who refers to Rabbi Sheila not as the head of the "yeshiva," but as the head of the "place of Torah."

merely repeat the Torah he hears. When Rabbi Sheila teaches the blessing about the One who gives discernment to the rooster, Rav explains that the crying of the rooster is actually a man. Rabbi Sheila asks him why he does not interpret this word as rooster. Rav answers him rather cryptically, "A flute that was played for nobles is not acceptable to weavers." Rav himself is the flute who used to play for nobles when he served as speaker in the beit midrash of Rabbi Ḥiya. There they knew how to appreciate his melodies. But now, in the beit midrash of the "weaver" Rabbi Sheila, his melodies are rejected.

Rav, who cursed Karna and Shmuel when he first arrived in Babylonia, now speaks derisively to Rabbi Sheila. He reserves his praise for the beit midrash of his uncle Rabbi Ḥiya.

### CONFRONTING SHMUEL'S FATHER

There are several sources that suggest that when Rav came to Babylonia, he stayed first in Nehardea, the major city of the Babylonian Jewish diaspora. There he had a fraught encounter with the leading sage of the previous generation, Abba bar Ba, who was also Shmuel's father. The Talmud relates that Shmuel's father was teaching halakha in his beit midrash when Rav began to challenge his claims by invoking the Mishna he had brought with him from the Land of Israel:

> Shmuel's father said: The wife of an ordinary Jew [a non-priest] who was violated is forbidden to her husband, for we are concerned that perhaps the beginning of the cohabitation was by coercion, but its end was with consent. Rav responded to Shmuel's father: "If you are captured, I shall ransom you and return you to me as a wife." Shmuel's father remained silent. Rav cited the following verse about Shmuel' father: "Ministers would withhold their words, and place their hand to their mouth" [Job 29:9]. What could he have said? They ruled leniently regarding a captive. (Ketubot 51b)

The discussion begins with Shmuel's father's assertion that a woman who was raped is forbidden to her husband because of the fear that even though she was at first taken against her will, it is possible that at some point she consented. Rav challenges Shmuel's father's statement based on a mishna in Ketubot (4:8), which stipulates that a husband is obligated to redeem his wife if she is taken captive. The mere mention of this mishna is enough to silence Shmuel's father. After all, if a man is obligated to redeem his captive wife, then surely there is no suspicion that she may have willingly submitted to her captors. And thus the woman who was raped, too, should be permitted to her husband.

Rav is pleased that Shmuel's father has nothing to say in response. He quotes a verse that describes ministers refraining from speaking when they have nothing to say. At this point the Talmud supplies the rejoinder that Shmuel's father could have offered: "They ruled leniently regarding a captive." That is, the mishna in Ketubot is referring to the specific case of a woman taken captive, and cannot be generalized to all cases of rape.

Rav has another confrontation with Shmuel's father that is depicted in the Jerusalem Talmud. A mishna in Yevamot deals with witnesses who attest to the death of a husband. The mishna's innovative ruling is that even one witness's testimony that the husband is dead is sufficient to free his wife to remarry. This leniency, which is unique to this area of halakha, serves as the backdrop to the following story:

> Rav Naḥman bar Yaakov said in the name of Rav: If she was married on the basis of the testimony of two witnesses [that her husband had died], then even if her husband should then come, they say to her: He is not with us. Rabbi Shmuel bar Yitzḥak asked: What if he was a well-known man, such as Imi? Rabbi Yose bar Rabbi Bun said: And is there no one here who is like Rabbi Imi?
>
> Such a case came before the rabbis in Babylonia. They said to him: You are not with us. Abba bar Ba [Shmuel's father] got up and whispered in his ear: By your life! Give her a divorce by reason of doubt. The disciples of Rav got up and hit him. He said: The strap for flogging is burnt, and the stool for the subject of the flogging is burnt. Shmuel said: I was there, and it is not so that the strap for flogging is burnt, and that the stool for the subject of the flogging is burnt. But it was my father [Abba bar Ba] who was flogged and went on his way.

> The case came before Rabbi Imi. He said to [the second husband, after the first had come back]: Yes, it is true that she is permitted to you. But you should know that the sons by that man [you] will be bastards in the eyes of heaven. And Rabbi Zeira praised him for laying out the matter with full clarity. (Y. Yevamot 15:4 [15a])

The first part of the story cites the halakha taught in Rav's beit midrash. If a woman's husband disappeared and two witnesses came and testified that he was killed, the woman may remarry based on the testimony of those witnesses. Even if the first husband then returns, they say to him, "It's not really you." This is clearly a complicated situation, but it was historically not uncommon. Throughout the halakhic literature we find various cases in which "chained women" were permitted to remarry based on the testimony of witnesses or based on a court ruling, only later to be confronted with the return of the first husband.[8] In any case, the Jerusalem Talmud seems uncomfortable with this story and questions whether the first husband would be turned away even if he were a great and famous man such Rav Imi, one of Rabbi Yoḥanan's students in Tiberias.

The second part of the story transfers this conversation from the theoretical realm of the beit midrash to the practical realm of the courtroom. In a case that comes before the court, a woman remarries after witnesses testify that her first husband has died, but then the first husband comes back on the scene. The court, led by Rav, refuses to recognize this husband and re-open the case: "You are not with us." Shmuel's father, known in the Jerusalem Talmud as Abba bar Ba, is also present. He hears Rav's ruling and whispers to the second husband, "Give her a divorce by reason of doubt." Rav's students hear him and fall upon him violently: "The strap for flogging is burnt, and the stool for the subject of the flogging is burnt."

The traditional commentators are divided as to what actually happened. According to the Penei Moshe, Rav's students merely spoke these

8. The responsa literature contains many cases of "chained women" who were permitted to remarry and were then confronted with a "dead man walking." See Y.Z. Kahane, *Sefer HaAgunot* (Jerusalem: 5714), the inspiration for a story by S.Y. Agnon.

words about flogging, and so the physical violence was in fact verbal. According to the Korban HaEda, the Talmud records an anonymous witness's account of what he saw in the courtroom: The strap with which Abba was lashed and the bench that he sat upon when he was lashed were both burned to show that he should not have been lashed. And finally, according to Rabbi S. Friedlander, Shmuel's father responded to the violence that the students sought to inflict on him by protesting, "May the strap and bench be burned."[9] The Talmud concludes with Shmuel's testimony that he was present during this incident and there was no actual fire that broke out; the students of Rav "merely" beat his father.

Most traditional rabbinic commentators have regarded this story as implausible and have therefore not engaged with it seriously.[10] If this story has any historical basis it may lie in the depiction of Rav, even at this early stage of his career in Babylonia, as stern and uncompromising, surrounded by a group of disciples who jealously guard his honor.

### FROM NEHARDEA TO SOUTHERN BABYLONIA

Rav does not manage to adapt to life in Nehardea and he sets off sparks all around him. The city is full of Torah, wisdom, and good deeds, but he cannot find a place for himself. His Torah is different from that of the locals, and the lessons he brings with him from his teachers in the Land of Israel prevent him from feeling comfortable among the sages of the city. And so he leaves Nehardea and heads south.

In the course of his travels, Rav arrives at places quite remote from the centers of Torah study. He stumbles upon villages populated by Jews ignorant of the most fundamental principles of Jewish living. The Talmud, in speaking of this stage of Rav's travels, writes, "Rav

9. S. Friedlander published *Ḥeshek Shlomo,* a commentary on the Jerusalem Talmud, in 5665. One year later he published a text of the Jerusalem Talmud to Seder Kodashim, which created a great storm in the rabbinic world. One luminary who was nearly convinced by the authenticity of this text was Rabbi Yisrael Meir Kagan (the Ḥafetz Ḥayim). For an account of this incident and for the story of how rabbis and scholars responded to this text, see my book *MiMaran Ad Maran* [Hebrew] (Tel Aviv: 2005), 134–136.
10. See Hyman, *Tanna'im and Amora'im,* 13. "This is difficult to understand," he writes, and then skips over the story completely.

found an open field and erected a protective fence around it." Wherever he went, Rav imparted rabbinic rulings that were intended to "make a fence around the Torah," to invoke the language of the Mishna in Tractate Avot (1:1). He understood that people who know nothing require guidelines that are as clear and simple as possible. And so, for instance, he prohibited the eating of the udders of an animal, presumably because they are made of meat but contain milk. This ruling was a legal innovation, since the udder is kosher according to the Mishna (Ḥullin 8:1). Indeed, even Rav's students were troubled by his ruling, and when one of his senior disciples, Rabbi Elazar, came to the Land of Israel, he tried to discover its source:

> When Rabbi Elazar ascended from Babylonia, he met Ze'iri. He said to him: Is the *Tanna* who taught Rav his ruling forbidding a roasted udder here? They pointed to Rav Yitzḥak bar Avudimi. Rav Yitzḥak bar Avudimi said to Rabbi Elazar: I did not teach Rav any prohibition whatsoever regarding a roasted udder. Rather, Rav found an open field and erected a protective fence around it. For Rav once visited Tatlafush. He overheard a certain housewife saying to her friend: How much milk is required to cook a quart of meat? Rav said: They have never learned that meat with milk is prohibited! So he tarried there and prohibited udders to them. Rav Kahana taught it this way: Rabbi Yose bar Abba taught that Rav Yitzḥak bar Avudimi said: I taught Rav that *baraita* only with respect to an udder of a nursing animal. But Rabbi Ḥiya, due to his sharpness of mind, taught this same *baraita* with respect to an udder, without elaborating. (Ḥullin 110a)

Rav Yitzḥak bar Avudimi was the Mishna instructor in the patriarchal house, where Rav received his training. Rabbi Elazar asks him about the source of Rav's ruling about the udder, and he responds, "It didn't come from me."[11]

It is clear that Rav is not ruling in accordance with the Mishna in this case, but is rather responding to the exigencies of the situation.

11. Epstein, *Text of the Mishna*, 169.

In this sense he may be compared to Neḥemia ben Ḥaklia, who ruled that "all utensils are prohibited on Shabbat" when he witnessed the widespread violation of the Sabbath laws. Both sages sought to build fences around the law in order to safeguard it.

This is true, too, of one of Rav's rulings regarding the laws of Eiruvin which is debated by Rav Huna and Rav Huna the son of Rabbi Yehoshua. Rav Huna rules stringently, insisting that it is necessary to close up any opening in a fence that is wider than four *tefaḥim*. Rav Huna the son of Rabbi Yehoshua rules leniently and says that only a wider opening requires attention. Rav Huna responds as follows:

> Rav Huna said to Rav Huna the son of Yehoshua: Do not disagree with me, for Rav happened to be in Camharya,[12] and he made an actual ruling as I have ruled [forbidding carrying in an alley whose side wall was breached four *tefaḥim*]. Rav Huna son of Yehoshua said to Rav Huna: Rav found an open field and erected a fence around it. (Eiruvin 6a)

Rav rules similarly regarding the prohibition of sitting on a tree on Shabbat. The Talmud (Eiruvin 100b) distinguishes between a fruit-bearing tree and a non-fruit-bearing tree; sitting on the former is prohibited on Shabbat, whereas sitting on the latter is permitted. The Talmud questions, "Is that so? But after all, Rav visited Apastia[13] and forbade sitting on a non-fruit-bearing tree." Once again, the Talmud invokes the same phrase: "Rav found an open field and erected a fence around it."

It seems that when Rav traveled south from Nehardea, he encountered a land full of Jews who were alienated from the center of Jewish learning. They acted as their fathers taught them, and whatever was forgotten was simply forgotten. And so Rav pitched his tent in the middle of this spiritual wasteland and began rebuilding Babylonian Jewry from the ground up.

12. This place is generally identified as Damar, which was a way station between Baghdad and the city of Kufa, six kilometers southwest of Sura. See Eshel, *Jewish Settlements*, 97.
13. The location of Apastia is uncertain. Some have identified it as the city Abusata, but this is problematic since Abusata is nowhere near Sura. See ibid., 26.

### THE FOUNDING OF A YESHIVA IN SURA

Rav Sherira Gaon writes in his epistle about the founding of the yeshiva in Sura:

> Rav purchased the orchard of Beit Rav in Sura, which was the property of a deceased convert. He assembled numerous students and taught them much Torah, and he established a court there. Babylonia already had a great court in Nehardea, and Rav established a second one in Sura. And this is what Shmuel meant when he said: "We do not write a *prozbul* except in the court at Sura or the court at Nehardea." (Gittin 36b)

The Talmud offers its own account in Tractate Bava Batra:

> Rav said: One who draws a picture on the ownerless property of a deceased convert acquires that property. For Rav did not acquire the garden adjoining his academy except by drawing a picture on it. (Bava Batra 54a)

This talmudic passage deals with the way in which a deceased convert's property is acquired. When a convert dies leaving no heirs, there is no one who has a rightful claim to his property. Rav teaches that this property can be acquired by marking it with a picture, and he gives the example of the academy at Sura, which he acquired in this manner.

We cannot know for certain exactly when Rav founded his yeshiva. As we have seen, at that time, Rabbi Sheila was the leader of the academy in Nehardea, which was then the center of Babylonian Torah scholarship.[14] Rav worked until his death in 247 to found the academy at Sura and transform it into a magnet for students of Torah from all

14. M. Beer dates the establishment of the yeshiva in Sura to shortly after Rav came to Babylonia. See Beer, *The Origins of the Babylonian Diaspora During the Period of the Mishna and the Talmud* [Hebrew] (Ramat Gan: 5771), 38–39. But Rav Meshulam Beer dates the establishment of the academy in Sura to 228 CE in *Divrei Meshulam* (Frankfurt: 5686), 64.

over Babylonia. Following his death, some of his disciples went up to the Land of Israel and joined Rabbi Yoḥanan's academy in Tiberias; others stayed in Babylonia and went on to shape the development of the Babylonian Talmud.

It seems that throughout his tenure in Sura, Rav continued to institute his own practices and customs, many of which were based on the learning he had brought with him from the Land of Israel. He was responsible for both the style of learning and the way of life in Sura, which bore his indelible stamp.

*Chapter Twelve*

# Rav and Shmuel I: Styles of Learning

## BIBLICAL EXEGESIS

At the academy in Sura, halakha was always supported by its biblical underpinnings. Rav and his students searched methodically for a biblical proof text for every law they codified. Rav Ḥananel quotes Rav's description of this approach:

> That which is written, "They read in the scroll, in God's Torah, elucidated, heeding the sense, and they understood the reading" [Neh. 8:8]. This is interpreted as, "They read in the scroll, in God's Torah" – this is Bible. "Elucidated" – this is the traditional Aramaic translation. "Heeding the sense" – these are the divisions of the text into verses. "And they understood the reading" – this alludes to cantillation. But some say of "and they understood the reading" – these are the traditions [i.e., the traditional spellings]. (Nedarim 37b)

This style of learning, which involves deriving halakha from biblical verses, is based heavily on received traditions. There are those who argue that Rav inherited this method of learning from his uncle Rabbi Ḥiya, who received it from the sages of the south (Lod); as such, it stood in contrast to the style of learning of the sages in the Galilee.[1] The difference between the two schools is demonstrated elsewhere in the Talmud:

> This is like what Shmuel inquired of Rav Huna: From where do we derive that the unwitting slaughter of sacrificial animals is invalid? Rav Huna said: It is known from [the words], "And he shall slaughter the young bull before God" [Lev. 1:5]. The offering is not valid unless the slaughtering is performed for the sake of the young bull. Shmuel told Rav Huna: That derivation was already in our hands. From where do we learn that intent is essential? He said to Shmuel: From the words, "You shall slaughter it according to your will" [Lev. 19:5], which means you shall slaughter it with awareness. Because the intent is determined only by the one who performs the slaughter. (Zevaḥim 47a)

It is a well-known principle that one who slaughters a sacrificial animal "unwittingly," that is, without the proper intent, renders the sacrifice invalid. The source of this principle is unclear. When Shmuel asks Rav Huna, he responds that the source is a verse from the beginning of Leviticus. But Shmuel replies that this source is already known. He is rather asking about the source of the law that if a person already sacrificed an animal without the proper intent, then the sacrifice is invalid. Rav Huna responds by quoting another verse which teaches that the intent of the one making the sacrifice must be proper in order for the sacrifice to be valid.

It seems strange that Shmuel asks this question of Rav Huna, who is not his teacher but his student, as the Tosafot have pointed out. They suggest that perhaps the Talmud is referring to a different Rav

1. Y.S. Tzuri based all of his research on Rav and the academy in Sura on this dichotomy between the traditions of the south and the Galilee. See Y.S. Tzuri, *The History of Styles of Learning in the Yeshivot of the South, the Galilee, Sura, and Nehardea* [Hebrew] (Jerusalem: 5674), and *Sefer Rav.* Tzuri's dichotomy did not withstand critical scrutiny, as Epstein clearly demonstrated in *Literature of the Tanna'im* [Hebrew], 537.

Huna.[2] More likely, Shmuel may be inquiring about the style of learning at Rav's academy in Sura, which involves finding textual support for all known rabbinic laws.

The following source explicitly distinguishes between the styles of learning of Rav and Shmuel:

> Rav said: Once a person goes from the study of halakha (Mishna) [to the study of Torah], he will no longer enjoy peace. And Shmuel said: This is so even in the case of one who goes from the study of Talmud to the study of Mishna. And Rabbi Yoḥanan said: This is so even in the case of one who goes from the study of one Talmud to the study of another Talmud.[3] (Ḥagiga 10a)

The sages of the first generation describe what happens to a person after he is exposed to various styles of learning. Rav regards halakha – that is, explicit proscriptive statements – as the ultimate form of learning. But for Shmuel, there is also the level of Talmud, which involves biblical exegesis. Once a student is exposed to Talmud, he cannot return to Mishna. Rabbi Yoḥanan adds an additional level, namely the passage from one Talmud to another. As Rashi explains, "From the Jerusalem Talmud to the Babylonian Talmud, which is deep, as we read in Tractate Sanhedrin, 'He has made me dwell in darkness like those long dead' (Lam. 3:6) – this is the Babylonian Talmud." Rabbeinu Ḥananel offers a similar explanation: "From the Babylonian Talmud to the Jerusalem Talmud, whose styles are not one and the same." It is clear that the disagreement among Rav, Shmuel, and Rabbi Yoḥanan reflects three different approaches to Torah study. We shall discuss Rabbi Yoḥanan's approach in a future chapter. At this point we will focus on the differences between Rav's approach as practiced in Sura, and Shmuel's approach as practiced in Nehardea.

2. Tosafot, Ḥullin 13a: "He asked him." If Shmuel is indeed inquiring of a younger student, this is not the only occasion in which he does so; in Makkot 3b, Shmuel asks his young student Rav Matna about the source of a particular law: "Don't sit down until you tell me the source of this law."
3. The words in brackets are missing from several of the manuscripts.

## MEMORIZING MISHNAYOT IN SURA, EXEGESIS IN NEHARDEA

Rav's approach represents the most basic level of Torah study, in which halakha is derived from biblical verses. At Rav's academy in Sura they would commonly ask, "Who taught this?" or "This mishna is according to whom?" in an effort to discover the source of various laws.[4] This approach was foreign to Shmuel and his disciples in Nehardea, who focused on interpreting the Mishna rather than uncovering its biblical roots. Shmuel and his students worked on finding ways of understanding the Mishna that accorded with the accepted and practiced halakha, and on completing those phrases in the Mishna that seemed to be missing words. It is among the sages of Nehardea that we find the origins of talmudic scholarship.[5]

In any case, it is clear that in Sura the Mishna served as the basis for halakha, whereas in Nehardea it was merely the basis for learning. "Shmuel's approach was to try to find a way of interpreting Rebbi's Mishna in accordance with the frameworks of learning in Babylonia, even if this was forced."[6]

Rabbi Zeira quotes two statements, one from Rav and one from Shmuel, which capture their views of the relationship between the Mishna and the Talmud. He quotes Rav as saying, "'All of the days of a poor man are wretched' – this is the master of Talmud. 'But contentment is a feast without end' – this is the master of Mishna [Prov. 15:15]" (Bava Batra 145b). And he quotes Shmuel as saying, "We do not learn from laws or from legends or from *baraitot*, but from the Talmud" (Y. Pe'ah 2:6 [15d]).

This difference in learning styles applies to their approach to dialectical reasoning as well. At Sura, Rav trained his students to memorize and master sources. In contrast, Shmuel's father trained his son to sharpen his mind, pay attention to subtle distinctions, and perform close analysis. In the Talmud's terminology, this is the difference between "Sinai" and "The Uprooter of Mountains."[7]

4. Y.S. Tzuri, *The History of Learning Styles*, 33.
5. Epstein, *Text of the Mishna*, 217–234.
6. A. Goldberg, "Rava's Use of the Tosefta" [Hebrew], *Tarbiz* 40 (5731): 144.
7. The dichotomy of Sinai (breadth of knowledge) and the Uprooter of Mountains (dialectical reasoning) is generally associated with the difference between the Land

**BETWEEN INTENTION AND ACTION**

The debate about whether to privilege intention or action can be traced back to the earliest *Tanna'im*: Shammai (action) versus Hillel (intention), and Rabbi Yehuda (action) versus Rabbi Shimon (intention).[8] This debate extends to Rav and Shmuel as well. Rav held like Rabbi Yehuda that an unintentional violation is nonetheless forbidden, whereas Shmuel held like Rabbi Shimon that an unintentional violation is permissible since "everything goes according to thought" (Beitza 23a). Likewise, Shmuel held that a person who is not familiar with the ways of idolatry cannot render his wine impure, whereas Rav held that even a one-day-old baby can contaminate wine (Avoda Zara 58a). And so in accordance with their general approaches, Rav was focused on tradition and therefore tended to privilege action; Shmuel was focused on interpretation and analysis, and therefore tended to privilege intention.

of Israel and Babylonia. See Y. Ben Shalom, "And I Took Two Staffs," 236, and the bibliography in note 8.

8. Rabbi S.Y. Zevin, "The Approaches of Beit Shammai and Beit Hillel," *In the Light of Halakha* [Hebrew] (Tel Aviv: 5717), 302–309. On Rabbi Yehuda and Rabbi Shimon see *Sages* III, Part Two.

*Chapter Thirteen*

# Rav and Shmuel II: The Attitude to Sasanian Rule

### RAV: THE BUNDLE IS UNRAVELED

As we learn from several sources, at first Rav was quite successful politically: He forged ties with the tolerant Parthian government headed by Ardavan, and he benefited from a general atmosphere of autonomy and religious freedom. But the Sasanian revolution rocked Babylonia approximately five years after Rav's arrival, and in 224 Ardavan was murdered by his successor Ardashir. The Talmud documents Rav's response to this event:

> Antoninus[1] waited upon Rebbi. Adarkan[2] waited upon Rav. When Antoninus died, Rebbi said: The bundle is unraveled. When Adarkan died, Rav said: The bundle is unraveled. (Avoda Zara 10b)

1. On the identity of Antoninus, see I. Zlotnick, "The Identification of Antoninus, Rebbi's Friend" [Hebrew], *Sinai* 11 (Spring–Fall 5707): 143–144.
2. Ardavan was the final Parthian king. The various manuscripts spell his name Adravan, Adarkan, and Ardavan. See A.S. Rosenthal, "The Talmudic Dictionary," 112–113. Rosenthal demonstrates the origins of the name based on middle Persian linguistic developments.

With the death of Ardavan, the last Parthian king, the bundle unraveled, as Rav put it. Rashi interprets this phrase as meaning that the love that bound their souls together had died.[3] The Sasanian dynasty rose to power and the situation did not look good for the Jews, particularly when Ardashir began to deprive them of their autonomy and jurisdiction.[4]

The clearest example of the fear instilled in Rav by the new Persian leadership can be found in the Talmud's story about Rav Kahana, a leading student of Rav. The Talmud tells of a Jew who informed on his friend for hiding straw, a form of tax evasion. The friend came to complain to Rav about the informer. In the context of the ensuing discussion, the informer spoke out harshly against Rav, and Rav Kahana, who was also present, stood up and killed the informer. Rav's response sheds light on the political reality of the day:

> Rav said to him: Kahana, until now, those in power were Greeks, who were not concerned with the spilling of blood. But now those in power are Persians, who are concerned with the spilling of blood. Arise and go up to the Land of Israel.[5] (Bava Kamma 117a)

Much has been written about this story, which speaks to the difference between an imperial government that granted the Jews judicial autonomy, and one that ruled all its subjects – including the Jews – with an iron fist.[6]

3. S. Riskin suggests that the phrase "the bundle is unraveled," which symbolizes the parting of dear friends, may be based on a symbol that was common in Rome and in the East, known as a fasces. A fasces was made out of a bundle of wooden rods and an axe with a protruding blade tied together with a red covering. The rods symbolized the punitive magisterial power, and the axe symbolized the power to decree death by beheading. See S. Riskin, "The Bundle is Unraveled – What Bundle?" [Hebrew], *Sidra* 23 (5768).
4. Many have written about Ardavan's relationship with the Jews. See Y. Dinari, "Rebbi Sent a Mezuza to Ardavan" [Hebrew], *An Epigram to David: A Book in Memory of David Oaks* [Hebrew] (Ramat Gan: 5738), 86–105.
5. This is the most authentic version of the text according to A.S. Rosenthal, "The Talmudic Dictionary," 54–58.
6. See especially Rosenthal, "The Talmudic Dictionary." This story became key to our understanding of the transition from Parthian to Sasanian rule. See Gafni, *The Jews of Babylonia*, 35.

Rav mentions the Greeks, a reference to the strong Hellenistic influence on the Parthian empire that preceded the Sasanians. The Parthians did not take interest in the internal judicial administration of the Jewish community, and the Jews enjoyed the right to adjudicate both civil and criminal cases and to enforce punishment. But the new Sasanian rulers forced the entire kingdom to be subject to a Persian-Sasanian legislative and judicial system, allowing for no autonomous courts of justice.[7]

## SHMUEL: THE LAW OF THE LAND IS THE LAW

### Accepting Persian Law and Legal System

In contrast to Rav, who lamented the loss of freedom and the rise of a new rule of law, Shmuel was pleased with the new political reality, which inspired him to coin a foundational principle regarding the relationship between the Jews and the governments under which they live: "The law of the land is the law."[8]

According to this principle, it is incumbent upon all citizens, including Jews, to obey the local law.[9] This principle is generally cited with regard to tax law and public administration. At four points in the Talmud, Shmuel quotes this statement in an effort to create a more conciliatory political atmosphere. We will offer just one example:

> Rava[10] said: Ukvan bar Neḥemia, the exilarch, told me the following three things in the name of Shmuel: The law of the land is the law; the Persians' ownership of land is not effective until

7. A.S. Rosenthal located an abridged version of this story that does not mention Rav Kahana. This version suggests that informants were killed according to the Jewish law of the time. The version in which Rav Kahana is forced to flee to the Land of Israel is also authentic, but it reflects a different time period with its own attitudes to crime and punishment. See Rosenthal, "The Talmudic Dictionary."
8. Gafni refers to several sources from the nineteenth century that frame the opposition between Rav and Shmuel in these terms. See Gafni, *The Jews of Babylonia*, 42, note 106.
9. S. Shilo, *The Law of the Land is the Law* [Hebrew] (Jerusalem: 5735), 4.
10. Some manuscript variants read Rava, and some read Rabba. G. Herman explains that "Rava" is preferable because of this sage's close ties to the central administration of Mehoza. See Herman, "The Exilarchs in Babylonia," 227.

> forty years have elapsed;[11] and the acquisition of those clerks[12] who acquire land by paying its property taxes is valid. But this ruling applies only to one who acquires land by paying its property tax, but not to one who acquires land by paying the poll tax of its former owners. What is the reason? The poll tax is placed upon the people themselves. (Bava Batra 55a)

Rava, a fourth-generation sage, quotes three laws in Shmuel's name, all of which he heard from the exilarch Mar Ukva.[13]

Shmuel's statement that "the Persians' ownership of land is not effective until forty years have elapsed" means that anyone who has occupied property for forty years is considered its legitimate owner. In contrast, Jewish law holds that just three years of occupancy are sufficient. Shmuel's statement that "the acquisition of those clerks who acquire land by paying its property taxes is valid" refers to land that was confiscated by the government from individuals who failed to pay their taxes. Shmuel distinguishes between land that was confiscated from those who owed property taxes, and land that was confiscated from those who owed the poll tax.[14] The former is permitted, since all property was regarded as belonging to the king. But the government may not confiscate land arbitrarily. This law seems fair and ethical, and Shmuel wishes for the Jewish community to accept it as binding upon itself as well.

11. The version in the printed text reads, "and the Persians' ownership of land is not effective...." The "and" is missing from most of the manuscripts, suggesting that this is an illustration of Shmuel's first principle rather than merely an additional statement. See *Dikdukei Sofrim*. Also see A. S. Rosenthal, "Toward a Talmudic Dictionary" [Hebrew], *Tarbiz* 40 (5731): 187–188.
12. For the definition of this term, see Shilo, *The Law of the Land is the Law*, 9 and notes.
13. Albeck identifies Ukvan bar Neḥemia, who is mentioned several times among the second generation of Babylonian sages, as the exilarch Mar Ukva. See Albeck, *Introduction to the Talmuds*, 205. G. Herman also discusses the identification of this figure in "The Exilarchs in Babylonia," 98–111. For our purposes, suffice it to say that there was a Jewish community leader during Shmuel's time named Ukvan, and he was an authoritative voice with regard to civil affairs.
14. On the tax system in Babylonia during the talmudic period, see M. Beer, *The Amora'im of Babylonia: Episodes in Economic Life* [Hebrew] (Ramat Gan: 5735), 228–230.

The influence of Persian law on Shmuel's halakhic reasoning is apparent throughout the Talmud. One example will suffice:

> Shmuel said: One who takes possession of land along the banks of a river is an impudent person, but we do not remove him from the property. But now that the Persians write to such people, "Acquire for yourself land into the river until the water reaches the height of a horse's neck," we can remove him. (Bava Metzia 108a)

As talmudic commentators have explained, this passage deals with a Persian law about the ownership of river banks.[15] But the details became clear only in recent years, as talmudic scholarship became increasingly aware of the influence of Iranian culture on Jewish life during the talmudic period. Yaakov Elman, a pioneer of this type of comparative study, showed that in Sasanian law, the public area of the riverbank was defined by the height of horses. And so Shmuel encouraged obedience to the Sasanian law and even changed his halakhic stance to accord with it.[16] In subsequent generations, all aspects of Jewish life were affected by Sasanian law and culture, as we will discover when we study the later Babylonian sages.

### Shmuel's Closeness with King Shapur

We have already introduced King Shapur I (241–272 CE) as a powerful and influential ruler whose aggressive foreign policy threatened Rome on the eastern front. At the climax of the war against Rome, the emperor Valerian was captured by the Persian king (259 CE). Shapur instilled discipline in the new leadership, and Shmuel, who was at the peak of his own power as a leader of Babylonian Jewry, took part in

15. Rashi and Tosafot disagree about whether this law is intended to protect the purchaser of riverfront property or to protect the public interest. See Jacob Neusner, *A History of the Jews in Babylonia – Part 2: The Early Sasanian Period* (Leiden, Netherlands: 1966), 116–117.
16. Y. Elman, "Up to the Ears in Horses' Necks (B.M. 108a): On Sasanian Agricultural Policy and Private Eminent Domain," *JSIJ* 3 (2004), 95–149.

the revolution. The Talmud speaks of the close relationship between Shmuel and King Shapur:

> Shmuel would sport in front of King Shapur with eight glasses of wine. (Sukka 53a)

One talmudic story depicts Shmuel acting as a dream interpreter for King Shapur:

> King Shapur said to Shmuel: You Jews say that you are exceedingly wise. Tell me what I will see in my dream tonight. Shmuel replied to him: You will see the Romans come and take you captive, and they will force you to grind date pits with a golden mill. The king thought about this vision the entire day, and at night he saw it in his dream. (Berakhot 56a)

This story is clearly mythical rather than historical. The image of a non-Jewish king consulting with a Jewish sage about his dream was likely inspired by the story of Nebuchadnezzar and Daniel in the second chapter of the biblical Book of Daniel. At the same time, this story reflects the tension that surely gripped the historical King Shapur during his war against the Romans. Why did Shmuel show Shapur a vision of his downfall? Was it a deliberate attempt to distress the king? After all, in reality the situation was quite the opposite: Shapur took the Roman emperor captive. Perhaps the talmudic story was even inspired by this very event.[17]

### Loyalty to Persian Rule Overrides Solidarity with Jews Around the World

The most interesting and complex source concerning the relationship between Shmuel and King Shapur is a story about Jews who were killed in the city of Metzigat Caesarea.

17. I am not suggesting that talmudic *Aggada* reflects historical events, but rather that several *aggadot* contain a historical kernel. See S. Friedman, "The Historical Aggada," 119–164.

A *baraita* teaches that when one hears about someone who has died far away, one rips one's garment in such a manner that it cannot be mended. The Talmud then asks the following question:

> Do we rend our garments over bad tidings? They reported to Shmuel: King Shapur killed twelve thousand Jews in Metzigat Caesarea, and Shmuel did not rend his garments. (Mo'ed Katan 26a)

The Talmud offers a technical response: The *baraita* requires rending one's garment for the news of a distant death only if the tragedy affects the majority of the population, as with the case of the death of Saul and his sons in battle, which the Talmud goes on to cite. But the deaths in Metzigat Caesarea were just a local occurrence, and so it was not necessary to rend one's garments. The Talmud now questions what in fact happened there:

> Did King Shapur kill Jews? After all, King Shapur said to Shmuel: I am deserving of a reward, for I never killed any Jews. There, the Jews of Metzigat Caesarea brought it upon themselves. As Rabbi Ami said: From the noise of the harpstrings of Metzigat Caesarea that were played when its citizens rebelled, the wall of the city of Ludka cracked. (Mo'ed Katan 26a)

The Talmud is dealing with the stuff of history, not legend. It seems there was a Jewish city called Metzigat Caesarea which suffered the blows of the Sasanian King Shapur, even as the king remained on friendly terms with Shmuel. By comparing the various sources, both rabbinic and extra-rabbinic, we can date this incident to King Shapur's second war against the Romans, during the 250s.[18]

18. King Shapur's second war against the Romans is recorded in an inscription known as the Kaba of Zoroaster. According to this source, King Shapur fought his second Roman war in the 250s in Syria, also destroying the greater area of Cappadocia (in Asia Minor, now Turkey) as well as Caesarea, referred to as Metzigat Caesarea. Though the inscription explicitly states that Caesarea was attacked in Shapur's third Roman war, it seems more likely that the passage in Mo'ed Katan is referring to the second war rather than the third. After all, Shmuel was no longer alive during the

The Talmud reports that Shmuel did not rip his clothes in mourning when he learned about the killing of the residents of Metzigat Caesarea. He regarded himself as a loyal Persian citizen who could not mourn one of his kingdom's victories. The Talmud justifies Shmuel's behavior with the declaration that the Jews "brought it upon themselves": Had the residents not rebelled, Shapur would not have responded with violence. This is an important statement about Babylonian Jewry's attitude toward rebellion. The Babylonian Jews inherited a tradition from their ancestors which was powerfully articulated by the prophet Jeremiah: "Seek the peace of the city to which I have carried you into exile. Pray to the Lord for it, because if it prospers, you too will prosper" (Jer. 29:7). Shmuel follows in the footsteps of his Babylonian forebears and remains loyal to his kingdom of residence and its ruler.

### RAV'S AND SHMUEL'S ATTITUDES TOWARD ZOROASTRIAN PRIESTS

According to Mazda theology, the head of the pantheon of deities, Ahura Mazda, was worshipped by guarding a holy fire in the temple and its environs. Every flame was lit carefully and deliberately, in accordance with a set of ritual laws. The priests were charged with guarding the fire, and anyone who was not part of the religion was regarded as contaminating the fire. Extinguishing it was considered a grave national offense.[19]

The Talmud preserves an account of a Zoroastrian priest's entrance into a Jew's home in order to remove a flame burning inside:

> Rabba bar bar Ḥana fell ill. Rav Yehuda and Rabba went to him to inquire about his welfare. They asked him: If two agents brought a *get* to the Land of Israel from abroad, are they required to say: The *get* was written in our presence and it was signed in our presence? ... Meanwhile, there came a Zoroastrian priest who brazenly took away their lamp. Rabba bar bar Ḥana exclaimed: Merciful

third Roman war, at least not according to Rav Sherira Gaon's epistle, which there is no reason to discredit. See Gafni, *The Jews of Babylonia*, 258–265.

19. Y. Yamamoto, "The Zoroastrian Temple Cult of Fire," *Archeology and Literature II, Orient* XVII (Tokyo: 1981), 81–98.

> One! Either conceal us in Your protective shadow, or exile us in the shadow of the sons of Esau. (Gittin 16b)

The priest in this story acts in accordance with his own religious dictates.[20] Rabba bar bar Ḥana responds with an expression of despair about the new leadership, which seems to him even worse than the rule of Rome, referred to as Esau. The sages of the Talmud question Rama bar bar Ḥana's response:

> Is this to say that Romans are better than Persians? But Rabbi Ḥiya taught: What is the meaning of that which is written, "God understood the Torah's way, and He knew its place" [Job 28:23]? The Holy One, Blessed Be He, knew that Israel could not withstand the Romans' decree, and so He rose and exiled them to Babylonia. This is not a difficulty. This verse reflects the Jews' situation before the Persians came to Babylonia, whereas the statement by Rabba bar bar Ḥana reflects their situation after the Persians came to Babylonia. (Gittin 17a)

The division into two different time periods makes sense historically. Rabbi Ḥiya, who lived one generation earlier, interprets the verse from Job as an expression of praise for the Parthian kingdom, which allowed Jews to live freely and autonomously. Remembering the horror of the Hadrianic persecutions, Rabbi Ḥiya thanks God for saving the rest of His people and exiling them to Babylonia. But it is all relative. Just one generation later, with the rise of the Sasanians during Rabba bar bar Ḥana's time, Roman rule no longer seems as terrible.

In rabbinic sources, the Sasanians are blamed for the collapse of Jewish autonomy in Babylonia.[21] This is evident, too, in the following source about Ḥanukka candle lighting:

20. A.S. Rosenthal discusses the practice whereby Zoroastrian priests would enter Jewish homes to remove any fires burning. See Rosenthal, "The Talmudic Dictionary."
21. M. Beer identifies the priest who removes Rabba bar bar Ḥana's candle as the Zoroastrian high priest Kartir Hangirpe, who was influential during the second half of the third century. See M. Beer, *The Sages of the Mishna and the Talmud* [Hebrew] (Ramat Gan: 5771), 329–343. A.S. Rosenthal supports this identification and argues that the

> They inquired of Rav: What is the law with regard to moving a Ḥanukka menora away from where it may be seen by the Habari on Shabbat, after the flames have gone out? Rav replied: It is fine to do so. A time of emergency is different. For Rav Kahana and Rav Ashi said to Rav: Is this really the law? And he replied: Rabbi Shimon is sufficiently worthy to be relied upon as an authority in a time of emergency. (Shabbat 45a)

The halakhic background to this story is a discussion in the second chapter of Tractate Shabbat about moving a candle on Shabbat. Rabbi Shimon holds that it is permissible to move a candle even if it is lit. Rav permits moving a Ḥanukka candle if there are Zoroastrian priests approaching, because this would constitute an emergency situation, and "Rabbi Shimon is sufficiently worthy to be relied upon as an authority in a time of emergency." Rav's students know that the law does not follow Rabbi Shimon, but their rabbi teaches them that an emergency situation demands special provisions. And the Sasanian revolution certainly qualified as a time of emergency.[22]

In contrast to the fear that guided Rav's halakhic decisions, we find no reference to these historical circumstances in Shmuel's beit midrash in Nehardea. The people of Nehardea, who had lived there for hundreds of years, presumably learned how to adapt to the ever-changing demographics, which shifted each time a new empire came to power. The difference between Rav's and Shmuel's attitudes to the Zoroastrian priests is reflected in the following source:

> What is *magoshta*? Rav and Shmuel disagreed. One said it means a sorcerer, and one said it means a blasphemer. It can be concluded that Rav is the one who said it means a blasphemer, for Rav Zutra

period of religious persecution did not begin until after the deaths of Rav and Shmuel. See Rosenthal, "The Talmudic Dictionary."

22. The early medieval talmudic commentators understood the Babylonian Talmud's use of the phrase "time of emergency" as referring to the rise of the Mazda priests. For instance, in the eleventh century the Arukh (Natan ben Yehiel of Rome) wrote, "They decreed that no one could light candles except for their own festival abominations, and the Jews would light in secret."

> bar Toviya said in the name of Rav: One who learns something from a *magosh* is liable to death. For if you think that Rav holds it means sorcerer, behold it is written, "You shall not learn to do [acts of sorcery]" [Deut. 18:9] – implying that you may not acquire this knowledge in order to commit acts of sorcery, but you may learn sorcery in order to understand and rule on such matters. And so it can be concluded that Rav was the one who said blasphemer. (Shabbat 75a)

Rav relates to the Zoroastrian priests, known as *magoshta* or *magi*, as blasphemers, and decrees that anyone who learns from them is liable for death. But Shmuel regards them as sorcerers, whose ways may be studied so as to know how to rule with regard to such matters. The Talmud relates that Shmuel even went to Zoroastrian religious gatherings in order to hear what they had to say:

> Rav would not go to Beit Avidan and certainly not to Beit Nitzrefei. Shmuel would not go to Beit Nitzrefei, but he would go to Beit Avidan. (Shabbat 116a)

Beit Avidan and Beit Nitzrefei were two Zoroastrian institutions. Beit Avidan was a place of intellectual discussion and debate about Zoroastrian religious matters, whereas Beit Nitzrefei was a fire temple. Neither sage would enter the latter, but they disagreed about the former: Shmuel would attend Beit Avidan to listen in on theological symposia, whereas Rav kept his distance.[23]

23. Shai Secunda, "The Talmudic Bei Abedan and the Sasanian Attempt to 'Recover' the Lost Avesta," *Jewish Studies Quarterly* 18 (2011), 1–24.

*Chapter Fourteen*

# Rav and Shmuel III: The Attitude to the Exilarch

The Sasanian rulers in Persia supported a Jewish leadership structure headed by the exilarch, who was responsible for tax collection, tax exemptions, and the regulation of economic stratification within Jewish society. Though we have no way of dating the origins of this institution, we know that Mar Ukva, who was probably one of the first exilarchs, held this position during the end of Shapur's reign, which coincided with Shmuel's final years.[1]

1. If Mar Ukva was not an official exilarch, then he was at least a member of the exilarch's court. On the position and purview of the exilarch, see M. Beer, *The Exilarchs*. On Shmuel's relationship with the exilarch, see "The Exilarch," *The Jewish Community: The Ancient Period* [Hebrew], ed. Y. Gafni (Jerusalem: 5761), 176–187. The most up-to-date and comprehensive work on the subject is G. Herman, "The Exilarchs in Babylonia." Herman devotes a full chapter (98–110) to Mar Ukva, in which he demonstrates that he is referred to only as "judge" and not as "exilarch" in all sources dating earlier than the Epistle of Rav Sherira Gaon. Herman contends that Mar Ukva later became a

Several sources refer to the leadership of Mar Ukva, who lived in Nehardea and served as the leader of the Jewish community. He is often described as being very close with Shmuel, as in the following source:[2]

> Shmuel and members of the household of Sheila would greet the patriarch every day. The members of the house of Sheila went in first and sat down first. They paid honor to Shmuel and sat him down in front. Then Rav came there, and Shmuel paid him honor and sat him down before himself. The members of the house of Sheila said: We have always been second. Shmuel agreed to be seated third in line. (Y. Taanit 4:2 [68a])

The purpose of visiting the exilarch, like the purpose of visiting the patriarch in the Land of Israel, was to pay respects. In exchange for this display of honor, the visitor could expect to be rewarded with a more prestigious public role.[3] In this story, Shmuel is depicted as a humble, deferential man who is prepared to put others first. Mar Ukva regarded him as his rabbi and his teacher, as the following source attests:

> Like the incident involving Shmuel and Mar Ukva. When they would sit and study Torah, Mar Ukva would sit before Shmuel at a distance of four *amot*. But when they sat in judgment, Shmuel would sit before Mar Ukva at a distance of four *amot*. And yet they dug out a place for Mar Ukva which they covered with a mat, and he sat on it, so that Mar Ukva could hear Shmuel's words.

legendary figure, but that the official position of exilarch can be dated only as far back as the middle of the third century, during the reign of King Shapur I.

2. Rav Sherira Gaon identifies Mar Ukva as the exilarch and states that he ruled alongside Shmuel. See *The Epistle of Rav Sherira Gaon*, Lewin edition, 77. Some scholars questioned the historical veracity of this epistle, but later scholars disputed their claims. See C. Fixler, "Shmuel: The Man and His Achievements" (M.A. thesis, Tel Aviv University, 5742), 86–91; Gafni, *The Jews of Babylonia*, 239–265; Herman, "The Exilarchs in Babylonia," 86–123.
3. Lieberman, *Yerushalmi Kifshuto* (Jerusalem: 5695), 175–176.

> Each day Mar Ukva would escort Shmuel to his lodging place. One day Mar Ukva was preoccupied with his court case, and so Shmuel was walking behind him. When they reached Mar Ukva's house, Shmuel said to him: Are your actions not clear to you? Let master release me from his dispute. Mar Ukva understood that Shmuel had been offended. He took upon himself a form of excommunication for one day. (Mo'ed Katan 16b)

In this rather idealized depiction, Mar Ukva and Shmuel respect one another's areas of expertise. Mar Ukva is Shmuel's student. Yet he is also the head of the court, which has jurisdiction over sages such as Shmuel. Their mutual deference serves as the background to the following story:

> Rav Yehuda was sitting in front of Shmuel and observing him judge cases of law. A certain woman entered the court and cried out before him about an injustice committed against her, but Shmuel paid no attention to her. Rav Yehuda said to Shmuel: Does master not hold that "he who closes his ears to the outcry of the poor, he too will call and not be answered" [Prov. 21:13]? Shmuel said to him: Sharp one! Your head is in cool water; it is your head's head that is in hot water, for Mar Ukva is sitting and judging cases, as it is written, "O House of David, thus said God: Execute judgment in the morning and rescue the robbed from the hand of the oppressor, lest My wrath go forth like fire, and consume that none can quench it, because of the evil of their deeds" [Jer. 21:12]. (Shabbat 55a)

This is a rather extreme story about Shmuel, the great leader of the Jews of Nehardea, who refuses to pay heed to a woman's cries of oppression. Like any good bureaucrat, he passes her onto someone else. He refers her to Mar Ukva who, as exilarch, is a descendant of the house of David. The text he cites as justification for doing so comes from the Book of Jeremiah, where the prophet rebukes the king for being deaf to the cries of those who are oppressed in his kingdom.

Rav Yehuda, who was educated in the beit midrash in Sura but transferred to Shmuel's beit midrash after the death of Rav, rebukes Shmuel for his behavior. Shmuel tells his student that he is fortunate that his head is only in cool water, which is harmless. In contrast, he, as the teacher, has his head in hot water, because he is responsible for responding to criticism of the exilarch's court, which is known to be violent and unforgiving.[4] Shmuel has the last word in the story, because this is how conversations in the beit midrash unfold. But in later sources, Shmuel is held accountable for his refusal to be receptive to the cries of others.[5]

### THE TENSION BETWEEN RAV AND THE EXILARCH: THE CASE OF THE AGRONOMOS

Unlike the special connection between Shmuel and Mar Ukva, Rav does not have any relationship with the exilarch or with any representatives of his court. The one source that describes any interaction between Rav and the exilarch reflects the tension between them, and perhaps also gives voice to Rav's resistance to the exilarch's authority. In this story, which appears in both Talmuds, we encounter Rav working as the agronomos, the supervisor of the markets. In order to understand the background to this story, we will first consider this position more generally.

4. There are several examples throughout the Talmud of the exilarch's cruel means of imposing the regime's norms on the Jewish community as a whole. See Beer, *The Exilarchs*, 160–170.
5. The Talmud (Bava Batra 10b) relates that Yosef the son of Rabbi Yehoshua fell deathly ill. When he recovered, his father asked him what he had seen. The son responded, "I saw an inverted world! The uppermost in this world are below in the World to Come, and the lowly in this world are above in the World to Come." The *Geonim* (Tosafot on Bava Batra) explained that there was a tradition passed down from teacher to student that the world appeared upside down because Shmuel was sitting before his student Rav Yehuda, instead of vice versa. According to this tradition, Shmuel had to surrender his place to his student Rav Yehuda, who protested his refusal to respond to the oppressed woman in our story. The *Geonim* are suggesting, then, that even if the administration of justice ultimately rests with the political system, the individual (and certainly the rabbinical authority) is not exempt from the responsibility to fight injustice on the local level.

## Background: The Role of the Agronomos in the Greco-Roman City

The agronomos, or market supervisor, was a member of the Greco-Roman city council responsible for overseeing prices, weights, and measures.[6] Agrippa is the first Jewish market supervisor documented in historical sources. Josephus describes his arrival in the Land of Israel, where he was appointed to this position before he became king:

> For these reasons he went away from Rome, and sailed to Judea, but in evil circumstances.... His wife Cypros...sent a letter to his sister Herodias, who was now the wife of Herod the tetrarch, and let her know Agrippa's present design.... So they sent for him, and allotted him Tiberias for his habitation, and appointed him some income of money for his maintenance, and made him the market supervisor of that city, as a way of honoring him. (Josephus, *Antiquities of the Jews*, 18)[7]

According to the descriptions in Greek and Roman literature, the market supervisor was responsible for regulating prices as well as weights and measures. He also had to supply merchandise, at his own expense, in times of scarcity.[8] The Talmud mentions this role as part of a discussion of tithing:

> Regarding bakers: From the *demai* produce which they sell, the sages required them to separate only *terumat maaser* and *ḥalla*. (Yoma 8b)

6. On the position of the agronomos in rabbinic literature, see A. Ben-David, *Talmudische Okonomie* (New York: 1974), 214–218; D. Sperber, *The City in Roman Palestine* (Oxford: 1998), 32–35; M. Beer, *The Exilarchs*, 123–125. For a survey of the role of the agronomos in the Greek city, see A.H.M. Jones, *The Greek City* (Oxford: 1971), 215–217. For a more recently published account of the job of overseeing the markets, see Y. Brenner, "Scales of Justice, the Law of Heaven and Earth: A Study of the Laws of Weights and Measures" [Hebrew], *JSIJ* 6 (2007).
7. D. Schwartz, *Agrippa I* [Hebrew] (Jerusalem: 5747), 57, note 50.
8. Lieberman, *Tosefta Kifshuta* Bava Metzia, 241.

The Talmud tries to clarify why the sages exempted the bakers from further tithings, especially *maaser sheni.* Ulla responds:

> Since these *parhedin* would beat the bakers every twelve months and tell them: Sell cheaply! Sell cheaply! So the sages did not trouble the bakers to separate *maaser sheni* from their *demai.* What does *parhedin* mean? Town council. (Yoma 9a)

The agronomos was the representative of the *parhedin,* the municipal workers and town council members. As the market supervisor, he would beat the merchants so as to force them to lower their prices. He seems to have been a non-Jew, as the Jerusalem Talmud suggests:

> There was a gentile agronomos who forced an Israelite traveling merchant to sell cheaply, and the sages permitted him to sell fully untithed produce with the understanding that the purchaser would look out for himself. (Y. Demai 2:1 [22c])

As these sources suggest, the merchants were under such severe economic pressure from the supervisors that they could not afford to satisfy the halakhic requirement to tithe. And so they were granted license to sell *demai,* untithed produce.

According to tannaitic sources from the Land of Israel, the supervisors were responsible only for weights and measures, but not for prices:

> There were market supervisors in Jerusalem, but they were not responsible for the prices, only for measures. (Tosefta Bava Metzia 6:14)

It seems that the sages in the Land of Israel scaled back the responsibilities of the market supervisors during the tannaitic period. This becomes clear from halakhic midrashim on the verses, "You shall have honest scales and honest weights" (Lev. 19:36) and "A perfect and just weight you shall have" (Deut. 25:15). Based on these verses, the sages of the

Land of Israel concluded that the responsibility for justice related only to the regulation of weights and measures:

> "You shall have" – this teaches that we appoint an agronomos.[9] An agronomos for measures, and not an agronomos for prices. (Midrash Tanna'im Deuteronomy 25:15)

As we shall see, however, the question of whether the agronomos was responsible for prices or just for weights and members became a contentious and divisive issue.

## Rav's Appointment as Agronomos and His Rebellion Against the Exilarch

The sages' injunction that only weights and measures – not prices – should be monitored created a fair and competitive open market. It is against this backdrop that we can understand Rav's clash with the exilarch. We start with the Jerusalem Talmud:

> The exilarch appointed Rav as market supervisor. Rav enforced the law[10] in regard to measures, but not in regard to prices.[11] The exilarch threw him into prison. Rav Karna came to him. Rav said to him: The market supervisor of which the sages have spoken is one for measures and not for prices. He said to him: And you

9. The term is spelled "agrodomos" in this source.
10. The Aramaic term used in the Talmud is most commonly translated as enforcing the law. But Shlomo Naeh raises the possibility that the Talmud is referring to checking the measures used in the market by comparing them to the agronomos's measures. See Naeh, "Checking Weights and Scales" [Hebrew], *Tarbiz* 59 (5750): 392.
11. The Escorial manuscript of the Jerusalem Talmud reads, "Rav enforced the law in regard to prices, but not in regard to measures." This version was corrected so as to accord with the Babylonian Talmud. See Lieberman's comment on this manuscript, p. 205, line 64. G. Herman assumes that this is Rav's position: He was responsible for prices but not measures. See Herman, "The Exilarchs in Babylonia," 271–272. This reading does not just run contrary to all the traditional commentators on the Jerusalem Talmud, but also makes no sense given the economic and social role of the market supervisor, who refused to intervene when it came to fair pricing.

> have taught: The market supervisor oversees both measures and prices. He went and said to them: Here is someone who teaches the law of weights and measures, and yet they throw him into prison?[12] (Y. Bava Batra 5:5 [15b])

According to this story, the exilarch appointed Rav as agronomos, presumably shortly after he arrived in Babylonia and before he developed a reputation as a great sage.[13] This position, in keeping with the accepted Babylonian practice, involved overseeing prices as well as weights and measures. But Rav instead wishes to fulfill this role in accordance with the dictates of the sages of the Land of Israel, who held that it is only weights and measures, and not prices, that should be monitored. In so doing, Rav undermines the authority of the exilarch, who responds by imprisoning him.[14] The Talmud presents their disagreement as centering on the nature of the accepted practice, which leads to a discussion of the tannaitic sources that define the role of the agronomos.[15] Rav

12. Lieberman notes that the Leiden and Escorial manuscript versions break up one of the Aramaic words in this sentence into two separate words, which makes this line difficult to interpret. See Lieberman's comments on the Escorial manuscript, p. 205, note 284 and p. 206, note 22. The Talmud explicitly states (Bava Batra 87a) that Rav taught the mishna about measures in Babylonia. But the phrase in question can also mean "police," so another possible reading is, "Here is someone who teaches the law of weights and measures, and yet they throw him into prison? The police imprison him?"
13. On Rav's appointment, see Y.A. HaLevi, *The Early Generations* 1 [Hebrew] (Jerusalem: 5727), 110; Gafni, *The Jews of Babylonia*, 102–103. On the tension between Rav and the exilarch, see Beer, *The Exilarchs*, 124.
14. According to M. Beer, the agronomos in the Land of Israel during the tannaitic period (as opposed to the amoraic period) was responsible solely for measures, unlike in Babylonia, where he was also responsible for prices. Rav remained faithful to the practice of the Land of Israel and refused to adapt to the Babylonian norm, which he even tried to alter by drawing on halakhic midrashim from the Land of Israel. See ibid., 16. G. Herman questions this source entirely, arguing that there was no position of agronomos whatsoever in Babylonia. See Herman, "The Exilarchs in Babylonia," 272–275.
15. The view represented here describes the overseeing of prices as an ethical norm. But there were those who explained it as an economic arrangement that depended on market conditions. See Weiss, *Each Generation and Its Interpreters*, 152. H. Albeck

teaches the sources from the Land of Israel as we encountered them in the halakhic midrashim and in the Tosefta. Karna counters his teachings by presenting the sources as they are studied in Babylonia, suggesting that there is an alternative "Babylonian *baraita*."[16]

When the story appears in the Babylonian Talmud, we are shown a different perspective:

> The rabbis taught: "A perfect and just weight you shall have" [Deut. 25:15]. This teaches that we appoint an agronomos for measures, but we do not appoint an agronomos for prices. The patriarchal house once appointed an agronomos for measures as well as for prices. Shmuel said to Karna: Go out and teach them: We appoint an agronomos for measures, but we do not appoint an agronomos for prices. Karna went out and expounded: We appoint an agronomos for measures as well as for prices. When Karna returned, Shmuel said to him: What is your name? He said: Karna. Shmuel said: Let it be the will of heaven that a horn emerge from his eye. A horn emerged from Karna's eye. And Karna, in accord with whom does he hold? In accord with that which Rami bar Ḥama said in the name of Rabbi Yitzḥak: We appoint an agronomos for measures as well as for prices, because of the swindlers. (Bava Batra 89a)

tries to bridge these two stances, arguing that "perhaps there were different practices in different places." See Albeck, *Studies in Baraita and Tosefta* [Hebrew] (Jerusalem: 5730), 23, note 3. M. Rostovtzeff contends that the agrnomos would supply merchandise at his own expense and oversee prices. See Rostovtzeff, *The Social and Economic History of the Roman Empire*, I (Oxford: 1957), 599. S. Lieberman suggests that during a period of inflation and price-fixing (during the time of Diocletian), the prices were monitored. See Lieberman, *Texts and Studies* (New York: 1974), 93, note 241, and 108. E.E. Urbach argues that during the period between the destruction of the Temple and the Bar Kokhba revolt, there were major economic shifts, as merchants took over from farmers. And so new laws developed to encourage this trend, including a decrease in the extent to which prices were monitored. See Urbach, *The Law, Its Sources, and Its Development* [Hebrew] (Givatayim: 1984), 161–162.

16. Epstein, *Text of the Mishna*, 174.

The Babylonian Talmud's version is problematic on several counts. First, it pitches Shmuel in Rav's camp, which seems unlikely: Like Rav, Shmuel teaches here that an overseer is appointed for measures but not for prices.[17] Furthermore, it seems unlikely that Shmuel would have said, "Let a horn emerge from his eye," a phrase attributed to Rav in the story of Rav's reception in Babylonia.[18] Nor does it seem plausible that Shmuel would have argued against price-fixing, since several other sources attest that Shmuel himself oversaw prices and fought actively against the merchants' attempts to take advantage of others:

1. *The myrtle market*

In the Mishna in Sukka, the sages disagree about the number of myrtles necessary to fulfill the mitzva of the four species on Sukkot. Rabbi Yishmael holds that three are necessary, but two of the three may be clipped. Rabbi Tarfon holds that three are necessary, but all three may be clipped. Rabbi Akiva contends that one full-grown myrtle alone is sufficient.

In talmudic Babylonia, damaged myrtles were plentiful, but full-grown myrtles were a rare and prized commodity. Everyone was aware of this reality, especially the merchants. And so full-grown myrtle prices skyrocketed on the eve of Sukkot. In response, Shmuel sent a warning to the merchants:

> Shmuel said to those who sell myrtles: Sell the myrtles in line with their true value, for if you do not, I will teach publicly in accordance with the opinion of Rabbi Tarfon. (Sukka 34b)

Rabbi Tarfon, as we have seen, held that all three myrtles could be clipped. Such a ruling would hurt the livelihood of the merchants. The Talmud explains the logic underlying Shmuel's threat:

17. M. Beer, "The Social and Economic Status of the Babylonian Amora'im" (PhD diss., Hebrew University of Jerusalem, 5723), 79.
18. The Rashbam (Rabbi Samuel ben Meir, 1085–1158) notes on Bava Batra 89a that this line does not belong in this context.

> What is the reason? If you say it is simply because Rabbi Tarfon is lenient, then Shmuel should have threatened to expound against them in accordance with the opinion of Rabbi Akiva, who is even more lenient. No, three clipped myrtles are commonly found, whereas one that is unclipped is not so commonly found. (Sukka 34b)

Shmuel had the authority to change the halakhic norm, thereby lowering the bar for the performance of the mitzva of taking myrtles on Sukkot. He threatened to adopt the ruling of Rabbi Tarfon, who held that clipped myrtles were sufficient. Given that there was no dearth of clipped myrtles, the merchants realized they would no longer be able to overcharge, and prices stabilized once again.

2. Ḥametz *dishes after Passover*

Regular pots are made of earthenware. When they are used to cook any food that includes *ḥametz*, the *ḥametz* is considered to have been absorbed by the sides of the pot, rendering it unfit for use after Passover. The Talmud cites a debate between Rav and Shmuel relating to this matter:

> Rav said: Earthenware pots used for *ḥametz* must be broken on Passover. Why? Could one not keep them until after Passover and prepare food that is not of the same kind? Rav issued his decree that they not be used lest people use them to prepare food that is of the same kind. But Shmuel says: They need not be broken. Rather, one may keep them until after Passover, when he can prepare any food with them, whether of the *ḥametz* kind or not of its kind. And Shmuel is consistent with his opinion, for Shmuel said to those who sell new pots after Passover: Set the price of your pots in line with their true value, and if you do not, I will announce that old pots are permitted after Passover in accordance with Rabbi Shimon. (Pesaḥim 30a)

The disagreement between Rav and Shmuel is based on economic considerations. Rav finds no halakhic grounds to permit the use of *ḥametz* pots after Passover. But Shmuel permits the owners to store and save the pots for use after the holiday. The Talmud explains that Shmuel's ruling enabled him to regulate market prices. So long as the people were permitted to reuse their *ḥametz* pots after Passover, there was no rush to buy new pots, and the vendors could not overcharge.

3. *Lowering prices by flooding the market*

> Shmuel's father would sell his produce early in the season, for the early market price. Shmuel, his son, would store his produce and sell it at the end of the season for the early market price. (Bava Batra 90a)

Shmuel and his father adopted different economic tactics. His father would bring the fruit to market as soon as it was picked and sell it at market price. But Shmuel adopted a more calculated approach. He would stockpile the fruit until it was no longer available in the market, and then he would flood the market with his produce and sell it cheaply.

The Talmud tells of the reaction to the practices of the father and son in the Land of Israel:

> They sent a message from the Land of Israel: The deeds of the father are better than those of the son. What is the reason? Once a market price has risen, it tends to remain high for the rest of the year. (Bava Batra 90a)

The residents of the Land of Israel had a tradition of an open market with unregulated competition. They did not want market supervisors to regulate prices. The Talmud quotes Rav:

> Rav said: A person may hoard his own small portion. A *baraita* teaches this as well: One may not hoard the kinds of produce that are the staples of life, such as wine, oil, and fine flours. However, one is allowed to hoard spices such as cumin and pepper. In regard to what was this stated? In regard to one who buys produce from the marketplace. But one who gathers produce from his own fields is permitted [to withhold it from the market]. (Bava Batra 90a)

There is nothing to prevent a person from stockpiling his produce in his home and bringing it to sell in the market whenever he desires – so long as he is not causing anyone to starve. Rav's statement that "a person may hoard his own small portion" stands in opposition to Shmuel's practice of hoarding all his produce and then selling it only when such items were no longer available in the market. Here, too, Shmuel takes it upon himself to oversee prices, and he does everything within his power to ensure economic stability as part of his concern for the general welfare in Babylonia. And so when it comes to price regulation, Rav and Shmuel reflect opposite ends of the spectrum.

For our purposes, we can conclude that it seems quite unlikely that it was Shmuel who told Karna that market prices should not be regulated. The version in the Jerusalem Talmud, in which Rav rebels against the exilarch, seems a more accurate reflection of the historical reality.

### RAV AND SHMUEL: CONCLUSION

As these sources indicate, Rav and Shmuel could not be more different when it came to their styles of learning, their relationship to the political authorities, their economic outlook, and their religious practice. A halakhic tradition notes the dichotomy between them and establishes the following principle:

> It is accepted that wherever Rav and Shmuel disagree, we hold in accordance with Rav in matters of prohibitory law and with Shmuel in matters of monetary law. (Bekhorot 49b)

Rav, who found an open field and erected a protective fence around it, became the arbiter in matters of prohibitory religious law. Shmuel, who adopted the local culture and its political and economic norms, became the arbiter in matters of civil jurisprudence. In other words, the law follows Rav with regard to affairs between man and God, and Shmuel with regard to affairs between man and his surroundings.

*Chapter Fifteen*

# Geniva's Rebellion Against the Exilarch

## GENIVA AS RAV'S CONTEMPORARY: I'M AN ELDER AND HE'S AN ELDER

The figure of Geniva, who is virtually unknown in the Talmud, serves to shed light on the relationships between the exilarch and the early sages of the Talmud.[1] In Rav's time, Geniva was a familiar figure who took part in the world of the sages, as we learn from the Jerusalem Talmud:

> What is the law regarding their lupin beans? Rebbi said they are forbidden, and Geniva said they are permitted. Rebbi said: I am an elder, and he is an elder. I intend to prohibit them, and he intends to permit them. (Y. Avoda Zara 2:8 [41d])

1. This chapter is based on M. Beer, "Geniva's Rebellion Against Mar Ukva" [Hebrew], *The Sages of the Mishna and the Talmud* (Ramat Gan: 5771), 45–50.

This source reads Rebbi rather than Rav, but it is clear from the historical and literary context that it is about Rav.[2] As we saw above, Rav instituted many stringencies in Sura and its environs, including the laws relating to crops grown by non-Jews. This passage deals with his prohibition on eating lupin beans. Rav is aware of his own tendency to rule stringently, and he declares, "I intend to prohibit them, and he intends to permit them." This is not an argument about halakhic sources, but about individual approaches to halakhic decision-making.

The law with regard to the eating of lupin beans came to represent a certain level of *kashrut*. Only those who were very stringent would not eat the lupin beans of non-Jews. The Babylonian Talmud describes Rabbi Yoḥanan's view on the matter:

> Rabbi Ḥiya bar Abba came to Gabla. He saw Jewish women who became pregnant from converts who were circumcised but had not immersed in the *mikva*. He saw idolaters who were serving Jewish wine. And he saw that idolaters were cooking lupin beans and Jews were eating them. But he did not say anything to them.
>
> He came before Rabbi Yoḥanan who said to him: Go and announce that their children are bastards, their wine is forbidden wine of libation, and their lupin beans are forbidden as food cooked by idolaters, because they are ignorant of Torah....
>
> Would their lupin beans have been permitted if they had been men of Torah? But Rav Shmuel bar Yitzḥak said in the name of Rav: Any food that may be eaten raw does not come under the prohibition of food cooked by idolaters, and since lupin beans cannot be eaten raw, this prohibition applies. Rabbi Yoḥanan holds by a different version of Rav's ruling. For Rabbi Shmuel bar Rabbi Yitzḥak said in the name of Rav: Whatever is not served on a royal table as a dish to be eaten with bread is not subject to the prohibition of food cooked by idolaters. The reason is because they were ignorant of Torah, for had they been men of Torah, their lupin beans would have been permitted. (Yevamot 46a)

2. See Beer, "Geniva's Rebellion Against Mar Ukva," 45, note 2.

The prohibition on the lupin beans of idolaters is typical of the stringencies instituted by Rav in the south, but Geniva takes issue with it. Rav maintains that Geniva has every right to challenge him: "He is an elder, and I am an elder." An elder is a term for a sage with the authority to make halakhic decisions – one who serves, perhaps, as a judge in Rav's court.[3]

## GENIVA ENCOUNTERS RAV HUNA AND RAV ḤISDA

There are two primary talmudic sources about Geniva, both in Tractate Gittin. If we study them in conjunction, we will gain a fuller sense of this sage.

In each of these sources, Geniva interacts with Rav Huna and Rav Ḥisda, two leading disciples of Rav who became leaders of their generation. They are still in the formative stage of their rabbinic training, whereas Geniva, a contemporary of Rav, is older.

### To Rise or Not to Rise Before Geniva?

> Rav Huna and Rav Ḥisda were sitting together. Geniva began to pass by. One said to the other: Let us rise before him, since he is a man of Torah. The other said: Shall we rise before one who is quarrelsome? In the meantime, he came up to them and said: Peace be unto you kings, peace be unto you kings. They said to him: From where do you learn that sages are called kings? He said: Because it is written, "By me, kings reign" [Prov. 8:15]. They said to him: From where do you learn that a double greeting is extended to kings? He said: From what Rav Yehuda said in the name of Rav: How do we know that a double greeting should be extended to kings? Because it says: "Then the spirit came upon Amasai who was chief of the captains. We are yours, David, and on your side, son of Jesse; peace, peace be unto you" [1 Chr. 12:19]. They said to him: Would you care to have a bite with us? He said: Thus said Rav Yehuda in the name of Rav: It is forbidden for a man to taste anything until he has given food

3. This is Beer's suggestion, though it seems to me more likely that it is just a reference to a wise person.

> to his cattle, as it says, "And I will give grass in your field for your cattle" [Deut. 11:15], and then it says, "You shall eat and be full" [Deut. 11:15]. (Gittin 62a)

**Rav Huna and Rav Ḥisda Learn from Geniva**

> Rav Huna and Rav Ḥisda were sitting together. Geniva passed by. One of them said: Let us rise before him, for he is a man of Torah. The other said: Shall we rise before a quarrelsome man? In the meantime, he came up to them. He said to them: What are you discussing? They said: The winds. He said to them: Thus said Rabbi Ḥanan bar Rava in the name of Rav: Four winds blow every day, and the north wind blows with all of them, for were it not so, the world would not be able to exist for a moment. The south wind is the most violent of all, and were it not that the son of the hawk holds it back, it would devastate the whole world, for it is said, "Does the hawk soar by your wisdom and stretch her wings toward the south?" [Job 39:26]. (Gittin 31b)

If we read these sources in conjunction, it seems that the two scenes unfold as follows: Rav Huna and Rav Ḥisda, of the second generation of sages at Sura, are studying together when Geniva passes by. They know Geniva as a great man but also a quarrelsome one. And so they are not sure whether it is appropriate to rise before him. While they are still debating, he comes before them and greets them with the strange words, "Peace be unto you kings."[4] They are surprised by this greeting. In our own day it has become common to refer to Torah scholars as kings, but apparently this was not so in Babylonia then. Indeed, this convention seems to have originated with Geniva.

When Rav Huna and Rav Ḥisda ask about this greeting, he responds by quoting verses from Proverbs (8:14–15): "Counsel is mine, and sound wisdom; I am understanding, power is mine. By me, kings reign, and princes decree justice." Perhaps Geniva is also offering a subtle

4. M. Beer writes about the significance of Geniva's use of the term "kings" to refer to the sages. See Beer, "Geniva's Rebellion Against Mar Ukva," 47, note 9.

critique of the exilarch, who conducts himself like a king. The real king, Geniva may be suggesting, is not the exilarch but those who offer counsel and wisdom. It is the sages and those of sound intellect who crown the political leaders, and not vice versa.

In the next part of the conversation, Geniva reproves the sages for not being more familiar with the Torah of their teacher Rav. He tells them that the proof text for the double greeting was taught by Rav, who quoted Chronicles, where Amasai greets David with the words, "Peace, peace be unto you." Rav Huna and Rav Ḥisda, though students of Rav, do not remember or are not familiar with this teaching. And so Geniva is also intimating that when it comes to Torah knowledge, he is their superior.

Their next encounter unfolds in a similar vein. Geniva asks Rav Huna and Rav Ḥisda what they are discussing. The honest answer would have been, "We were discussing you," since in fact they were talking about whether to rise in his presence. To avoid having to admit the truth, they say they were discussing the winds, which could mean meteorology, ecology, metaphysics, or something else entirely.[5] Geniva's response teaches them something about the winds, and this teaching, too, has its origin in Rav's beit midrash. There is a northern wind that blows with all the others, but the southern wind is the most violent, and were it not for the "son of hawk," it would destroy the world. Perhaps this is a reference to Babylonian political geography. The north was the site of the capital and the adjacent city of Mehoza. Not far was the city of Pumbedita, which rose to prominence after the fall of Nehardea. These cities comprise the northern region. The south lacked leadership until Rav arrived and "found an open field." And so Geniva's comment may be an allusion to the winds of political change.

At the end of this passage Rav Huna and Rav Ḥisda invite Geniva to sit and dine with them, but he turns them down, once again invoking a teaching of Rav. His refusal to eat with them leads to a parting of ways.

5. M. Margaliot suggests that they meant that they were studying the teaching that "anyone who is pleasing to his fellow men is pleasing to God" (Avot 3:10). The phrase used for "pleasing" literally means "the spirit is at peace with him," and the Hebrew words for "spirit" and "wind" are the same. See Margaliot, *Studies in the Ways of Learning and Its Riddles* [Hebrew] (Jerusalem: 5749).

### THE EXILARCH CONFRONTS GENIVA

We learn about Geniva's relationship with the exilarch from another source in the Babylonian Talmud. The exilarch felt threatened by Geniva and sought advice on how to deal with him from Rabbi Elazar ben Pedat, who previously lived in Babylonia and then moved to the Land of Israel:

> Mar Ukva sent a message to Rabbi Elazar, saying: Certain men are distressing me and I am able to get them in trouble with the government. Should I do so? He traced lines on which he wrote, quoting: "I said, I will take heed to my ways, that I sin not with my tongue. I will keep a curb on my mouth while the wicked is before me" [Ps. 39:2]. Even though the wicked is before me, I will keep a curb on my mouth. Mar Ukva sent to him, saying: They are distressing me very much, and I cannot stand them. He said: "Resign yourself unto the Lord, and wait patiently for Him" [Ps. 37:7]. Resign yourself, and He will cast them down before you. Go to the beit midrash every morning and evening, and there will soon be an end of them. As the words went forth from Rabbi Elazar's mouth, Geniva was placed in chains. (Gittin 7a)

It seems that all of this correspondence took place covertly and in code. Instead of answering the exilarch directly, Rabbi Elazar responds by quoting a verse from Psalms that speaks of guarding one's speech so as to avoid sin. The Talmud explains that the exilarch is meant to understand that even when confronted by evil, he must not speak ill of others. But the exilarch grows only more distressed, so he appeals once again to Rabbi Elazar. Here, too, he does not explicitly state what is distressing him. Rabbi Elazar's response is consistent with his previous message. He quotes another verse from Psalms, which the Talmud explicates: If the exilarch resigns himself to his enemies, God will take care of them for him. He must wake up early and stay late at the beit midrash, and God will deal with the rest. Rabbi Elazar's response seems to suggest that the exilarch's enemies are present in the beit midrash, rather than outside its walls.

The story concludes with Geniva's arrest. Here the Talmud's language echoes a verse from the Book of Esther about Haman's downfall.

By invoking the story of Esther, the Talmud makes a statement about who is the king and who is the villain in this story.

### THE EXECUTION OF GENIVA

Geniva's arrest leads to his execution, as we learn elsewhere in Gittin. The Mishna (Gittin 6:4) discusses the case of a person who wishes to divorce his wife while he is on death row. The Talmud relates the following anecdote:

> Geniva was being led out to execution. On his way out, he said: Give four hundred *zuz* of the wine of Naharpania to Rabbi Avina. (Gittin 65b)

Before he dies, Geniva pays off all his debts. He instructs that four hundred *zuz* of wine should be paid to Rabbi Avina.

### A POSSIBLE INTERPRETATION OF THE DIFFICULT STORY OF GENIVA

One possible interpretation of Geniva's story takes into account the political and religious leadership in his day. We have already discussed Mar Ukva's leadership of the Babylonian Jewish community in the third century. Shmuel was close with Mar Ukva, but the administration of civic affairs was beyond his jurisdiction.

In the transition from the first to the second generation of Babylonian sages, the world of Torah scholarship became increasingly established. But several years passed between Rav's death in 247 CE and the appointment of his successor. Rav's students made their way to Shmuel's beit midrash in Nehardea, and only after Shmuel's death in 254 CE was Rav Huna appointed head of the beit midrash in Sura.

Over the next five years, Mar Ukva involved himself in appointing the rabbinic leadership. But Geniva was very opposed to his intervention and insisted on autonomy for the rabbis, whom he regarded as the true kings. He also fomented widespread social protest against Mar Ukva, who grew increasingly distressed. Rabbi Elazar advised the exilarch to refrain from taking action, and eventually the Persian government arrested Geniva for a capital crime.

With the death of Geniva, the first generation of Babylonian sages came to a close. The next generation would be led by Rav Huna, Rav Ḥisda, Rav Naḥman, and Rav Yehuda, and Torah scholarship would continue to take root and flourish. As time passed, the gap between the yeshivot of Rav and Shmuel only continued to widen, and Babylonian Jewry became increasingly split into these two camps.

# Part Three

## *The Early Talmudic Period in the Land of Israel*

| | | |
|---|---|---|
| The Elders of the Generation after Rabbi Yehuda HaNasi | The Early Years of the Babylonian Sages<br>Shmuel in Nehardea and Rav in Sura | The Early Years of the Talmud in the Land of Israel<br>The World and Teachings of Rabbi Yoḥanan |
| 199–235 | 226–254 | 235–279 |
| The Beginning of the Anarchic Period in the Roman Empire | The Sasanian Revolution in the East | Anarchy in the Roman Empire and the Rise of Palmyra |

*Historical Background*

# Jewish Life in Israel in the Anarchic Period

In Part One, we studied the sages of the transitional generation between the Mishna and the Talmud, who lived during the patriarchy of Rabban Gamliel III and the early years of his son and successor Rabbi Yehuda. We now turn to the height of the anarchic period, which lasted until the rule of Diocletian (284). The economic hardship of this era took its toll throughout the Roman Empire, and the Land of Israel was no exception.

Throughout this period, Caesars rose and fell in quick succession, the army was busy quelling rebellion, and inflation was rampant. In the east the Parthian empire expanded under Sasanian leadership, and in the northwest the Gothic tribes gained force. The Roman Empire began to collapse. Valerian was the last emperor from the old aristocracy. During his reign, in the 250s, revolts broke out throughout the empire. Desperate, the aging emperor decided to head to the eastern front himself, and after a difficult battle, amidst plague and famine, he surrendered to the Persian king Shapur I, known in rabbinic literature as Shavur Malka. The Caesar's capture became a powerful symbol of the empire's decline, and left an indelible impression on the history, literature, and art of the period.

During the anarchic period, the residents of the Land of Israel, like those living throughout the empire, were subjected to forced labor, military conscription, and an unbearable tax burden. Many were plagued by famine, as Rabbi Yoḥanan recounts:

> Rabbi Yoḥanan said: I remember when the price of four *se'ah*s of wheat stood at a *sela,* yet Tiberias abounded with people swollen from hunger, because there was no money. And Rabbi Yoḥanan said: I remember when workers would not hire themselves out to work to the east of the city because they would die from the smell of bread. (Bava Batra 91b)

Rabbi Yoḥanan's colleague and student Reish Lakish describes a similar reality. When Rabbi Yoḥanan, in speaking of the Messiah, declares, "May he come, but may I not see him," Reish Lakish responds by trying to guess the motive for this assertion:

> Reish Lakish asked Rabbi Yoḥanan: Why do you not want to see the Messiah's arrival? Is it because it is written, "When a man flees from a lion, a bear meets him, and entering his house, he leans his hand on the wall and a snake bites him" [Amos 5:19]? Come and I will show you an example of this in this world. When a man goes out to his field and an official[1] meets him, it is as though he had been approached by a lion. When he enters a town and a tax collector approaches him, it is as though he had been approached by a bear. When he comes home and finds his

1. The term used for an official is *santeir,* which Rashi defines (in Bava Batra 68a) as a bureaucrat responsible for recording the boundaries of private land holdings. Such a bureaucrat had the authority to appropriate property from one person and transfer it to another, thereby altering the distribution of land. And so when a landowner encountered a *santeir,* it was like stumbling upon a lion.

> sons and daughters lying in hunger, it is as though he had been bitten by a snake. (Sanhedrin 98b)

Reish Lakish's statement gives voice to the distressing economic reality of the anarchic period.[2]

2. D. Sperber, "The Economic Reality in the Land of Israel During the Third Century CE" [Hebrew], *Proceedings of the Fifth World Congress of Jewish Studies* (5729), 370–374; M. Avi-Yonah, *Rome and Byzantium*, 74–135; Y.L. Levine, "The Land of Israel in the Third Century," 116–136.

*Chapter Sixteen*

# Rabbi Yoḥanan bar Nappaḥa

The sages of the Land of Israel, some of whom were born there and many of whom emigrated from Babylonia, flourished during the difficult anarchic period. The leading sage of the period was Rabbi Yoḥanan, who is regarded as the editor of the Jerusalem Talmud.[1] Historians of the Talmud compare Rabbi Yoḥanan to Rabbi Yehuda HaNasi in significance and stature. As Hyman writes:

> At the same time that our holy rabbi awarded Israel with his ordered Mishna, a giant was born, as if heaven-sent, who gave us commentaries on that Mishna. And like our holy rabbi, who was the leader of the entire generation, so too was Rabbi Yoḥanan the leader of his entire generation, and almost all the amoraic laws in the Jerusalem Talmud originated from him. And it is not just the Jerusalem Talmud, but also the Babylonian Talmud

1. See Maimonides' introduction to the *Mishneh Torah*. Z. Frankel writes, "Maimonides meant that he began compiling the Jerusalem Talmud." See Frankel, *Introduction to the Jerusalem Talmud*, 95b.

that teems with his teachings. After the death of Rav and Shmuel he was the leader of the entire generation, and his words were regarded as oracles.[2]

### RABBI YOḤANAN'S CHILDHOOD: THE WORLD CHANGED IN HIS TIME

Rabbi Yoḥanan's surname "Bar Nappaḥa" may indicate that he grew up in the village of Nappaḥa, to the east of Tiberias.[3] But we know very little about his background. The only story about his birth appears in Tractate Yoma:

> There was a pregnant woman who smelled food and craved it on Yom Kippur. They came before Rebbi [and asked him what to do]. He said to them: Go whisper to her that it is Yom Kippur. They whispered it to her, and her craving subsided. Rebbi applied the following verse: "Before I formed you in the womb, I knew you" [Jer. 1:5]. From her came Rabbi Yoḥanan. (Yoma 82b)

According to another talmudic source, Rabbi Yoḥanan did not merit to meet his parents. His father died when his mother became pregnant with him, and then his mother died in childbirth (Kiddushin 31b). As a young child he would sit on his grandfather's shoulders and listen to the lectures of Rabbi Shimon ben Elazar, a student of Rabbi Meir (Y. Maasrot 1:2 [48d]).[4] He went on to study with and serve Rabbi Yehuda HaNasi in his beit midrash in Tzippori, where Rav was also a student. Years later, he once heard students in Tiberias speaking insultingly of Rav, and he rebuked these students who were ignorant of the scholar's greatness:

2. Hyman, *Tanna'im and Amora'im*, 653. For the most comprehensive study of the figure of Rabbi Yoḥanan, see R. Kimelman, "Rabbi Yoḥanan of Tiberias: Aspects of the Social and Religious History of Third-Century Palestine" (PhD diss., Yale University, 1977).
3. Epstein, *Text of the Mishna*, 238, note 6.
4. Rabbi Shimon ben Elazar was Rabbi Yehuda HaNasi's study partner. His beit midrash was in Tiberias, which seems to suggest that Rabbi Yoḥanan was born there.

> I remember when I used to sit seventeen rows behind Rav, who sat in front of Rebbi, and when they would debate, sparks would fly out of Rav's mouth to Rebbi's mouth, and from Rebbi's mouth to Rav's mouth, and I could not comprehend what they were saying. (Ḥullin 137b)[5]

This source suggests than Rabbi Yoḥanan began studying in Rebbi's beit midrash before 219 CE, the year that Rav relocated to Babylonia. Based on this fact, we can date Rabbi Yoḥanan's birth to approximately 210 CE. In his introduction to the *Mishneh Torah,* Maimonides counts Rabbi Yoḥanan among Rebbi's youngest students. But Rabbi Yoḥanan's primary teachers were the members of the transitional generation, including Rabbi Yannai, Rabbi Oshaya, and Rabbi Ḥanina. He drank thirstily from the teachings of the generation that preceded him, and he went on to transmit their wisdom. He also mastered collections of mishnayot, including Rebbi's Mishna and all the circulating *baraitot.*[6]

In Rabbi Yoḥanan's dotage, during the height of the Roman anarchy, he recalled his childhood during the early years of the century, which he describes as a time of abundance:

> Rabbi Yoḥanan said: The simple fruit that we ate as children was better than the peaches we now eat in our old age, for in our own lives, the world has changed. (Y. Pe'ah 7:3 [20a])

Rabbi Yoḥanan recalls that even the wild, uncultivated fruit of his youth surpassed the best summer fruit of his later life. In the next source, too, Rabbi Yoḥanan shares fond memories of the plentiful harvests of his youth:

> And Rabbi Yoḥanan said: I remember that when a child would slice a carob, a thread of honey would spread over his hands. (Y. Pe'ah 7:3 [20a])

5. Also see Ḥullin 54a. It is clear from these sources that Rabbi Yoḥanan was significantly younger than Rav, and was part of the outermost circle in Rav's beit midrash.
6. Epstein, *Text of the Mishna,* 238–245.

## RABBI YOḤANAN AND THE STUDY OF TORAH: WALKING IN THE FOOTSTEPS OF RASHBI

Rabbi Yoḥanan's spiritual life was strongly influenced by the towering figure of Rabbi Shimon bar Yoḥai, known as Rashbi. As we have seen, Rashbi inhabited an otherworldly realm and became the object of veneration and awe among later generations of Torah scholars. Throughout his life, Rabbi Yoḥanan wrestled with the figure of Rashbi. He was drawn to him even as he recognized the differences between them.

### Rabbi Yoḥanan Chooses to Study Torah in Times of Hardship

> Ilfa and Rabbi Yoḥanan were studying Torah in dire financial straits. They said to themselves: Let us go and do some business, and fulfill in ourselves the verse, "But among you there will be no destitute" [Deut. 15:4]. They set out, and sat alongside a dilapidated wall and ate. Two ministering angels came by. Rabbi Yoḥanan overheard one angel saying to his fellow: Let us topple this wall on them and kill them, for they forsake the pursuit of the life of the World to Come and occupy themselves instead with the transitory life. The other angel said: Leave them alone, because there is one among them whose hour is at hand. Rabbi Yoḥanan overheard them, but Ilfa did not. Rabbi Yoḥanan said to Ilfa: Did you, master, hear anything? He answered him: No. Rabbi Yoḥanan said to himself: Since I overheard and Ilfa did not, it must be for me that the hour of greatness is at hand. Rabbi Yoḥanan said to Ilfa: Let me return to study Torah, and I will fulfill in myself the verse, "The poor will never cease from the midst of the land" [Deut. 15:11]. Rabbi Yoḥanan returned, and Ilfa did not. (Taanit 21a)

This story is set during a time of economic hardship, presumably at the beginning of the Roman anarchic period.[7] Rabbi Yoḥanan and Ilfa sit in the beit midrash, but aware that they are in dire financial straits, they

7. M. Beer, *The Babylonian Amora'im: Episodes in Economic Life* [Hebrew] (Ramat Gan: 5742), 181–183.

feel the need to forsake the world of Torah study to earn a living. It is not clear who financed their learning until this point; presumably in calmer, more prosperous times there were donors who supported Torah scholars.[8] But in times of hardship, the donations dwindled, and members of the yeshiva began to worry about their future. Rabbi Yoḥanan and Ilfa decide to take matters into their own hands, in fulfillment of the biblical verse, "But among you there will be no destitute."

The two sages sit alongside a dilapidated wall and eat bread. This scene pits the world of the beit midrash against the "outside world," like the story of Rashbi in the cave (Shabbat 33b).[9] In that story, Rashbi and his son sit in the cave, free from economic concerns and sustained by the miraculous carob tree and spring of water. When they leave the cave they encounter a man working a field and criticize him for forsaking the world of Torah study to occupy himself with the transitory world. In contrast, Ilfa and Rabbi Yoḥanan choose to leave the beit midrash and make a living in the transitory world. They choose bread and sustenance over Torah. But a sense of worthlessness and desperation envelops them in spite of their resolve.

At this point, two ministering angels come on the scene. One suggests killing these two sages who have forsaken the world of Torah study, but the other restrains him with the claim that one of the two is destined for greatness. Both the reader and the hero of the story know which of the two it is, heightening the dramatic irony. Rabbi Yoḥanan, who overhears the angels' conversation, ascertains that Ilfa did not hear a thing. Rather than relating to Ilfa what he heard, he simply informs him of his change of plan. He returns to the beit midrash and abandons his business venture, basing his decision on words of Torah: "The poor will never cease from the midst of the land." He chooses poverty for the sake of Torah in the hope that Heaven will take mercy on him. Meanwhile, Ilfa, who did not overhear the angels' conversation, sets out to make a living.[10]

8. M. Beer, "Issaḥar and Zevulun" [Hebrew], *Bar Ilan Annual*, 6 (5728), 174–177.
9. Y. Frankel, *The Aggadic Story*, 58–61.
10. A. Kosman argues that the fact that Ilfa did not overhear the angels' conversation reflects that he was wholly at peace with the decision to leave the beit midrash:

**Ilfa at the Top of the Mast: Whose Hour Is at Hand?**

Anyone who has studied a page of Talmud has encountered Rabbi Yoḥanan, because there is almost no talmudic *sugya* in which he does not appear. In contrast, his childhood friend Ilfa is virtually unknown to students of Torah. Apparently, Ilfa's decision to leave the world of Torah scholarship in order to make a living meant that he would not have a significant role in the shaping of the Oral Torah. Still, it is not clear from the rest of the story that the storyteller frowns upon Ilfa's choice:

> By the time Ilfa came back, Rabbi Yoḥanan was reigning. They said to Ilfa: If you, master, had sat and studied Torah, the other master would not have reigned as head of the yeshiva. Ilfa went and hung himself on the mast of a ship. He said: If there is anyone who can ask me about a *baraita* from Rabbi Ḥiya and Rabbi Oshaya and I am not able to demonstrate its basis in a mishna, I will allow myself to fall from the mast of the ship and drown in the sea below. An old man came and quoted the following *baraita* to him: If someone said [to the trustee of his estate]: Give a *shekel* to my sons each week, and it would be appropriate in their case to give them a *sela*, we give them a *sela*. But if he said explicitly: Give them only a *shekel*, we give them only a *shekel*. If he said: Should they die, let others inherit in their stead, then whether he said to give them a *shekel* or whether he said to give them only a *shekel*, we give them only a *shekel*. He said to him: Who is the *Tanna* of this *baraita*? It is Rabbi Meir, who states: It is obligatory to fulfill the will of the deceased. (Taanit 21a)

The second half of this story begins with Ilfa's return. It is not clear how many years elapsed in the interim. Rabbi Yoḥanan already reigns

"He does not doubt that he made the right decision.... The fact that Ilfa did not hear [the angels] is not just a technical matter, but reflects something more fundamental: Ilfa cannot overhear the angels' conversation overheard by his friend Rabbi Yoḥanan because it does not take place in his consciousness.... Ilfa did not sense any danger, because for him there was none." See A. Kosman, *Men's Tractate* [Hebrew] (Jerusalem: 2002), 121–126.

as king of the yeshiva.[11] No sooner has Ilfa shown his face than rabble-rousers come along to foment jealousy: "If you, master, had sat and studied Torah, the other master would not have reigned as head of the yeshiva."

Upon hearing this, Ilfa climbs to the top of the mast of a ship and declares that if there is someone who can ask him about a *baraita* that has no correlate in the Mishna, he will jump into the water. Ilfa's challenge is fascinating; he proposes that a major literary output of the beit midrash, the *baraitot* of Rabbi Ḥiya and Rabbi Oshaya, does not contain any insights beyond those already included in the Mishna. Ilfa, who left the world of Torah scholarship, seeks to prove that although he now spends his time earning a living, there is no one who surpasses him in knowledge of Torah.

Ilfa is challenged with a *baraita* that deals with the case of a trustee who departs slightly from the will of the deceased. This *baraita* is not selected at random, but is related to the larger context of the story in which it appears: The father who instructs that his sons be given only a *shekel* (and not a *sela*) does not want to starve them, but rather teach them to take responsibility for their own economic welfare, which is the same message that Ilfa wishes to impart to the world.

Does the storyteller prefer Rabbi Yoḥanan to Ilfa? The answer at first seems obvious: Surely the one who merits to overhear the conversation of the angels saying that his hour is at hand is the chosen one, whereas the one who prefers the transitory life of business is not. But on closer examination, it becomes clear that Ilfa, who opted to make a living in fulfillment of the verse, "But among you there will be no destitute," has not forsaken Torah, but mastered it. After all, when challenged with a *baraita,* he immediately responds by quoting Rabbi Meir's Mishna: "It is obligatory to fulfill the will of the deceased." And so even though he no longer spends his days in the beit midrash, no one can best him when it comes to Torah. It seems that this story wishes to teach that every person should follow his own path, whether this involves dedicating

11. On the use of the term "king" to refer to a sage, see the discussion of Rav and Geniva in Part Two. There, too, we encountered a sage who left the world of Torah scholarship and referred to the sages as "kings."

oneself exclusively to Torah study or leaving the beit midrash to make a living. Each has merit.[12]

The Talmud in Tractate Taanit speaks of Ilfa as one of the righteous members of his generation, in whose merit rain fell in time of drought:

> Rebbi decreed a fast but the rain did not come. Ilfa went down before the ark, and some say it was Rabbi Ilfai. When he said, "He makes the wind blow," the wind blew. When he said, "He makes the rain fall," the rain came. Rebbi said to him: What do you do? He said to him: I live in a poverty-stricken village which lacks wine for Kiddush and Havdala. I make it my business to bring wine for Kiddush and Havdala, and thereby discharge their obligations for them. (Taanit 24a)

Ilfa chooses to live in a poor neighborhood, where he provides the residents with wine for Shabbat. He engages in acts of loving-kindness reminiscent of Rabbi Yehoshua ben Levi, who sat among the lepers. Though he left the beit midrash, he continues to master and embody Torah.

12. Y. Frankel argues that Ilfa did not overhear the angels because he did not leave the world of Torah study entirely; for him, Torah learning could take place alongside business pursuits. In contrast, Rabbi Yoḥanan adopted Rashbi's all-or-nothing approach, and so he was haunted by the angels' words. See Y. Frankel, *The Aggadic Story*, 58–61. Rabbi M. Margaliot used the story of Ilfa and Rabbi Yoḥanan in the introduction to his book *Pearls of the Sea* [Hebrew] on Tractate Sanhedrin (Jerusalem: 5618). His choice of this story reflects his own biography: He grew up as a gifted student of Torah in Galicia, received rabbinical ordination as a young man, and was widely known as a great Torah scholar, but he chose instead to pursue business and management. For dozens of years, he ran Rambam Library in Tel Aviv, and he wrote several books which attest to his mastery of all aspects of Torah. But he never served as a rabbi or returned to yeshiva. He concludes his introduction as follows: "Ilfa never reigned, but he had no desire to do so. He wished to learn and to teach, to make Torah accessible, to draw from the wellsprings of early sources and sate those who thirst for words of Torah through conversations with friends and by publishing words of Torah that he wrote in his notebook." I am grateful to Rabbi Aryeh Stern for bringing this citation to my attention.

**Rabbi Yoḥanan Renounces Everything for Torah**

The choice to give oneself over entirely to Torah study and live a life of penury was not for everyone.[13] But it is another point of commonality between Rabbi Yoḥanan and Rashbi.[14] In addition to giving up on making a living and dedicating himself to Torah study, Rabbi Yoḥanan was also entirely unconcerned about his finances, as the following source attests:

> Rabbi Yoḥanan was once walking from Tiberias to Tzippori, accompanied by Rabbi Ḥiya bar Abba. As they passed a certain field, Rabbi Yoḥanan said: This field used to belong to me, and I sold it so that I could devote myself to the study of Torah. They came to a vineyard and Rabbi Yoḥanan said: This vineyard used to belong to me, and I sold it so that I could devote myself to the study of Torah. They passed an olive press and he said the same thing. Rabbi Ḥiya began to weep. He asked: Why are you weeping? He said: I am weeping because you have not left yourself anything for your old age. He said to him: Ḥiya, my son, do you think so little of what I have done in selling a thing which was given after six days, as it says, "For in six days the Lord made heaven and earth" [Ex. 20:11]? But the Torah was given after forty days, as it says, "And he was there with the Lord forty days" [Ex. 34:28], and it is also written, "Then I stayed in the mountain forty days" [Deut. 9:9]. (Song of Songs Rabba 8:7)

In this story, Rabbi Yoḥanan points out everything he sold so as to support his life of study. Rabbi Ḥiya bar Abba, his close disciple, knows that

13. On the study of Torah as a religious value in the period of the early Ashkenazi sages, see Y.M. Ta-Shma, "The Commandment to Study Torah as a Religious and Social Problem in Sefer Hasidim," *Halakha, Custom, and Reality in Ashkenaz* [Hebrew] (Jerusalem: 5756), 112–129. On Rashbi's way of life and its influence on Jewish life in general, see *Sages* II.

14. Epstein, *Text of the Mishna*, 239. However, Rabbi Yehuda Brandes cautioned me that often when the Talmud speaks of "Rabbi Yoḥanan in the name of Rashbi," the Rashbi invoked is actually Rabbi Shimon ben Yehotzadak, who was Rabbi Yoḥanan's teacher. The matter requires further investigation.

Rabbi Yoḥanan has nothing to bequeath to his children. He imagines all the wealth they would have inherited if only Rabbi Yoḥanan had not renounced the things of this world. But in spite of his disciple's lamentation, Rabbi Yoḥanan remains confident in his decision. He contrasts the six days of creation with the forty days in which the Torah was given to Moses on Sinai, which he interprets as a sign that Torah is superior to material possessions. Even so, the story's enumeration of the field, vineyard, and olive press serves as a testament to just how great a sacrifice he made.

### Breaking from the Study of Torah: Between Rabbi Yoḥanan and Rashbi

We learn about the difference between Rabbi Yoḥanan and Rashbi from a passage in Tractate Berakhot that deals with the obligation to break from the study of Torah to recite the *Shema* and the *Amida*. This source suggests that the study of Torah serves as a direct connection to God, both on the level of the heart and the mind.[15] A person in the middle of studying Torah does not need to break to recite the *Shema* because he is already "accepting the yoke of the commandments." Even the *Amida* pales in comparison to the study of Torah, since Torah study is part of the life of the World to Come, whereas prayer belongs to this world.[16]

The Babylonian Talmud teaches:

> Scholars who are studying Torah have to interrupt their studies for the recitation of the *Shema*, but they do not have to interrupt their studies for the *Amida*. Rabbi Yoḥanan said: They taught this only in regard to people such as Rabbi Shimon bar Yoḥai and his colleagues, whose sole occupation is the study of Torah. But people such as ourselves must interrupt their studies for both the recitation of the *Shema* and for the *Amida*. (Shabbat 11a)

15. See Rabbi Meir's teaching on this subject in *Sages* III, Part Three.
16. This is how the Talmud speaks of the dichotomy between Torah study and learning, a formulation clearly based on Rashbi.

Rabbi Yoḥanan distinguishes himself from Rashbi. Unlike Rashbi, he and his disciples do not live in a cave and God does not miraculously supply them with food. Their life of penury is a reflection of their economic reality rather than a conscious retreat from the world, and so they interrupt their Torah study for prayer.

In the Jerusalem Talmud, Rabbi Yoḥanan compares his approach to that of Rashbi with regard to this question:

> Rabbi Yoḥanan said in the name of Rabbi Shimon bar Yoḥai: "Like we who occupy ourselves with the study of Torah" – we do not break even for the recitation of the *Shema*. Rabbi Yoḥanan said about himself: "Like we who occupy ourselves with the study of Torah" – we break even for the *Amida*. (Y. Berakhot 1:2 [3b])

Rabbi Yoḥanan is well aware of the difference between Rashbi's experience of a miraculous world in which all is provided, and his own very difficult challenge of living in the real world, coping with poverty, and nonetheless remaining committed to Torah.

### The One-Day Student

After examining the tension between the world of Torah study and the world beyond the walls of the beit midrash, we now turn to consider the figure of Rav Idi, known in the Talmud as "the father of Rabbi Yaakov bar Idi."

> Rav Idi, the father of Rabbi Yaakov bar Idi, used to set out on a three-month journey and then spend only one day at the rabbinical academy. The rabbis would mockingly call him "a one-day student of the rabbinical academy." He felt dejected and applied to himself the verse, "I will be as one who is a mockery to his friend" [Job 12:4]. Rabbi Yoḥanan entreated Rav Idi, "I beg of you, do not bring punishment upon the rabbis who have insulted you." Rabbi Yoḥanan went out to the beit midrash and expounded: "To be sure, they seek Me daily, eager to learn My ways" [Is. 58:2]. Is it only by day that they seek Him, and by night they do not seek Him? Rather, this comes to tell you that

> anyone who learns Torah for even a single day is considered as if he studied it all year long. (Ḥagiga 5b)

This is a story about a man who is known by the name of his son, Rabbi Yaakov bar Idi, a leading and close disciple of Rabbi Yoḥanan.[17] The storyteller describes Rav Idi spending three months on the road and then one day studying Torah. According to Rashi's explanation, his home was a three-month journey from the beit midrash:

> It was a three-month journey from his home to the beit midrash, and he would leave his house after Passover and learn for one day, and then return home to gladden his wife on Sukkot.

Some scholars contend that Rav Idi was not alone in traveling so far for such a brief period of study. But we have no parallel sources that speak of sages leaving home to study Torah during this period. Perhaps, as other scholars contend, Rashi was projecting the reality of his own experience in medieval Ashkenaz.[18]

The Maharsha (Rabbi Shmuel Eidels, 1555–1631) suggests a simpler explanation, namely that Rav Idi spent three months making a living, and then took a day off each quarter to study Torah. The students in the beit midrash, who see him arriving once every three months to learn for just a single day, make fun of "the one-day student." It is not hard to imagine how students immersed in the study of Torah for extended periods would mock a man whose level of learning was so basic, and who acted like a stranger in their midst. For them, anyone who does not spend all his time studying Torah amounts to a "one-day student."

Rav Idi is insulted by the students' behavior and recites a verse from Job: "I will be as one who is a mockery to his friend" (Job 12:3). In this verse, Job curses his friends who think themselves better than him:

17. Hyman, *Tanna'im and Amora'im*, 776–777.
18. D. Herman, "The Study and Teaching of Torah During the Roman Anarchic Period in the Land of Israel" [Hebrew], *Asufot* 4 (5750): 37.

> Then Job responded: Truly then, you are the people and wisdom will die with you! But I have intelligence as well as you; I am not inferior to you. And who does not know such things as these? I will be as one who is a mockery to his friend, the one who called on God and He answered him. The just and blameless man is a joke. (Job 12:1–4)

The students in the beit midrash do not understand that even the man who must travel far to make a living is deserving of their respect. Their attitude is a far cry from what we are told of the beit midrash in Yavneh:

> The following was a familiar lesson in the mouths of the rabbis at Yavneh: I, who am engaged in Torah study, am a human being, and my unlearned friend is a human being. My work is in the city and his work is in the field. I arise early to perform my work, and he arises early to perform his work. Just as he does not aspire to distinguish himself by doing my work, so I do not aspire to distinguish myself by doing his work. And perhaps you will say that I am able to study extensively whereas he is able to study only minimally; this is not so, for we have learned that both the one who does much and the one who does little are equally rewarded, provided that each directs his heart toward heaven. (Berakhot 17a)

Rabbi Yoḥanan's students are not aware of the distress they have caused. Only Rabbi Yoḥanan is sensitive to Rav Idi's plight and recognizes that this one-day student has the ability to destroy the entire beit midrash. He pleads with Rav Idi not to speak poorly about his students, and Rav Idi agrees. Then Rabbi Yoḥanan goes out to rebuke his students. He invokes verses from Isaiah in which the prophet chides the people for sitting and seeking out God day after day: "To be sure, they seek Me daily, eager to learn My ways, like a nation that does what is right, that has not abandoned the laws of God" (Is. 58:2). Learning devoid of action is worthless. The people sit there day after day, yet they do not understand how a servant of God is judged. It is Rav Idi who merits Rabbi Yoḥanan's blessing: Anyone who learns Torah for even a single day is regarded as if he studied it all year long.

### Rabbi Yoḥanan and Rabbi Oshaya of Teria

Another figure who sheds light on Rabbi Yoḥanan is featured in a source that appears in close proximity to the midrash about how Rabbi Yoḥanan sold all his possessions to study Torah.[19] According to this midrash, Rabbi Yoḥanan stood out among his contemporaries as a man who devoted himself wholeheartedly to Torah, such that there was nothing else he wanted of the world. With his death, he became a model of total devotion to Torah study, like Rabbi Shimon bar Yoḥai and Rabbi Meir before him. [20] The midrash closes with an impassioned eulogy for Rabbi Yoḥanan offered by his contemporaries:

> When Rabbi Yoḥanan died, his generation applied to him the verse, "If a man offered all his wealth for love" – for the love which Rabbi Yoḥanan bore for the Torah – "he would be laughed to scorn." (Song of Songs Rabba 8:7)

But the editor of the midrash was not content to leave it at that. He appended the eulogy for Rabbi Oshaya of Teria, who merited a similar – but not identical – description:

> When Rabbi Oshaya of Teria died, they saw his bier suspended in the air, and his generation applied to him the verse, "If a man would give his wealth for love" – for the love which the Holy One, Blessed Be He, bore to Rabbi Oshaya of Teria – "he would be laughed to scorn." (Song of Songs Rabba 8:7)

We must pay close attention to the difference between these two eulogies that invoke the same verse. Rabbi Yoḥanan gave away all his wealth because of his love of Torah. No one loved Torah more than he. But Rabbi Oshaya's bier was suspended in the air as a sign of God's love for him.

19. I am grateful to my cousin Rabbi Moshe Haim Hagar-Lau who called this extraordinary figure to my attention.
20. Their love for Torah was compared to the love between a man and a woman. See *Sages* III, Part Three.

What did Rabbi Oshaya do to merit such divine love? We know almost nothing about this sage. In the Jerusalem Talmud, he is described as a launderer who took care that all his actions should place him above suspicion:

> Abba Oshaya of Teria was a launderer. He made himself a garment from only one kind of wool, so that people should not say: He is wearing clothes made of our garments! (Y. Bava Kamma 10:10 [7c])

Abba Oshaya did not want other people to be able to claim that he pulled out wool from their clothes and wove it into his own. Another story speaks of a lost item that he returned to a queen:

> Abba Oshaya was a launderer. The queen came to wash there and lost her bathing clothes. He found them and held them out to her.[21] She said: They are yours. As for me, what are these worth to me? I have many which are even better than those. He said to her: The Torah has decreed that we should return what we find. She said: Blessed be the God of the Jews. (Y. Bava Metzia 2:5 [8c])

Rabbi Oshaya is depicted as an honest, upright man who does not put on airs or act with ulterior motives. He does not seem to be part of the sages' circle, but all his actions are for the sake of heaven.[22] This simple individual merits divine love, and in this sense he may be compared to Ilfa and Rav Idi the father of Rabbi Yaakov. Taken together, these three individuals in Rabbi Yoḥanan's circle represent an alternative way of life.

21. This version is based on the Escorial manuscript of Y. Nezikin, published with an introduction by A.S. Rosenthal (Jerusalem: 5744). See Lieberman's commentary on the difficult words in this story on page 135.
22. Hyman counts Oshaya among the sages of the period, which is how he arrives at over one thousand sages. See Hyman, *Tanna'im and Amora'im*, 115–116.

## RABBI YOḤANAN'S MOVE FROM TZIPPORI TO TIBERIAS

Rabbi Yoḥanan is associated with Tiberias, though he spent his early years in Tzippori in the beit midrash of Rabbi Yehuda HaNasi and then Rabbi Ḥanina. The Jerusalem Talmud preserves a record of this period in his life:

> Rabbi Yoḥanan was sitting and reciting before a Babylonian synagogue in Tzippori. A Roman archon passed by but Rabbi Yoḥanan did not stand for him. The archon's guards went to strike him. The archon said to them: Let him be! He is busy paying homage to his Creator. (Y. Berakhot 5:1 [9a])

This story depicts Rabbi Yoḥanan studying in a synagogue of Babylonian immigrants in Tzippori.[23] He is so absorbed in his studies that he does not notice the Roman archon passing before him. Fortunately, the Roman archon understands that Rabbi Ḥanina is not being rude, but is merely oblivious to his presence. For this sage, the world consists only of Torah study.

It seems there was a degree of tension between Rabbi Ḥanina, who was chosen as the head as per Rebbi's will, and his student Rabbi Yoḥanan, a rising star. On the one hand, it is rare for a person to grow jealous of his own son or disciple. But on the other hand, no one wants to see his son or student inherit his position while he is still alive. The following story demonstrates Rabbi Ḥanina's complicated relationship with his students:

> Rabbi Ḥanina was living in Tzippori, and cases would come before him again and again. Rabbi Yoḥanan and Rabbi Shimon ben Lakish were living there, but Rabbi Ḥanina did not add them to his court. They said: That old man is wise, and his knife

23. The phrase "Babylonian synagogue" may have been derogatory, a reflection of the biases of the residents of Tzippori. On the historical evidence for a Babylonian beit midrash in Tzippori, see D. Rosenthal, "On the Annual Torah Reading Cycle in the Land of Israel" [Hebrew], *Tarbiz* 53 (5744): 144–148. Also see Lieberman, *The Land of Israel During the Period of the Mishna and the Talmud* [Hebrew] (Jerusalem: 5751), 334, note 15.

> is sharp. One time he added them to his court. They said: Why does Rabbi pay attention to us today? He said to them: May something bad come upon me if it is not so that every case I adjudicate, I do not rule in accordance with a law that I learned from my teacher as a valid law as many times as there are hairs on my head, and if I did not see my teacher apply these laws in practice at least three times. But this particular case did not come before my teacher as a matter of law or practical decision more than twice, and therefore I have joined you with me to make the decision. (Y. Nidda 2:7 [50b])

Rabbi Ḥanina is a humble man who does not try to pretend he is something he is not. If he previously heard a judge rule on the matter at hand, then he offers his ruling. If there is no precedent, then he invites his two leading disciples to help him investigate the matter. His disciples, unaware of his modus operandi, are concerned about all those occasions in which Rabbi Ḥanina does not seek out their opinion. They worry that he does not take them sufficiently into consideration.

As Rabbi Yoḥanan became increasingly learned, he found himself at loggerheads with his teacher Rabbi Ḥanina, as the following source relates:

> Rabbi Ḥanina gave a decision to the people of Tzippori concerning the aftergrowth of mustard in the sabbatical year and concerning an egg in accordance with the view of Rabbi Yehuda. Rabbi Yoḥanan went in and taught them in accordance with the rabbis here, and in accordance with the rabbis there. Rabbi Abba bar Zimna said in the name of Rabbi Yehotzadak: On account of these two things, Rabbi Yoḥanan went down from Tzippori to Tiberias. He said: Why do you bring me the opinions of that elder? What I permit, he prohibits, and what I prohibit, he permits. (Y. Shevi'it 9:1 [38c])

We can understand what is at stake in this story even without going into the details of the halakhic issue under discussion, which relates to the laws of the sabbatical year and the laws of festivals. The presiding elder,

Rabbi Ḥanina, offers his ruling on these matters, but then the young Rabbi Yoḥanan offers a contradictory opinion. At this point Rabbi Yoḥanan realizes that he cannot continue to grow as a scholar in the shadow of Rabbi Ḥanina's overhanging presence. As the commanding elder, Rabbi Ḥanina cramps his style and prevents him from leading the community as he sees fit.

When we studied the figure of Rabbi Ḥanina, we saw how kindly he looked upon his disciples. As an old man, he watched joyously as everyone ran to listen to the rising star of Tzippori, like a tree witnessing its own flowers bloom. But in spite of his teacher's encouragement, Rabbi Yoḥanan found it difficult to blossom in his shadow, and so he relocated to Tiberias.

Rabbi Yoḥanan became the leader of the Jewish community in Tiberias. Students from all over the Land of Israel flocked to him, and eventually the entire Jerusalem Talmud bore his imprint. It would be impossible to imagine Rabbi Yoḥanan without his Torah learning, and it would be impossible to imagine Torah learning without Rabbi Yoḥanan. This powerful symbiosis became the cornerstone of the talmudic enterprise.

### ARE THESE AFFLICTIONS DEAR TO YOU: AN EPISODE IN THE LIFE OF RABBI YOḤANAN

It is worth devoting a few pages to the pain that beset Rabbi Yoḥanan throughout his lifetime. The Talmud speaks on several occasions of his physical afflictions. According to one source, he was absent from the beit midrash for three years on account of illness.[24]

> Rabbi Yoḥanan spent three and a half years without going to the meetinghouse of the sages because of his anguish. Finally Rabbi Elazar saw in his dream:[25] Tomorrow Sinai will come down

24. In the famous story about the breach between Rabbi Yoḥanan and Reish Lakish, which we will consider at the end of this volume, Rabbi Yoḥanan is described as being absent from the beit midrash on account of a broken heart. According to the Jerusalem Talmud, however, his absence was due to physical affliction.
25. I translated this line in accordance with the reading of the Penei Moshe (Rabbi Moshe Margalit) and the Korban HaEda (Rabbi David ben Naftali Hirsch Frankel,

> and teach you something new. He returned to the beit midrash. (Y. Megilla 1:11 [72b])

Elsewhere in the Talmud we learn that Rabbi Yoḥanan had ten sons who died in his lifetime. This information is related in the context of Rabbi Yoḥanan's visit to his ailing student, Rabbi Elazar ben Pedat:

> Rabbi Elazar fell ill. Rabbi Yoḥanan went in to visit him. He saw that Rabbi Elazar was lying in a dark room. Rabbi Yoḥanan exposed his arm and light fell. He saw that Rabbi Elazar was crying. Rabbi Yoḥanan asked him: Why are you crying? If it is because you did not accumulate as much Torah as you wanted, haven't we learned in a mishna: Both the offering of one who gives much and the offering of one who gives little are equally pleasing to God, provided he directs his heart to heaven? And if you are crying because of a lack of food, not everyone merits two tables. And if you are crying because of your children who died, this is the bone of my tenth son that I lost. Rabbi Elazar said to Rabbi Yoḥanan: It is on account of this beauty which will be ravaged to dust that I am crying. Rabbi Yoḥanan said to him: For this you should certainly cry. And they both cried. In the meantime, Rabbi Yoḥanan asked him: Are these afflictions dear to you? Rabbi Elazar said to him: Neither they nor their reward. Rabbi Yoḥanan said to him: Give me your hand. Rabbi Elazar gave him his hand, and Rabbi Yoḥanan pulled him up. (Berakhot 5b)

Rabbi Yoḥanan arrives at a dark house, hoping to lift the spirits of his sick and dejected student. He is aware of the brilliance that is hidden within him, so he exposes his arm, filling the house with light. Rabbi Elazar responds with tears, and Rabbi Yoḥanan challenges him: Who are you to cry? If you think you didn't learn enough Torah, well, you learned as much as you could. If you think you didn't have enough

1707–1762). But it is also possible to read it as, "Rabbi Yoḥanan saw Rabbi Elazar (Sinai) in his dream." We will consider this alternative reading at the conclusion of this volume.

money, well, not everyone does. And if you are concerned about the children you lost, well, here is the bone of my tenth child to die! And with that, Rabbi Yoḥanan shows Rabbi Elazar the bone that he carries around in his pocket.

Rabbi Yoḥanan, who spent his whole life immersed in Torah, found himself suffering the greatest pain of all – the loss of his children. The Talmud relates that a *Tanna*, someone who would memorize and then quote back earlier sources to the sages, tried to teach Rabbi Yoḥanan a lesson.

> A *Tanna* taught before Rabbi Yoḥanan: Whoever engages in studying Torah and in bestowing kindness and buries his sons is forgiven for all his sins. (Berakhot 5b)

Rabbi Yoḥanan is skeptical:

> Rabbi Yoḥanan said to him: It is understandable that studying Torah and bestowing kindness cause one's sins to be forgiven, for it is written, "Through kindness and truth, iniquity will be forgiven" [Prov. 16:6]. "Kindness" is a reference to bestowing kindness, as it is said, "One who pursues righteousness and bestows kindness will find life, righteousness, and honor" [Prov. 21:21]. "Truth" is a reference to studying Torah, as it is stated, "Purchase truth and do not sell" [Prov. 23:23]. But from where does the *baraita* derive that one who buries his sons has his sins forgiven? (Berakhot 5b)

An old man responds to him by quoting Rabbi Shimon bar Yoḥai, who drew this conclusion by linking a word used in two different biblical contexts:

> A certain elder taught him in the name of Rabbi Shimon bar Yoḥai: It is derived from a link between the two mentions of the word "iniquity." It is written here, "Through kindness and truth, iniquity will be forgiven" [Prov. 16:6], and it is written there, "And who repays the iniquity of the fathers into the bosom of their children" [Jer. 32:18]. (Berakhot 5b)

Rabbi Yoḥanan refuses to accept this teaching and refutes the old man firmly:

> Rabbi Yoḥanan said: Leprosy and loss of children are not afflictions of love. (Berakhot 5b)

Back in the dark room with Rabbi Elazar, Rabbi Yoḥanan takes out the bone of his tenth son as a way of telling the ailing man that suffering is all relative. He can teach Rabbi Elazar a lesson about how to accept afflictions, even when they are not afflictions of love.[26]

The student offers a surprising response. He is crying because he sees the beauty of Rabbi Yoḥanan and realizes that it is transient. Rabbi Yoḥanan's beauty is mentioned throughout the Talmud. At one point he says about himself, "I alone remain from the beautiful people of Jerusalem" (Bava Metzia 84a). The Talmud instructs that someone who wants to see the beauty of Rabbi Yoḥanan should bring a goblet of refined silver, fill it with red pomegranate seeds, crown it with rose petals, and rest it between the sun and the shade. The rays of light that emanate will resemble the beauty of Rabbi Yoḥanan.

Rabbi Yoḥanan responds sympathetically, joining in his student's tears. All the beauty of this world will ultimately decay, and we have nothing to hope for but the World to Come. Then he asks his student if his afflictions are dear to him, and Rabbi Elazar responds, "Neither they nor their reward." This response stands in stark contrast to the rabbinic tradition that afflictions are dear, attributed to Naḥum Ish Gamzu and his student Rabbi Akiva. Their notion of lovingly accepting one's fate had a profound influence on the rabbinic worldview.[27] But it is not

26. For more on accepting affliction, see E.E. Urbach, *The Sages: Their Beliefs and Opinions*, 394–395. The question of whether Rabbi Yoḥanan accepted the death of his sons as an affliction of love preoccupied the early medieval commentators. (See Tosafot on Berakhot 5b.) In my humble opinion, this story espouses Rabbi Yoḥanan's view that the death of sons is not an affliction of love, though Urbach argues otherwise (see note 90).

27. For more on Rabbi Akiva's teachings about affliction and his influence on his own and subsequent generations, see E.E. Urbach, "Asceticism and Affliction in Rabbinic Teaching" [Hebrew], *The World of the Sages*, 347–458.

the approach we find here. For Rabbi Elazar, afflictions must be borne, but they are not beloved.

### RABBI YOḤANAN'S APPROACH TO JOB

Rabbi Yoḥanan's attitude toward suffering afforded him a unique perspective on the figure of Job.[28] Unlike Rabbi Akiva, who criticized Job for his unwillingness to accept his afflictions, Rabbi Yoḥanan understood Job's response and cited verses in his praise. One of Rabbi Yoḥanan's most difficult rabbinic exegeses appears in an extended talmudic passage (Ḥagiga 4b–5b) which describes the verses that would make various sages weep. It is a verse from Job that moves Rabbi Yoḥanan to tears:

> When Rabbi Yoḥanan would come to the following verse, he would weep: "You have incited Me against him, to destroy him for no reason" [Job 2:3]. A slave whose master is incited and turns against the slave, is there any remedy for him? (Ḥagiga 5a)

This verse from Job raises a difficult theological question. The description of the Holy One, Blessed Be He, as being incited to turn against His holy people suggests that Satan has seized control over the Creator Himself. According to this reading, it is not Job who is at fault, but the world that has gone awry. Rabbi Yoḥanan makes a similar claim elsewhere:

> "God said to Satan: Have you paid attention to My servant Job? For there is none like him in all the world…and you incited Me against him, to destroy him for no reason" [Job 2:3]. Rabbi Yoḥanan said: Were this verse not written, it would be impossible to say it. It describes God like a mortal, whom others urge and He is persuaded by them. (Bava Batra 16a)

In the continuation of the passage in Ḥagiga, the Talmud cites another verse that moved Rabbi Yoḥanan to tears:

28. Hananel Mack has written about Rabbi Yoḥanan's unique attitude toward the figure of Job. See H. Mack, *But Rather Just a Parable: Job in Second-Temple Literature and in the Eyes of the Sages* [Hebrew] (Ramat Gan: 5765), 168–190.

> When Rabbi Yoḥanan would come to the following verse, he would weep: "Behold, He cannot have any faith even in His holy ones" [Job 15:15]. If in His holy ones He cannot have any faith, then in whom can He have faith? (Ḥagiga 5b)

Rabbi Yoḥanan depicts Job as one of God's holy ones, perhaps seeing himself, too, reflected in Job. He cries because he spent his whole life trying to cleave to Torah, believing that in doing so, he was cleaving to God. But suddenly he realizes that God does not believe in him. If God has no faith in His holy ones, then in whom can He have faith? The Talmud then cites the following story about Rabbi Yoḥanan:

> One day Rabbi Yoḥanan was going on a journey. He saw a certain man who was gathering figs. He would leave those that were ripe, and take those that were not ripe. Rabbi Yoḥanan said to him: Are these ripe ones not better? He said: I require these figs for provisions during my journey. These unripe figs will keep for the journey, while those that are ripe now will not keep for the journey. Rabbi Yoḥanan said: This is the meaning of that which is written, "Behold, He cannot have any faith even in His holy ones" [Job 15:15]. (Ḥagiga 5a)

The parable is simple, but the lesson it seeks to impart is devastating. God is depicted as the owner of a great field who gathers figs and sets out on a journey. He picks the unripe fruit but leaves the ripe ones. Rabbi Yoḥanan questions the fig-gatherer: Why pick unripe fruit when there is ripe fruit to be had? The notion of unripe fruit that is plucked before its time suggests that the Creator has lost faith in creation, and the image moves Rabbi Yoḥanan to tears. And so Rabbi Yoḥanan is left sunk in his afflictions, mourning the loss of his sons but continuing to serve God by studying His Torah – even while failing to understand His ways.

*Chapter Seventeen*

# The Authority of the Mishna

## CANONIZING THE MISHNA IN RABBI YOḤANAN'S BEIT MIDRASH

The sages of the transitional generation possessed collections of mishnayot that were taught in their own *batei midrash*. They also had access to Rabbi Yehuda HaNasi's Mishna, which compiled all the collections into a single document that was regarded as significant but not yet authoritative. Rebbi's Mishna was taught, but not as a binding halakhic code,[1] and dispute in matters of halakha was considered desirable and fruitful.

Rabbi Yoḥanan brought his beit midrash into a new era in which the curriculum was based on a single text, the Mishna. All other mishnaic collections became secondary, drawing their authority from that of the Mishna. The following example, like countless others, demonstrates

1. A. Goldberg has written, "All those who sought to find in Rebbi's Mishna a halakhic code have labored in vain." See A. Goldberg, *Commentary on Tractate Eiruvin* [Hebrew] (Jerusalem: 5746), 24, note 38. Also see Y. Brandes, "The Origins of the Laws of Halakhic Ruling," 175–186.

how the Mishna came to assume such a central place in Rabbi Yoḥanan's beit midrash.

The background to this story is a debate among the sages of the Usha generation about the status of food that was cooked on Shabbat. Three sages took part in the debate: Rabbi Meir, Rabbi Yehuda, and Rabbi Yoḥanan the Sandal-Maker. According to Rabbi Meir, one who cooks on Shabbat may eat from the food only if he cooked by accident. Rabbi Yehuda, presumably worried that people would take advantage of this allowance, rules that one who cooks inadvertently on Shabbat may eat from his food only after Shabbat has ended. Rabbi Yoḥanan the Sandal-Maker is even stricter, and rules that one who inadvertently cooked on Shabbat may not eat from his food at all, but may serve it to others after Shabbat is over.[2] Rabbi Yehuda HaNasi's Mishna presents only Rabbi Meir's lenient ruling, namely that one who cooks on Shabbat inadvertently may eat from that food.

The Jerusalem Talmud, in its discussion of this mishna, describes the process by which halakhic decisions were made by the first generation of talmudic sages:

> Shmuel agreed with Rabbi Yoḥanan the Sandal-Maker. As for Rav, when he would teach his colleagues, he would teach in accordance with the opinion of Rabbi Meir. But in public he would teach according to the opinion of Rabbi Yoḥanan the Sandal-Maker.... They asked in the presence of Rabbi Yoḥanan: What do you say? He said to them: I know only what it says in the Mishna: One who tithes his produce or who cooks on the Sabbath – if he did this inadvertently, he may eat of the food he has prepared. But if he did this deliberately, he may not eat. (Y. Terumot 2:1 [41c])

Rav and Shmuel disagree about the halakha in this case. It is clear to both of them that they cannot rule in accordance with Rebbi's Mishna, which cites only the opinion of Rabbi Meir. They both understand the fences that the other sages build around Rabbi Meir's opinion to ensure that people would not transgress the law. Such fences are crucial when

2. This dispute is preserved in Tosefta Shabbat 2:15 and at several points in the Babylonian Talmud.

teaching the masses in a public setting. But they disagree about the case where the sage is teaching the matter to a group of colleagues, who can be trusted not to take advantage of a lenient ruling to circumvent the law. Whereas Rav shares Rabbi Meir's more lenient opinion with his colleagues, Shmuel does not.

Unlike Rav and Shmuel, Rabbi Yoḥanan does not hesitate for a moment. He holds like Rabbi Meir's opinion in the Mishna. He teaches everyone – not just his colleagues – that if one cooks on Shabbat accidentally, the food is permitted. His ruling seems dangerously lax and irresponsible. But it is typical of Rabbi Yoḥanan to put an end to all debate by accepting Rabbi Yehuda HaNasi's Mishna as authoritative.

In contrast, Rav rejects the Mishna's ruling:

> A teacher of *baraitot* taught the following in the presence of Rav: If one cooked on Shabbat inadvertently, he may eat. If he did so deliberately, he may not eat. Rav silenced him. (Ḥullin 15a)

Rav hears his *Tanna* quote Rabbi Meir's opinion and silences him.[3] But it is not clear why he does so. For him, Rabbi Yehuda HaNasi's Mishna was already "our Mishna," and even if Rav was not bound to it, he clearly recognized its authoritative nature. The Talmud asks this question:

> Why did Rav silence him? If you will say it was because Rav subscribes to the view of Rabbi Yehuda, whereas the teacher of *baraitot* taught something that accords instead with Rabbi Meir, this cannot be, for just because Rav himself subscribes to Rabbi Yehuda's view, is that a reason to silence someone who taught in accordance with Rabbi Meir? (Ḥullin 15a)

Why can't Rav bear to listen to the opinion of a sage who disagrees with him? It seems that Rav understood the implications of the widespread

3. This source sheds light on the role of the *Tanna* in talmudic times. The *Tanna* was an individual with a prodigious memory who served as the sage's "open book," able to quote passages on demand. See A. Amir, *Institutions and Titles in Talmudic Literature* [Hebrew] (Jerusalem: 5737), 9–37.

acceptance of Rebbi's Mishna. He realized that if he did not silence his *Tanna* and erase Rabbi Meir's opinion, it would soon become authoritative.

The Talmud continues:

> And moreover, does Rav really subscribe to the view of Rabbi Yehuda? When Rav would rule for his students in private, he would rule for them in accordance with Rabbi Meir's view. But when Rav would expound at his public discourse,[4] he would expound in accordance with Rabbi Yehuda's more stringent position, because of the unlearned masses. And if you say, it was at Rav's public discourse that this *Tanna* taught Rabbi Meir's view in Rav's presence, does everyone present listen to a *Tanna*? They listen rather to the speaker! (Ḥullin 15a)

This talmudic passage speaks to the tension that was associated with the acceptance of Rebbi's Mishna. Whereas Rabbi Yoḥanan regarded Rebbi's Mishna as the source of his halakhic decision-making and moved on to creating commentary, Rav was unwilling to accept the Mishna's exclusive authority.

In any case, by the next generation, it would be clear that the Mishna belonged to all of Israel. Rabbi Yoḥanan documents how this came to be:

> It was taught: Those who engross themselves in the study of Torah accomplish a measure, but it is not a large measure. Those who engross themselves in the study of Mishna accomplish a large measure, and they receive reward for studying it. And for those who delve into the study of Talmud, there is no greater measure than this, yet one should always run to study Mishna more than Talmud. Rabbi Yoḥanan said: This first statement was taught in the name of Rebbi. Then everyone abandoned the study of Mishna and pursued the study of Talmud. So he expounded to

4. The term used for the public discourse is *pirka*. The *pirka* was intended for the masses, which meant that only clear halakhic rulings were presented so as not to lead anyone astray. See Gafni, *The Jews of Babylonia*, 204–213.

> them that one should always run to study Mishna more than Talmud. (Bava Metzia 33a)

In Rebbi's day, when there was an abundance of mishnaic collections from all the various *batei midrash*, students abandoned the Mishna and pursued Talmud instead. Rabbi Yoḥanan's mission was to teach them to "always run to study Mishna." He focused his scholarly work on commenting on and correcting the Mishna, until it became a canonical text for subsequent generations.

### RABBI YOḤANAN'S REVOLUTION: THE MISHNA AS A HALAKHIC BOOK

In addition to his pervasive presence throughout the Talmud, where he rules in all matters of halakha, Rabbi Yoḥanan was also responsible for establishing the rules by which halakhic decisions are made.[5] His foundational principle was that the law follows the anonymous voice in the Mishna. He then developed a method of clearing a path through the thicket of contradictory opinions that characterize Rebbi's Mishna. In order to appreciate the impact of Rabbi Yoḥanan's contribution, we will take a few steps back and consider how halakha was decided before Rabbi Yoḥanan came on the scene.

#### The Opening Scene: A World Without Dispute

Rabbi Yose, the presiding rabbi in Tzippori in the generation before Rebbi, speaks of the idyllic early days of the Oral Torah, in which the sages sat in the chamber of hewn stone and produced halakhic rulings for all of Israel without any dispute or debate:[6]

> Rabbi Yose said: In the beginning there was no dispute in Israel, but the court of seventy-one was in the chamber of hewn stone....

5. I am indebted to Rabbi Yehuda Brandes for the ideas in this section. See Brandes, "The Origins of the Laws of Halakhic Ruling."
6. A parallel source appears in Sanhedrin 11b without the opening phrase, "In the beginning there was no dispute," as a description of how the judicial system was run in the past.

> When there was an inquiry about a matter of law, if they had heard the correct ruling, they delivered it to them, and if not, they rose to take a vote. If those who declared the matter to be unclean formed the majority, they declared the matter unclean. And if those who declared it to be clean formed the majority, they declared it clean. From there the law went forth and was disseminated in Israel. Once the disciples of Shammai and Hillel who did not adequately serve their masters had multiplied, dispute multiplied in Israel, and there became two Torahs. (Tosefta Ḥagiga 2:9)

This source describes two different historical periods, one that precedes and one that follows the students of Hillel and Shammai. Before Hillel and Shammai, there was no dispute because everyone was humble and disciplined. Each judge, wherever he found himself, knew what he had learned and knew how to admit what he had not previously encountered. When he didn't know the answer to a particular question, he would appeal to a higher authority. If this higher authority did not know the answer, that court would say so and the matter would be appealed to an even higher court. This would continue until the case reached the chamber of hewn stone. There, in the absence of precedent, the sages would debate and vote upon the matter, and their decision would be publicized throughout all of Israel. Matters began to deteriorate with the proliferation of disciples of Hillel and Shammai, who did not learn from their masters properly, resulting in differences of opinion. According to Rabbi Yose, this was an unfortunate turn of events and a rupture in the transmission of Torah. As he saw it, dispute is a consequence of the "decline of the generations," with later generations lacking the requisite humility to admit their ignorance and defer to others who might know more.[7]

7. Maimonides accepts Rabbi Yose's view of the historical development of dispute in his introduction to the Mishna, Shilat edition, p. 41. He attributes the decline of the generations to the caliber of the students. In contrast, Rav Sherira Gaon writes in his epistle that the generations have declined due to external causes such as plague and persecution. On Rabbi Yose's statement and on the phenomenon of dispute, see B. De Price, "Dispute," *Studies in Talmudic Literature* (Jerusalem: 5728), 172–178.

**The Halakha Follows Beit Hillel at Yavneh**

With the proliferation of differing opinions and the rise of dispute, there was a fear that there would no longer be just one Torah for all of Israel. In the time of Rabban Gamliel, the patriarch of the Yavneh generation, the first rules of halakhic decision-making were established and an authoritative tradition took shape. Rabban Gamliel did not allow anyone to diverge from the straight line of his rule. As he often declared: "Not for the sake of my own honor and not for the sake of my father's honor, but for the sake of Your honor – so that dispute should not proliferate in Israel."[8] Rabban Gamliel ruled decisively on matters of halakha, leaving no room for appeal.

The alternative approach to dispute and to halakhic decision-making was that of Rabbi Elazar ben Azarya, who contended that there should be no guard policing entry to the beit midrash and everyone should be welcome to contribute to the halakhic conversation.[9] He sought to give voice to any and all opinions in the beit midrash, entrusting the listener with the responsibility of deciding between them. As Rabbi Elazar ben Azarya understood, both the ability to listen to a multiplicity of voices and the ability to decide between them were necessary to establish the requisite climate in which Torah could be preserved and enriched with new insights.

At Yavneh, these two major approaches to halakhic decision-making became intertwined. At a certain point, a heavenly voice went forth and declared, "These and these are the words of the living God, but the halakha follows Beit Hillel" (Eiruvin 13b). The decision to follow Beit Hillel at Yavneh was an institutional one. The Talmud explains that Beit Hillel was chosen because its members were "easy and forbearing." This is a fascinating claim: Beit Hillel's views were accepted not because of their content, but because of the character of those who espoused them.[10]

8. Bava Metzia 59b. For more on Rabban Gamliel of Yavneh, see *Sages* II.
9. See *Sages* II.
10. On the process by which this principle gained widespread acceptance, see S. Safrai, "The Halakha is Like Beit Hillel in Yavneh" [Hebrew], *Proceedings of the Seventh World Congress of Jewish Studies*, 3 (5741): 21–44.

The establishment of the halakha in accordance with Beit Hillel had already begun, gradually, during Rabban Gamliel's time. Rabbi Elazar is credited with allowing for "these and these" voices to participate in the halakhic conversation. This was a momentous shift. According to rabbinic tradition, every mention of the phrase "on that day" in the Babylonian Talmud refers to the day that Rabban Gamliel was replaced with Rabbi Elazar ben Azarya and Tractate Eduyot was taught in the beit midrash.

Tractate Eduyot is a collection of all the sages' statements.[11] The tractate brings together all the different halakhic opinions and allows the student to hear them all. The Talmud relates that everyone at Yavneh was part of this discussion, including Rabban Gamliel. Rabbi Elazar made room for all to sit in his beit midrash, which became known as the "vineyard at Yavneh," an attempt to gather all the branches of Torah that had been taught since Temple times. This is not to say that with the compilation of Tractate Eduyot, the sages at Yavneh did away with halakhic decision-making. Rather, the principle that the halakha follows Beit Hillel served as an appropriate counterweight to the sweeping inclusivity for which Rabbi Elazar ben Azarya strove.

### The Mishna Project at the Patriarchal House of Rashbag

The generation following the Bar Kokhba revolt was characterized by a proliferation of legal opinions, all of which could be traced back in some way to Rabbi Akiva. The heroes of this generation were Rabbi Yehuda, Rabbi Shimon, Rabbi Yose, and Rabbi Meir, with Rabban Shimon ben Gamliel (Rashbag) at their helm. During this generation, decisions were not made in favor of one camp or another, and "those who followed this one acted well, and those who followed that one acted well" (Berakhot 27a).

Rashbag's work in editing the Mishna, like that of Rebbi who followed him, suggests that there were no fixed laws of halakhic decision-making, but rather a collection of opinions that encompassed the full

11. On the origins of Tractate Eduyot and the creation of the Mishna, see H. Albeck, *Introduction to the Mishna* [Hebrew] (Tel Aviv: 5719), 82–84, and Appendix, 257.

range of tannaitic thought. The Mishna in Tractate Eduyot questions why all opinions are cited in the Mishna, including those that were not accepted as halakhic practice:

> And why do we mention an individual opinion along with the majority, though the halakha follows the majority? So that a court may approve the view of an individual and rely on him. For a court cannot overrule a decision of its fellow court unless it is greater in wisdom and number. If it was greater in wisdom but not in number, or in number but not in wisdom, it cannot overrule its decision, unless it exceeds it in wisdom and number. (Mishna Eduyot 1:5)

According to this source, the Mishna was intended not just for those interested in the final ruling, but also for those interested in the raw materials of halakhic decision-making. And so all the words of the sages were collected and organized by topic and sub-topic to create the Mishna as we know it.

### Rebbi's Mishna: A Collection of Opinions or a Means of Deciding Halakha?

The question of the nature and goals of Rebbi's Mishna has preoccupied students and scholars from the geonic period until our own day.[12] Even if Rebbi wanted his Mishna to be useful in determining halakha, he nonetheless included conflicting halakhic opinions, sometimes quoting sages by name and sometimes simply prefacing their remarks with, "the sages said." And so anyone who studies the Mishna encounters a diversity of opinions, not just the majority view. The Talmud explains the advantage of this approach:

> This once happened and Rebbi acted according to the opinion of Rabbi Elazar. After he remembered that the law does not follow

12. The first to discuss this question was Rav Sherira Gaon, who suggested that the Mishna is comprised of sources drawn from various *batei midrash* which Rebbi did not edit or select. Epstein makes a similar claim in his vast scholarship on the Mishna. See Epstein, *Introduction to Tannaitic Literature* [Hebrew] (Jerusalem: 5717).

> Rabbi Elazar, he said: Rabbi Elazar is worthy enough to be relied upon in times of emergency. What is the meaning of "after he remembered"? If you say it means: After he remembered that the halakha does not follow Rabbi Elazar but rather the rabbis, then even in a time of emergency, how could Rebbi act according to Rabbi Elazar? Rather, you must say that it had not been stated whether the halakha followed Rabbi Elazar or the rabbis, and the Mishna means that after Rebbi remembered that it is not merely an individual who disagrees with Rabbi Elazar but rather the majority who disagree with him, he nevertheless said: Rabbi Elazar is worthy enough to be relied upon in a time of emergency. (Eiruvin 46a)

Often the sages of the transitional generation ruled in accordance with their own halakhic opinions, and not in accordance with any established norms of halakhic decision-making. The Mishna project associated with the patriarchal house (both Rashbag and then Rebbi) served as a resource to them, but it did not compel them to rule in a particular way. Some sages even attacked those who made halakhic rulings based on the Mishna:

> If one has studied Torah and Mishna but has not served Torah scholars, Rabbi Elazar says: He is a commoner. Rabbi Shmuel bar Naḥmani says: He is a boor. Rabbi Yannai says: He is a Cuthean. Rav Aḥa bar Yaakov says: He is a sorcerer. Rav Naḥman bar Yitzḥak said: It is reasonable to say that the truth is in accordance with Rav Aḥa bar Yaakov, for people commonly say, "As a sorcerer incants and does not know what he is saying." So too a reciter of Mishna recites and does not know what he is saying. (Sota 22a)

This source criticizes those sages who study Mishna without serving Torah scholars, who would teach them how to comprehend its logic.[13]

13. Rashi explains that someone who merely recites mishnayot "makes noise" as if he were a Talmud scholar, when he is in fact "naked."

But it also suggests that the Mishna is not the final arbiter in matters of halakha, a view that appears in the Jerusalem Talmud as well:

> Rabbi Zeira said in the name of Shmuel: We do not derive rulings for new cases from laws, legends, or additional laws, but only from the Talmud.... Rabbi Ḥanania said in the name of Shmuel: We do not derive rulings for new cases from special dispensations. And all agree that we not derive rulings from particular cases. (Y. Pe'ah 2:4 [17a])[14]

The Mishna is a collection of halakhic opinions, not a distillation of approved halakhic practices. Even when the Mishna lists majority and minority opinions, it did not obligate the sages of the transitional generation or those who immediately followed them to rule in accordance with the majority.[15] The principle that the halakha follows Hillel, too, did not obligate all the sages to rule accordingly, and as we have seen, there were certain sages who continued to hold like Shammai.[16]

**Rabbi Yoḥanan's Rules of Halakhic Decision-Making**

Rabbi Yoḥanan began to formulate the rules of halakhic decision-making. These rules may be divided into two groups: Rules related to individual sages, and methodological rules.

1. *Rules related to individual sages:* These rules establish an internal hierarchy among the sages. They primarily reference the sages of the Usha generation. Rabbi Yose is at the top of the hierarchy when it comes to the sages of his generation; the halakha is always decided in his favor because "he has his reasons with him." He is followed by Rabbi Yehuda bar Ilai, then Rabbi Meir, and then

14. Urbach, *The Law, Its Sources, and Its Development*, 91–92.
15. Brandes, "The Origins of the Laws of Halakhic Ruling," 175–188.
16. Most famously, Rabbi Tarfon endangered himself on at least two occasions so as to follow Beit Shammai's view. But Rabbi Tarfon belonged to a generation in which the principle that the halakha follows Hillel was just gaining force. There were later sages, too, who ruled like Beit Shammai. See ibid., 200–208.

Rabbi Shimon (as per Eiruvin 46b). It is clear that this is just the skeletal structure, with many other sages involved as well.

2. *Methodological rules:* The foundational methodological rule is that "the halakha follows the anonymous source in the Mishna." This rule reflects the attitude toward the Mishna in Rabbi Yoḥanan's generation. We have already seen that when Rabbi Yoḥanan's colleague Ilfa wished to demonstrate that he had not forgotten any Torah knowledge, he gave the Mishna primacy above all other collections of tannaitic statements, arguing that the Mishna contained them all. Likewise, when Rabbi Abahu was asked about the relationship between the Mishna and the *baraitot,* he responded: If Rebbi didn't teach it, how would Rabbi Ḥiya know it? (Yevamot 42b). It is this view that lent the Mishna its foundational role in halakhic decision-making.

After Rabbi Yoḥanan formulated his rules, they then had to be ratified by the *Amora'im,* the sages of the Talmud. These rules became so widely accepted that the entire Mishna was explained so as to accord with them. For instance, in the *sugya* in Tractate Shabbat that deals with carrying a lamp on Shabbat, we find the following statement:

> Rabbi Zeira said: Let the implication of our mishna be interpreted as dealing with a case where there was no money on it throughout twilight at the onset of the Sabbath, in order not to break the words of Rabbi Yoḥanan. (Shabbat 46a)[17]

The mishna under discussion was interpreted in a manner that would be consistent with Rabbi Yoḥanan's rules of halakhic decision-making. Rabbi Yoḥanan was thus a revolutionary figure who established the rules of how halakha is decided, safeguarding against a reality of "two Torahs."

17. This phrase, "in order not to break the words of Rabbi Yoḥanan," appears elsewhere in Shabbat 112b in the name of Rabbi Yitzḥak bar Yosef.

*Chapter Eighteen*

# Was the Mishna Written Down?

Now that we have considered how the Mishna gained widespread acceptance as a book, we can turn our attention to one of the most fascinating questions in the study of Talmud and in the history of Jewish learning, namely whether the Mishna was written down. The earliest sources dealing with this question appear in the two Talmuds, where the first generations of *Amora'im* assert that it is forbidden to convert the Oral Torah into written form:

> Rabbi Yehuda bar Naḥmani, the speaker for Rabbi Shimon ben Lakish, expounded: It is written, "Write for yourself these words" [Ex. 34:27], and it is written, "For on the basis of these words" [Ex. 34:27]. How is this? Teachings that were handed down to Moses in writing, you are not permitted to transmit orally. Teachings that were given to you orally, you are not permitted to transmit in writing. In the academy of Rabbi Yishmael, they taught the following *baraita*: "These" – these words you may

> write, but you may not write laws. Rabbi Yoḥanan said: The Holy One, Blessed Be He, established a covenant with Israel only on the basis of oral teachings. As the verse states, "For on the basis of these words, I have established a covenant with you and with Israel" [Ex. 34:27]. (Gittin 60b)

This source articulates three different views. Rabbi Shimon ben Lakish distinguishes between oral and written learning based on the verse, "For on the basis of these words." The phrase used in the Torah for "on the basis of," *al pi*, literally reads, "by the mouths of," which is understood as a reference to oral learning. Rabbi Yishmael derives the prohibition on writing down the Oral Torah from the Torah's specification that "these" words may be written down; he argues that "these" words refer to the Written Torah alone. Rabbi Yoḥanan, whose statement also appears in the Jerusalem Talmud (Y. Megilla 4:1 [17d]), does not refer at all to any difference between the Written Torah and the Oral Torah, but rather explains that the Torah that is studied by the sages, namely the Oral Torah, is the basis for the covenant between God and Israel, and this covenant was intended to remain oral. The reason for this strict prohibition on writing down the Oral Torah becomes clear when we consider several midrashic passages that allude to the polemic between Jews and other sects.

Midrash Tanḥuma states that "the Mishna is the mystery of the Holy One, Blessed Be He, and He does not transmit His mystery to anyone except the righteous, as it is written, 'God's secret is for His righteous ones (Ps. 145).'" This midrash and other related midrashim base the prohibition on writing the Oral Torah on the polemic between Jews and Christians. Elsewhere in Midrash Tanḥuma this is stated even more explicitly:

> Rabbi Yehuda bar Shalom said: When the Holy One, Blessed Be He, said to Moses: "Write for yourself" [Ex. 34:27], Moses wanted to write the Mishna as well. The Holy One, Blessed Be He, foresaw that the nations of the world would translate the Torah and read it in Greek, and would say: We are the Israelites. Until now the scales are balanced. The Holy One, Blessed Be He, can

> say to the nations of the world: You say that you are My children? I know that only those who know My secrets are My children. What are His secrets? The Mishna, which was given orally, and from which everything can be derived. (Tanḥuma, *Ki Tissa* 34)

This source gives voice to the polemic with the Christian church, which adopted the Written Torah and claimed that it was the true Israel. Rabbi Yehuda bar Shalom expresses the fear that Christians will adopt the Oral Torah as well. He therefore insists that this text must remain a "mystery" that reflects the intimate link between Israel and its God.[1]

In the following talmudic passage, the sages discuss the extent of the prohibition on writing down the Oral Torah:

> When Rav Dimi went up from Babylonia to the Land of Israel, he found Rav Yirmiya sitting and speaking in the name of Rabbi Yehoshua ben Levi: From where do we know that libations brought with an animal sacrifice are offered only by day? The Torah therefore states, "And for your libations and for your peace offerings" [Num. 29:39]. Just as the peace offerings are brought by day, so too the accompanying libations are brought by day. Rav Dimi said: If I would find people going to Babylonia, I would write a letter and send it to Rav Yosef. It would say that the words "libation offering" should not be erased from the *baraita*. (Temura 14a)

The Talmud then asks:

> But if Rav Dimi would have had the opportunity to send the letter, would it have been permitted for him to send it? For Rabbi Abba son of Rabbi Ḥiya bar Abba said in the name of Rabbi Yoḥanan: Those who write down the laws of the Oral Torah are like one who burns the Torah, and one who studies from these gains no reward. (Temura 14a)

1. M. Alon, *HaMishpat HaIvri*, 1, 200.

The Talmud responds:

> They said: Perhaps the law regarding a novel matter is different, for Rabbi Yoḥanan and Reish Lakish would study a book of *Aggada* on the Sabbath, and they expounded a verse to justify their actions: "When it is a time to act for God, nullify your Torah" [Ps. 119:126]. They said that it is preferable for one letter of the Torah to be uprooted so that the Torah itself should not be forgotten from Israel. (Temura 14b)

The Talmud's response suggests that new insights may be written down so that they will not be forgotten. But the Talmud also quotes Rabbi Yoḥanan's assertion that writing the Torah is tantamount to burning it, a view that appears in tannaitic sources as well:

> From here they said: Those who write down blessings are like those who burn the Torah. (Tosefta Shabbat 13d)

Rabbi Yoḥanan's exegesis compares writing down halakhot, the laws of the Oral Torah, to burning the Torah. The parallel source in the Tosefta suggests that perhaps he means to say that it is forbidden to write down holy words such as blessings. If so, then writing down the novel insights of the sages was not necessarily forbidden.

In another version of the source from Tractate Temura that appears in the *Shita Mekubetzet*, the Talmud's response continues as follows:

> They said: The rabbis depended upon their memorized texts. Since forgetfulness exists, they write down the texts they have learned and put them someplace.

Rashi understands the permission to write down new insights in a similar manner: "When they hear new insights that had not been taught in the beit midrash, they write them down so that they will not be forgotten" (Shabbat 6b).

It appears that it was common to record new insights in the letters that were sent back and forth between Babylonia and the Land of Israel.

Perhaps with time, as the literary output of the talmudic sages continued to grow, these letters became longer and more numerous and the prohibition on writing down the Torah lost its force.[2] But we have still not answered our question about whether the Mishna was written down.

The matter is first debated by the *Geonim* and then the *Rishonim*. Rav Sherira Gaon assumes in his famous epistle that Rebbi wrote down the Mishna.[3] But Rashi and the commentators in France and Germany assert that the Mishna was not recorded in its time, and only during the final generations of the amoraic period was permission granted to write it down lest it be forgotten.[4]

Amidst all this historical debate, there is one passage in the Jerusalem Talmud that was seized upon as proof that the Mishna was indeed written down in its time:

> A certain man brought a basket of leek heads to Rabbi Yitzḥak bar Tablai. Rabbi Yitzḥak asked Rabbi Yoḥanan about the status of the produce. He replied: Go ask Ḥanania ben Shmuel, whom I taught. He went and asked him. He replied: I have not seen a tannaitic tradition on this matter, but I have heard a later tradition. (Y. Demai 2:1 [22d])

Rabbi Yoḥanan's *Tanna* states that although he never saw this particular tannaitic tradition written down, he heard a later tradition from Rabbi Yoḥanan about the matter. Based on this source, some of the greatest talmudic scholars have argued that the Mishna was recorded in Rebbi's generation.[5] But just a few years ago, Yaakov Zussman reawakened this debate when he found a Geniza fragment of the Jerusalem Talmud for

2. C. Czernowitz, *The History of Halakha* 1 (New York: 5695), 9.
3. See *The Epistle of Rav Sherira Gaon*, French recension, 71.
4. It is important to note that no one would argue that all sources were oral during the mishnaic and talmudic periods. For instance, Megillat Taanit was a written book dating back to Temple times. Although it was not a book of law, it was without a doubt part of the Oral Torah. See V. Noam, *Megillat Taanit* [Hebrew] (Jerusalem: 5764), 19–21.
5. Epstein, *Text of the Mishna*, 701. Prior to Epstein, there was also Weiss' *Each Generation and Its Interpreters*, as Zussman notes in "The Oral Torah Interpreted: The Power of the Tip of the *Yud*" [Hebrew], *Talmudic Studies* 3 (Jerusalem: 5765).

Tractate Demai that contains a different version of this critical source. Instead of the words, "I have not seen," this fragment reads, "He did not tell me," which calls the proof text into question.[6]

Zussman's finding lent credence to those who argued that the Mishna was transmitted orally and was continuously edited and commented upon. According to this view, there were some individuals known as *Tanna'im* who knew parts of the Mishna by heart and would recite it on demand. These *Tanna'im*, whom Lieberman describes as "walking books,"[7] took pains to preserve the precise version of the Mishna, such that the *Tanna*'s memory had the same authority as a written text. The sages themselves did not remember everything they taught, but sometimes they would question or challenge the version of the Mishna they heard from a *Tanna*.

It is difficult to enter into this debate, which has preoccupied sages, commentators, and academic scholars for generations. Perhaps the most we can say with certainty is that the Mishna was accepted as a book, regardless of whether it was written down or inscribed in the hearts and minds of the sages.

6. Zussman, "The Oral Torah Interpreted: The Power of the Tip of the *Yud*."
7. Lieberman, "The Publication of the Mishna," 216–218, 223.

*Chapter Nineteen*

# Rabbi Shimon ben Lakish

## RABBI SHIMON BEN LAKISH IN SOURCES FROM THE LAND OF ISRAEL

When we study Rabbi Yoḥanan, we must also consider his close colleague and disciple, Rabbi Shimon ben Lakish. According to the aggadic tradition of the Babylonian Talmud, which influenced the way in which these individuals were depicted and understood by later generations, the lives of these two sages were inextricably bound up in one another, connected by strong bonds of friendship and study which were ultimately and tragically severed.[1]

When we try to sketch the figure of Rabbi Shimon ben Lakish (also known by the acronym Rashbal), it becomes clear that there is a

1. Any biographical study raises fundamental questions about the nature of the sources that shape our understanding of a particular rabbinic figure. When the gaps between various sources are not highlighted, the picture blurs into a single coherent figure. Once we are aware of these differences and inconsistencies, we can better understand the literary biases that shaped the way in which rabbinic biography is written. There have been several studies of the figure of Rabbi Shimon ben Lakish. See T. Ziv, "Rashbal: The Man and His Accomplishments" (PhD diss., Tel Aviv University, 5741); Y. Giat, "Reish Lakish: The Man and His Public Life" (M.A. thesis, Bar Ilan University, 5759); S. Tov, "Rabbi Shimon ben Lakish (Reish Lakish)" [Hebrew], *Mabua* 29: 53–91.

stark contrast between the sources from the Land of Israel and those from Babylonia. The Babylonian sources (in which he is known as Reish Lakish) paint a bold, vivid picture of a criminal who reformed his ways and ultimately died of a broken heart. The sources from the Land of Israel (in which he is always known as Rabbi Shimon ben Lakish), depict him in softer hues. These differences emerge strikingly from any comparative study of the two Talmuds.

According to the Jerusalem Talmud, Reish Lakish spent his entire life in the beit midrash, from his earliest days to his last.[2] He even exiled himself from home so as to live in a place of Torah. This detail is related as part of a story that describes his yearning to see a vision of Rabbi Ḥiya the Great:

> Rabbi Shimon ben Lakish fasted three hundred fasts in order to see Rabbi Ḥiya the Great, but he did not see him. Finally he grew so upset that he said: Did he labor in Torah more than I did? They said to him: He taught Torah in Israel more widely than you did. Moreover, he went into exile in order to do so. He said to them: But did I not also go into exile? They said to him: You went into exile to learn, but he went into exile to teach. (Y. Kilayim 9:3 [32b])

Rashbal traveled far from home to study Torah, as opposed to Rabbi Ḥiya, who traveled far from home in order to teach.[3] Only after he had considerable learning under his belt did he allow himself to stay put. This story does not specify where he spent his earliest years, but another source relates that he started out in Tiberias:

> Rabbi Shimon ben Lakish was studying Torah with all his might in a cave in Tiberias, and a gatekeeper used to prepare a drink

2. This section was heavily informed by B.Z. Bacher, *Legends of the Amora'im*, 1, 120–196.
3. Bava Metzia 85b includes a parallel to this story which is consistent with the Babylonian Talmud's image of Reish Lakish. According to this source, Rabbi Ḥiya taught Torah widely whereas Rabbi Shimon ben Lakish amassed much Torah but did not teach it like Rabbi Ḥiya.

> of water for him every day. He used to come in feeling very tired and drink it. On one occasion the gatekeeper entered, sat down by his side and engaged him in conversation. He said to him: Master, do you remember that you and I used to sit in the beit midrash together, but whereas you were worthy, I was not so worthy? Pray for me that my portion may be with you in the World to Come. He replied to him: What should I pray for you? That you should enter there with your fellow craftsmen? Because they do not allow a man to enter except with his fellow craftsmen. (Ecclesiastes Rabba 3:9)

This is not the place to discuss Rashbal's relationship with common people who did not make Torah study their primary occupation. Relevant for our purposes is that the story alludes to Rashbal's youth spent in the beit midrash. It seems that his first exile was to Bar Kappara's yeshiva in Lod. He went on to teach halakhot in the name of Bar Kappara, though it is unclear to what extent he interacted with Bar Kappara himself.[4] One of his teachers was undoubtedly Rabbi Abba Kohen Bardala.[5] He also knew Rabbi Oshaya Rabba, whom he referred to as "the father of the Mishna" and quoted frequently. Rabbi Oshaya, as we have seen, took over Rabbi Ḥiya the Great's yeshiva in Tiberias before moving to Caesarea. And so presumably Rashbal returned from his southern wanderings to the yeshiva in Tiberias. He then encountered Rabbi Ḥanina bar Ḥama and Rabbi Yannai, who were the elders of the generation.

As a student of Rabbi Oshaya, Rashbal studied the Mishna of Rabbi Yehuda HaNasi very closely. In addition to Rabbi Oshaya, his primary teachers were the members of the transitional generation. Only as an adult did he make his way to Rabbi Yoḥanan's yeshiva, at which point he and Rabbi Yoḥanan became inseparable.

4. Epstein writes that Reish Lakish first studied with Bar Kappara, but his only proof consists of the laws that he transmitted in this sage's name. See Epstein, *Text of the Mishna*, 285. Bacher writes that although the Talmud never explicitly states that Reish Lakish was a student of Bar Kappara, he quotes many sources in his name, so it is likely that he learned from him as well. See Bacher, *Legends of the Amora'im*, 1, 130.
5. Epstein, *Text of the Mishna*, 286.

## REISH LAKISH IN THE STORIES OF THE BABYLONIAN TALMUD

The Babylonian Talmud paints a very different picture of Rashbal, who is referred to instead as Reish Lakish. He is depicted as a figure of unique strengths and talents who grew up outside the world of Torah study but reformed his ways and found a home in Rabbi Yoḥanan's yeshiva. There he ultimately came to challenge and question his teacher, with fatal consequences.

The story of Reish Lakish's repentance and his return to the beit midrash appears only in the Babylonian literature, which has led academic scholars to question its historicity.[6] Unlike the sources from the Land of Israel, which portray him spending his entire life within the walls of the beit midrash, the Babylonian sources describe him as a mythical figure who underwent a significant conversion process and made the conscious choice to dedicate his life to Torah.

We will now consider three Babylonian stories that vividly depict this sage:

### Story 1: His Sale to the Gladiators

> Reish Lakish sold himself to the gladiators. He took with him a bag with a stone inside. He said: They have a tradition that on the last day [of their victims' lives], everything that I ask of them, they will grant, so that I will forgive them for shedding blood. On the last day of his life, they asked him: What is your request? He said: I wish to tie you up and set each of you down and strike each one of you a blow and a half with my bag. He tied them up and sat them down. When he struck each one, their souls departed, and

6. Z. Frankel notes that the Jerusalem Talmud makes no mention of the fact that Rabbi Shimon ben Lakish forsook a criminal past for the world of the beit midrash. See Z. Frankel, *Introduction to the Jerusalem Talmud,* 130. Y. Frankel similarly notes that the Babylonian story has no parallel in any sources from the Land of Israel. See Y. Frankel, *Issues in the Spiritual World of the Sages* [Hebrew] (Tel Aviv: 5741), 168. Most biographers of Rabbi Shimon ben Lakish combine the accounts that appear in the two sets of sources. See Margaliot, *Encyclopedia of the Sages,* 791–797. Also see Tov, "Rabbi Shimon ben Lakish," 53–90.

> as their souls departed they gnashed their teeth [and appeared as if smiling]. Reish Lakish said to them: Are you still laughing at me? I still owe you half a blow. He slew them all, left, and ate and drank freely. His daughter said to him: Do you not want something to sleep on? He said to her: My daughter, my stomach is my mattress. When Reish Lakish died, he left behind him only a measure of saffron for his heirs. He applied to himself the verse, "And they leave their possessions to others" [Ps. 49:11]. (Gittin 47a)

This mythic story, which has no parallel in any other sources, depicts Reish Lakish as a neighborhood thug who manages to outwit his captors. It is hard to imagine where this account originated, since the Jerusalem Talmud paints such a different picture. But the story was accepted as authentic and all the biographies of Reish Lakish begin with his gladiatorial past.

### Story 11: His Entry into the Beit Midrash

> One day Rabbi Yoḥanan was swimming in the Jordan. Reish Lakish saw him and jumped into the Jordan after him. He said to him: Your strength should be for Torah! Reish Lakish said to him: Your beauty should be for women! Rabbi Yoḥanan said to him: If you will repent, I will give you my sister, who is more beautiful than I. He accepted. Reish Lakish then went to retrieve his clothes but he was unable to return. Rabbi Yoḥanan taught him Torah and he taught him Mishna and he made him into a great man. (Bava Metzia 84a)

This story is among the most famous and most frequently studied aggadic tales, though it too has no parallel in other rabbinic sources.[7]

7. It would be impossible to list all the articles and studies that have been written about this story. As Admiel Kosman wrote, "The following talmudic story is one of the deepest and most fascinating stories in rabbinic literature. It seems that nearly everyone who studies it finds his own way of reading it, and the more this story is read and analyzed, the more new insights and understandings are gleaned." See *Men's Tractate,* 34. For a partial bibliography, see Ruth Calderon, *A Bride for One Night,* trans. Ilana Kurshan (JPS: 2013), 30.

As we shall see, this fateful encounter between two great men in the Jordan river becomes a model for all their future interactions. Rabbi Yoḥanan initiates the conversation when he says, "Your strength should be for Torah." Reish Lakish responds impudently, "Your beauty should be for women." But Rabbi Yoḥanan has the last word when he invites Reish Lakish to accept the yoke of Torah upon himself in exchange for Yoḥanan's beautiful sister.

Reish Lakish accepts Rabbi Yoḥanan's offer and immediately loses his strength. He cannot even retrieve his clothes from the river bank. Instead, he follows Rabbi Yoḥanan into the beit midrash and becomes his protégé. The Talmud summarizes Reish Lakish's long career in Rabbi Yoḥanan's beit midrash in a single sentence: "He taught him Torah and he taught him Mishna and he made him into a great man." As this line suggests, it is through the study of Torah that men achieve greatness. We will consider the rest of this story, which involves the collapse of the beit midrash in Tiberias, when we discuss the death of Rabbi Yoḥanan at the end of this section of this volume.

**Story III: Hanging Onto the Coattails of the Sages**

The third story, which has received less scholarly attention than the previous two, describes Reish Lakish pushing his way to join two sages who are traveling to intercalate the year in a place called Asia.[8]

> Rabbi Ḥiya bar Zarnokei and Rabbi Shimon ben Yehotzadak were traveling to Asia to intercalate the year. Reish Lakish met them and joined them, saying: I will go along and see how they perform the procedure of the intercalation. As they traveled, Reish Lakish saw a man plowing. He said to them: This man is a priest and yet he is plowing? They said to him: He might say: I am merely working as an employee on the field. Further on, he saw a man pruning

8. See my analysis of this story: "*Da Aka*: The Obligation to Protest, or the Right to Remain Silent," in *Between Authority and Autonomy*, ed. Z. Safrai and A. Sagi [Hebrew] (Tel Aviv: 1997), 464–481. I learned how to analyze stories such as this one from Professor Yonah Frankel, who taught that studying the form and structure of a talmudic story is the key to unlocking its content and message.

> in the vineyard. Reish Lakish said to him: This man is a priest, and yet he is pruning? They said to him: He might say: I am cutting vines because I need them to use as netting in an olive press. Reish Lakish said to them: The heart knows whether his intent is for netting or for nettlesome perversity.... They said: This fellow is argumentative. When they arrived there, they ascended to the upper floor and pulled the ladder out from under Reish Lakish [so he would not be able to climb up after them].
>
> Reish Lakish came before Rabbi Yoḥanan and said to him: Are people who are suspected of violating the laws of the sabbatical year qualified to intercalate the year? Then he said: It is not difficult for me to understand. For there is a precedent in which three cattle herders aided the rabbis in their intercalation. The rabbis, though, relied on their own calculations to intercalate. Then Reish Lakish reconsidered and said: No, this case is not similar. For there it was the sages who voted and intercalated the year. Here, it is a confederacy of wicked men, and a confederacy of wicked men cannot be counted as part of a quorum. Rabbi Yoḥanan said: This is distressful.
>
> When they came before Rabbi Yoḥanan they said to him: He called us cattle herders and yet the master did not respond at all? Rabbi Yoḥanan said to them: And if he would have called you sheep herders, what could I have said to him? (Sanhedrin 26a)

The tension in this story revolves around Rabbi Yoḥanan's response to Reish Lakish's insulting comments. The only words he speaks, "*da aka*," are translated above as "this is distressful," though the meaning of this phrase is ambiguous.[9] Was Rabbi Yoḥanan persuaded by Reish Lakish, or did he remain loyal to the messengers sent to intercalate the year? In any case, there is no uncertainty about Reish Lakish's feelings. He

9. Most commentators understood Rabbi Yoḥanan as agreeing with Reish Lakish that it is forbidden to allow sinners to continue in their sinful ways. Only a few commentators agreed with Rashi that Rabbi Yoḥanan's response is a criticism of Reish Lakish. See my article cited above.

reproaches the sages who avert their eyes from sinners, calling them a confederacy of wicked men.

Although there are many good reasons to question the historicity of this source,[10] it nonetheless serves to flesh out our image of Reish Lakish as one who abandons his sinful ways and expects others to conform to his new standard. Coming from another world, he seeks to learn how the sages intercalate the year. But he cannot bear to witness these sages focusing only on the task at hand and averting their eyes from the sinners they pass along the way. Reish Lakish wishes to see the whole world run in accordance with the divine will. He tries to walk beside the sages in paths of righteousness, but ultimately the ground falls out from beneath him.

### REISH LAKISH'S SUBSERVIENCE TO RABBI YOḤANAN

The following story, which both the Babylonian and Jerusalem Talmuds reference, describes the newly repentant Reish Lakish:

> Reish Lakish visited Batzra. There he saw that the Jews were eating fruit that was not tithed, and he forbade it to them. He saw public waters that idol worshippers bowed down to and Jews then drank, and he forbade it to them. He came before Rabbi Yoḥanan and related this to him. Rabbi Yoḥanan said to him: While your cloak is still on you, go back and retract both rulings. Betzer is not Batzra, and public waters do not become prohibited through idolatrous worship. (Avoda Zara 58b)

Here is the parallel that appears in the Jerusalem Talmud:

> Rabbi Shimon ben Lakish was in Batzra. He saw them [idol worshippers] pouring out libations in honor of Aphrodite. He said to them: Is it not forbidden? He came and asked Rabbi Yoḥanan. Rabbi Yoḥanan said in the name of Rabbi Shimon ben Yehotzadak: Nothing done by the public causes it to become forbidden for Jews. (Y. Shevi'it 8:11 [38b])

10. The Tosafot question how they could be intercalating the year during the sabbatical year as well as outside the borders of the Land of Israel.

This story seems more historically plausible, both because it has a parallel in the Jerusalem Talmud and because it does not contain the literary flourishes we encountered previously. The two Talmuds relate that Reish Lakish went to Batzra, a city in the northeastern part of the Land of Israel.[11] According to the Jerusalem Talmud's version, he saw the people of Batzra making libations at a public water fountain which featured a statue of Aphrodite. This seemed to him like a form of idolatry, so Reish Lakish forbade the Jews from using the fountain. When he returned, Rabbi Yoḥanan taught him that he had learned from his own teacher, Rabbi Shimon ben Yehotzadak, that anything that belongs to the public does not become forbidden to Jews. In other words, the law distinguishes between the private domain, in which it is forbidden to use and benefit from forbidden idolatrous objects, and the public domain, in which all is permitted so that people can go on with their lives. This is a reasonable halakhic norm that Jews can realistically be expected to follow, and it accords with a well-known story about Rabban Gamliel that appears in the Mishna:

> Proclus son of Philosophus asked Rabban Gamliel in Akko, while he was bathing in the bathhouse of Aphrodite. He said to him: In your Torah it is written, "And there shall cleave nothing of the devoted thing to your hand" [Deut. 13:18]. Why are you bathing in the bathhouse of Aphrodite? He said to him: One does not respond in the bathhouse. When he went out, he said to him: I did not come into her place; she came into my place. They do not say: Let us make a bathhouse as an adornment for Aphrodite. Rather they say: Let us make Aphrodite an adornment for the bathhouse. (Avoda Zara 3:4)

Aphrodite is the Greek goddess of love and beauty. As this story suggests, the Roman Empire renovated the public bathhouse in Rabban Gamliel's neighborhood in Akko and decorated the water fountain with

11. G.J. Blidstein, "Rabbi Yoḥanan: Idolatry and Public Privilege," *Journal for the Study of Judaism* v (1974): 157. According to Blidstein, Batzra is the largest Syrian city south of Damascus.

a statue of Aphrodite. A Roman named Proclus is surprised when Rabban Gamliel continues to frequent the bathhouse after the renovation, but Rabban Gamliel justifies his behavior by invoking the distinction between public and private spaces.[12] Reish Lakish, unfamiliar with this distinction, forbids the people of Batzra from using the bathhouse. But Rabbi Yoḥanan corrects him and teaches him the halakhic tradition.

In the Babylonian Talmud, too, Rabbi Yoḥanan rebukes Reish Lakish for his stringent ruling. Like a teacher correcting a student, he says that "Betzer is not Batzra, and public waters do not become prohibited through idolatrous worship." According to Rashi's explanation, Reish Lakish confused Batzra in the north with Betzer in the south. Betzer in the south is considered part of the Land of Israel, whereas Batzra in the north is decidedly outside its borders.

In this story we can sense the gulf between Rabbi Yoḥanan, the senior teacher, and Reish Lakish, his student in need of instruction.

### REISH LAKISH'S EQUALITY WITH RABBI YOḤANAN

In spite of the clear hierarchy we have seen between Rabbi Yoḥanan and Reish Lakish, there are other sources in the Babylonian Talmud that depict Rabbi Yoḥanan as subservient to his student.

The background to one of these passages is a talmudic discussion about a man who died and left behind a wife, children, and creditors. The Mishna (Ketubot 9:2) cites a dispute between Rabbi Tarfon and Rabbi Akiva about who takes priority when it comes to dividing up the property of the deceased. Rabbi Tarfon argues that the estate is given to the one who needs it most. But Rabbi Akiva contends that the law leaves no room for compassion, and the estate should be given to the orphans because they are the only ones who are not required to take an oath before collecting. The Talmud (Ketubot 84b) relates that Reish Lakish did not allow the judges in his area to act mercifully in accordance with

12. A. Friedheim, "The Tale of Rabban Gamliel in Aphrodite's Bathhouse in Akko: A Study of the Eretz-Israel Realia" [Hebrew], *Cathedra* 105 (5763): 7–32; A. Wasserstein, "Rabban Gamliel and Proclus" [Hebrew], *Zion* 45 (5740): 257–267; D. Zlotnick, "Proclus ben Philosophus," *A Book in Memory of Saul Lieberman*, ed. S.Y. Friedman (New York: 5753), 49–52. A. Yadin, "Rabban Gamliel, Aphrodite's Bath, and the Question of Pagan Monotheism," *JQR* 96 (2006): 149–179.

Rabbi Tarfon's view, but instead followed Rabbi Akiva's ruling. Rabbi Yoḥanan responded angrily, "You treated Rabbi Akiva's ruling like a biblical law!" After all, Rabbi Tarfon's opinion, too, was included in the Mishna. At this point the Talmud relates a story that took place in the local court of Rabbi Yoḥanan and Reish Lakish:

> Relatives of Rabbi Yoḥanan whose debtor had died seized a cow inherited by the debtor's orphans from a public alley. They came before Rabbi Yoḥanan. Rabbi Yoḥanan said to them: You seized it properly. Then they came before Rabbi Shimon ben Lakish. He said to them: Go return the cow. They again came before Rabbi Yoḥanan. He said to them: What shall I do? The one who is opposite me disputes me. (Ketubot 84b)

This passage discusses a case in which a debtor seizes a cow from the orphans who have inherited it. The seizure takes place in a quiet alley on the outskirts of the marketplace. Rabbi Yoḥanan congratulates his relative, the creditor of the deceased, for successfully seizing the cow. But Rabbi Shimon ben Lakish holds like Rabbi Akiva that the orphans take priority over the creditors, and thus a creditor may not seize the deceased's property. Rabbi Yoḥanan does not challenge Reish Lakish's ruling, which contradicts his own. Instead he responds with resignation: "What shall I do? The one who is opposite me disputes me."[13]

It seems that this source offers a more nuanced depiction of the relationship between these two giants in the world of Torah study. Rabbi Yoḥanan was older and more influential, but Rabbi Shimon ben Lakish was an independent thinker who did not hesitate to disagree with his teacher and rule as he saw fit.

13. Rabbi Y. Eidelberg of early seventeenth-century Poland and Italy cited this story as proof that a student is not always forbidden to disagree with his teacher's ruling. See *Sefer Be'er Sheva*, Sanhedrin 110a.

# *Chapter Twenty*

# Rabbi Yehuda Nesiya

### RABBI YEHUDA NESIYA: CHRONOLOGICAL PROBLEMS

At the end of Part One, we discussed the relationship of the sages of the transitional generation to the young patriarch, Rabbi Yehuda Nesiya, who was Rebbi's grandson. The peak of his career coincided with the middle of the third century, just after the death of Rabban Gamliel III. But it is difficult to date Rabbi Yehuda Nesiya's tenure because of various conflicting accounts. It seems that he grew up at the end of the 230s, during the final years of Rabbi Yannai's life. He remained active following Rabbi Yoḥanan's death and had a relationship with Rabbi Ami and Rabbi Asi, who lived at the end of the third and the beginning of the fourth centuries. The Talmud relates, for instance, that Rabbi Yehuda Nesiya told Rabbi Ami and Rabbi Asi that Rabbi Yoḥanan would teach them all the days of his life (Rosh HaShana 20a). The Tosafot insist that this cannot possibly be the same Rabbi Yehuda Nesiya who lived during Rav and Shmuel's time. But if the Talmud is indeed referring to the same Rabbi Yehuda Nesiya, then he enjoyed tremendous longevity and served as the leader of the Jewish people for three generations.

The author of *Sefer Yuḥasin* assumes such longevity in describing the genealogy of the patriarchs:

> [There was] Rebbi's son Rabban Gamliel and his grandson Rabbi Yehuda Nesiya, who lived during the time of Rabbi Ami and Rabbi Asi, and Rabbi Hillel HaNasi, who was the son of Rabbi Yehuda Nesiya, who established a fixed calendar for all of Israel before the authority to do so was lost until the coming of the Messiah. These are ten generations, beginning with Hillel and ending with Hillel. (*Sefer Yuḥasin*, article 2, 10)

On the other hand, academic scholars generally enumerate several patriarchs between Rabbi Yehuda Nesiya and Hillel: Rabban Gamliel the son of Rabbi Yehuda Nesiya, Rabbi Yehuda Nesiya II, another Rabban Gamliel, another Rabbi Yehuda Nesiya, and then Hillel II.[1] For our purposes we will accept the earlier account according to which only one patriarch, Rabbi Yehuda Nesiya, ruled for several generations. Based on this assumption, we will examine how he came to achieve such prominence among the Jewish people.

### FIRST STEPS: PERMITTING THE OIL OF NON-JEWS

We can date the start of Rabbi Yehuda Nesiya's tenure based on the names of the sages with whom he came into contact. He assumed the mantle of leadership following the death of his father, Rabban Gamliel III. We already encountered him as a young patriarch when we studied the figure of Rabbi Yannai, who felt the new patriarch's fancy cloak and mocked him for his finery (Bava Batra 111a). We also discussed his attempt to send Purim treats to Rabbi Oshaya, who responded harshly: "You have fulfilled through us the commandment to give gifts to the poor" (Megilla 7a). These two sages were contemporaries of Rabbi Yehuda HaNasi, but they enjoyed long lives, and so it is entirely plausible that the young patriarch, too, could have encountered them years after the death of his grandfather.

1. L.I. Levine dates these patriarchs as follows: Rabbi Yehuda HaNasi (175–225); Rabban Gamliel III, son of Rebbi (225–235); Rabbi Yehuda Nesiya, grandson of Rebbi (235–260); Rabban Gamliel IV, great-grandson of Rebbi (260–265); a period of collective leadership (265–275); Rabbi Yehuda Nesiya, great-great-grandson of Rebbi (275–305); Rabban Gamliel V (305–320). See L.I. Levine, "The Jewish Patriarch (Nasi) in Third-Century Palestine," *Aufstieg und Niedergang der mischen*, II, 19.2 ed. H. Temporini and W. Haase (Berlin and New York: de Gruter, 1979), 649–688.

One of Rabbi Yehuda Nesiya's first rulings was to permit the oil of non-Jews, which was forbidden in a Mishna in Tractate Avoda Zara that deals with economic distinctions between Jews and non-Jews.

> These things belonging to non-Jews are forbidden, but benefit from them is not prohibited: milk which was milked by a non-Jew without being seen by a Jew, and their bread and oil. (Mishna Avoda Zara 2:6)

As background to this story, we must understand that the residents of the south (Lod) were accustomed to receiving their oil from the hills of Jerusalem. Following the Bar Kokhba revolt this oil was difficult to obtain and it became a scarce commodity in the south. The Jerusalem Talmud speaks of how dangerous it was to venture to the Jerusalem hills in search of oil: "They would go to the king's hill and be killed there." And so the southerners, wishing to avoid the reliance on the oil of this region, sought to permit the oil of non-Jews. Rabbi Yehuda Nesiya agreed and ruled accordingly, continuing the patriarchal tradition of intervening in economic affairs. Rebbi's Mishna offers an account of the patriarch's decision: "Rebbi and his court permitted the oil."[2]

The early commentators pointed out that this line was an addition to Rebbi's Mishna and refers not to Rebbi but to his grandson Rabbi Yehuda Nesiya. We know this is so because both Talmuds attest that it was Rabbi Yehuda Nesiya who permitted the oil of non-Jews. The Babylonian version reads as follows:

> Rabbi Yehuda Nesiya was leaning on the shoulder of his attendant Rabbi Simlai while walking along the way. Rabbi Yehuda Nesiya said to him: Simlai, you were not in the beit midrash yesterday when we permitted the oil. Rabbi Simlai said to him: In our days, you should permit even the bread. (Avoda Zara 37a)[3]

2. This line does not appear in all versions of the Mishna. See Epstein, *Text of the Mishna*, 22 and note 6.
3. Rashi comments, "It was not he [Rebbi] who permitted the oil but rather Rabbi Yehuda Nesiya his grandson, that is, Rabbi Yehuda HaNasi the son of Rabban Gamliel

We have already encountered Rabbi Simlai as Rabbi Yannai's assistant. In this story, he assists the patriarch as well.[4] The patriarch tells Rabbi Simlai what he missed: "You were not in the beit midrash yesterday when we permitted the oil." His comment suggests that permitting the oil was an event of considerable significance. Rabbi Simlai's reaction sounds obsequious: "In our days, you should permit even the bread." The prohibition of eating non-Jewish bread, stipulated in Mishna Avoda Zara, was among those intended to keep Jews apart from non-Jews. This was a particularly difficult prohibition to observe, and so Rabbi Simlai expressed his hope that the new patriarch would go even further and permit non-Jewish bread as well.

As we will see, all of these events can be dated to the early years of the patriarch's tenure.

### Reactions of the Babylonian *Amora'im* to the Permitting of the Oil

At the beginning of the amoraic period, Rav and Shmuel disagreed about the original source of the law prohibiting the oil of non-Jews:

> "And their oil" – Rav says: Daniel decreed against it. Shmuel says: The emission of flavors from impure utensils renders the oils forbidden. (Avoda Zara 35b)

According to Rav, the prohibition dates back to the days of Daniel in the sixth century BCE, before the Second Temple period. According to Shmuel, this prohibition was instituted by the sages. In order to substantiate his claim, Shmuel tells Rav about a teaching he learned from Rabbi Simlai in Netzivin:

> [Shmuel said to Rav:] When Rav Yitzḥak bar Shmuel bar Marta came from the Land of Israel, he said: Rabbi Simlai announced at

son of Rebbi, who lived during the time of the *Amora'im*." The same claim is made by Rashbam, Rashi's grandson, cited in Tosafot on Avoda Zara 36a.

4. Rabbi Simlai belonged to a family that served as representatives of the patriarchal house. His father lived in Nehardea, where he was a contemporary of Shmuel and served as representative of the previous patriarch. See B.Z. Rosenfeld, "The Figure of Rabbi Simlai," *Zion* 48: 227–239.

a public lecture in Netzivin: Regarding oil, Rabbi Yehuda and his court voted on it and permitted it. This is understandable according to me, because we can say that Rabbi Yehuda Nesiya holds that where a forbidden substance imparts a flavor to the detriment of the mixture, it is permitted. But according to you, who say that Daniel decreed against it as a safeguard against intermarriage, is it possible that Daniel made a decree and Rabbi Yehuda came and nullified it? Why, we learned in a mishna: A later court cannot abolish the edicts of another, earlier court unless it is greater in wisdom and number. He said to Shmuel: Are you telling me the view of Simlai the Ludean? The Ludeans are different, for they treat rabbinic matters lightly. Shmuel said to Rav: Would you agree that I should send word to Rabbi Simlai and tell him what you said? Rav became embarrassed. (Avoda Zara 36a)

Shmuel explains how the court could have permitted the oil according to his stance by invoking the talmudic principle that in a case where a forbidden substance imparts a flavor to the detriment of the mixture, it is permitted. But if the prohibition dates back to biblical times, as Rav suggests, how could Rabbi Yehuda HaNasi have had the authority to lift it? Rav responds disparagingly, questioning whether the patriarchal court in fact authorized the oil of non-Jews as per Simlai the Ludean's report. He states that the Ludeans cannot be trusted because they treat rabbinic matters lightly.

Nonetheless the story about permitting the oil makes its way to Babylonia, where Rav and Shmuel debate the nature of the patriarch's authority. What are the consequences of transgressing a ruling of the patriarchal court?[5]

Yitzḥak bar Shmuel bar Marta went down to Netzivin. He found Simlai, the southerner, sitting and expounding: Rebbi and his court permitted the oil of non-Jews. Shmuel accepted the teaching

5. See D. Rosenthal, "Mishna Avoda Zara," 166–174. Rosenthal discusses the relationship between the Land of Israel and Babylonia as it pertains to the reception of Rabbi Yehuda Nesiya's ruling.

> and ate oil prepared by non-Jews. He did the same before Rav, who did not accept the ruling for himself and would not eat such oil. He said to him: Shmuel ate. If you do not do the same, I shall decree concerning you that you are a rebellious elder. Rav said to him: When I was still there, I learned that Simlai the southerner rejected this prohibition against oil, so I do not trust this report. Shmuel said to him: Did Simlai say this in his own name? Did he not say it in the name of Rebbi and his court? Shmuel nagged him about the matter until he too ate oil prepared by non-Jews. (Y. Shabbat 1:4 [3d])

According to this account, Rabbi Yehuda Nesiya's ruling reached Netzivin during the time of Rav and Shmuel. Rav died in 247, so we can date the patriarch's ruling to the period between his assumption of the patriarchal title in 235 and Rav's death. Since no patriarch would overturn such an established ruling at the very beginning of his tenure, we can probably date this story more precisely to the early 240s, a good five to seven years after Rabbi Yehuda Nesiya became patriarch.

Rabbi Yehuda's ruling made its mark on the next generation as well. The Talmud discusses the case of a man who gives his wife a divorce on the condition that he does not return within twelve months. What happens if he dies in the twelfth month? According to the tannaitic sources, such a woman is not regarded as divorced. But the Talmud quotes a *baraita* that states the opposite: "Our rabbis permitted her to remarry" (Gittin 76b). The Talmud asks about the identity of these rabbis who offered such a lenient ruling. And Shmuel responds, "The court that permitted the oil." This stinging response serves to undermine the ruling about divorce by equating it with the ruling about oil. Shmuel is implying that this ruling was issued by a court that derived its authority not from its greatness in Torah learning, but from the patriarch's domination.

The Jerusalem Talmud lists three laws issued by the patriarchal court of Rabbi Yehuda Nesiya:

> In three settings Rabbi Yehuda Nesiya is referred to as "our rabbi": in the context of rules covering writs of divorce, oil, and

> producing an abortion in the shape of a sandal. They referred to his court as "the court that permitted oil made by non-Jews." Any court that gives a lenient ruling in three matters is called a permissive court. (Y. Avoda Zara 2:8 [41d])

Rabbi Yehuda Nesiya's court earned a reputation for being permissive, and not all its rulings were held in the highest regard.

### THE PATRIARCH'S INVOLVEMENT IN RELIGIOUS LIFE: FASTS FOR RAIN

During the period we are studying there was a clear division of labor between the patriarch and the sages. The sages were responsible for teaching Torah and educating the next generation; the patriarch was responsible for societal affairs and for representing the nation's leadership to the Roman authorities. In times of drought, it was the patriarch who led people in fasts for rain, as the Talmud describes:

> Rabbi Yehuda Nesiya decreed a fast. He prayed for mercy but the rains did not come. He said: See how much of a difference there is between Shmuel the Ramati and Yehuda ben Gamliel. Woe to the generation that has been put in such a state. Woe to him in whose days such a thing has occurred. Rabbi Yehuda Nesiya became dejected, and the rains came. (Taanit 24a)

Rabbi Yehuda Nesiya, appointed leader of the people, is all too conscious of the gap between his own stature and that of his forebears. He feels unfit for the task even as he realizes that he has no choice but to stand at the helm during a time of crisis.

The Talmud describes a political struggle between the patriarchal house and the great sages of Tiberias, Reish Lakish and Rabbi Yoḥanan:

> The court of the patriarch decreed a fast but no one notified Rabbi Yoḥanan and Reish Lakish until the morning. Reish Lakish said to Rabbi Yoḥanan: But we did not accept this fast upon ourselves yesterday evening. He said to him: We are drawn after them. (Taanit 24a)

The conversation between Reish Lakish and Rabbi Yoḥanan gives voice to the tension regarding patriarchal authority. Reish Lakish seeks to challenge the patriarch's decree on the basis of a technicality: They were not informed about the fast in time. Rabbi Yoḥanan, who is more mature and more active politically, tempers his student's outrage and insists that they must obey the patriarch. As we have seen, Rabbi Yoḥanan occupies the more senior position in the beit midrash. No one can tell him what to do; he is the king within its walls. But he recognizes his subservience to the patriarchal court. He understands that in order to raise a generation of Torah scholars who can immerse themselves in learning, it is crucial to remain on good terms with the authorities. As he tells Reish Lakish, the sages do not have a secure enough footing that they can afford to jeopardize their relationship with the patriarch. In contrast, Reish Lakish is depicted as a stubborn idealist. By harping on a technicality, he is essentially declaring that he regards himself as subject to the authority of Torah alone.[6]

### MONEY AND POWER: THE STRUGGLE OVER CLOSENESS TO THE PATRIARCH

While the sages were debating the patriarch's decrees and his leadership style, others vying for political and economic power sought to become members of the patriarch's circle. The Jerusalem Talmud documents this phenomenon:

> There were two families in Tzippori, Bulvati and Pagani. They would go up and greet the patriarch every day. And the Bulvati family would go in first and come out first.[7] The Pagani family went and acquired merit in learning. Then they came and sought the right to go in first. So they appeared before Rabbi Shimon ben Lakish.

6. R. Kimelman, "The Disagreement Between Rabbi Yoḥanan and Reish Lakish about the Patriarch's Seniority," *Proceedings of the World Congress of Jewish Studies*, Studies in Talmud, Halakha, and Midrash (5741), 1–20.
7. Other manuscripts read, "And the Bulvati family would go in first and sit before them." Lieberman demonstrates that "and come out first" is the authentic version based on a comparison with a passage in Tractate Taanit, and so this is the version I used. See *Yerushalmi Kifshuto*, 175.

> Rabbi Shimon ben Lakish asked Rabbi Yoḥanan. Rabbi Yoḥanan went and expounded in the beit midrash of Rabbi Benaya: Even a bastard who is a disciple of the sage takes precedence over a high priest who is an ignoramus. They thought that this teaching applied just to redeeming captives or to providing charity or clothing, but not to the order in which one approached the patriarch. Said Rabbi Abun: It does apply also to the patriarchal court. What is the basis for this opinion? "Happy is the man who finds wisdom, and the man who acquires understanding, for the gain from it is better than the gain from silver, and its profit better than gold. It is more precious than pearls" [Prov. 3:13–15]. And wisdom is more precious even than the entrance to the Holy of Holies. (Y. Shabbat 12:3 [13a])

In the Roman Empire, the ritual of entering the court of an important patron was known by the Latin term "*salutatio*." Whoever came first would win public office.[8] The entrance before the patriarch was no different.[9] And so the competition between the Bulvati and Pagani families was essentially a power struggle.

The Bulvati family was part of the city council, which existed in every city throughout the empire.[10] The members of the Pagani family were residents of the city who did not belong to the council but nonetheless sought positions of money and influence.[11] It seems obvious that the members of the city council should take priority over ordinary residents of the city. And so the Bulvati family passed on their roles from father to son for generations, and the Pagani family stood no chance.

8. Lieberman demonstrates that the order in which the families entered before the patriarch was not simply a matter of honor, but was related to the system of political appointments.
9. L. Friedlander, *Roman Life and Manners* (London: 1908), 207–208. Also see Herman, "The Exilarchs in Babylonia During the Sasanian Period" [Hebrew] (PhD diss., Hebrew University of Jerusalem, 5765), 155 (bibliographic notes).
10. G. Alon, *Studies in Jewish History* 1, 50–51.
11. R. Kimelman disputes the view that the members of the Pagani family were simple peasants, as several commentators suggest. Rather, he argues that they were a powerful group with no official public role. See Kimelman, "The Priestly Oligarchy and the Sages During the Talmudic Period" [Hebrew], *Zion* 48 (5743): 137.

At some point the Pagani family seeks to gain recognition by virtue of Torah study. They turn to Rabbi Shimon ben Lakish and ask him to change the order of entry before the patriarch so that they would precede the members of the city council. Rabbi Shimon ben Lakish is not sure how to respond, so he inquires of Rabbi Yoḥanan, who invokes a mishna from Tractate Horayot: "Even a bastard who is a disciple of the sage takes precedence over a high priest who is an ignoramus." By comparing the Pagani family to bastards, he implies that they were on the margins of society without connections to the centers of power. But in his eyes, they take priority. The Talmud seeks to mitigate the force of Rabbi Yoḥanan's statement, questioning whether the preference for the learned bastard applies only when it comes to redeeming captives and offering charity. But Rabbi Abun responds decisively that Torah learning is more valuable than pearls, *peninim*. He offers a play on words with the Talmud's term for the Holy of Holies, *lifnai velifnim*, to teach that Torah study is regarded as more precious than even the high priest's entry into the Holy of Holies.

This source gives voice to the sages' attempt to achieve recognition for their Torah learning even when they lacked political connections. Rabbi Yoḥanan campaigned aggressively to raise the status of the sages who were busy "building the world" (Shabbat 114a). At the same time, he realized that in order to be appointed as a judge or city councilman, one needs the patriarch's approval. Here and elsewhere, Rabbi Yoḥanan was responsible for the revolutionary understanding that the sages are a powerful group deserving of patriarchal and public recognition.

## APPOINTED BY MONEY: ACQUIRING AUTHORITY IN RABBI YEHUDA NESIYA'S COURT

> The patriarchal court once appointed a judge who was not learned. The patriarch said to Yehuda bar Naḥmani, the spokesman of Reish Lakish: Stand as a spokesman for him. Yehuda bar Naḥmani stood and bent over the judge, but the judge did not say anything to him at all. Yehuda bar Naḥmani began by teaching: "Woe to him that says to wood, 'awaken'; to dumb stone, 'arise.' Can it teach? Behold it is overlaid with gold and silver and there

> is no breath in it at all" [Hab. 2:19]. And the Holy One, Blessed Be He, will eventually take retribution from those that appoint unqualified judges, as it is stated in the next verse: "But God is in His holy Temple, O entire earth be silent before Him" [Hab. 2:20]. Reish Lakish said: If anyone appoints an unqualified judge over the community, it is as if he planted an Ashera tree in Israel, as it is stated, "Judges and officers you shall appoint for yourself" [Deut. 16:18], and near that verse it is written, "You shall not plant for yourself an Ashera of any tree" [Deut. 16:21]. (Sanhedrin 7b)

In this parodic account, the patriarchal administration appoints an unlearned judge. Yehuda bar Naḥmani, who is used to working hard as the spokesman of Reish Lakish, finds himself out of a job because the new appointee has nothing to say. He quotes a verse that suggests that the new judge is no better than a piece of wood or stone. He then adds his own exegesis which links two adjacent verses from Deuteronomy, one about appointing judges and one about planting a tree for idol worship. "If anyone appoints an unqualified judge over the community, it is as if he planted an Ashera tree in Israel," he states, leveling harsh criticism at the patriarchal administration for choosing such a judge.

We do not know how the patriarch himself felt about the appointment of the unlearned judge. As Gedalia Alon has noted, all the rabbinic sources at our disposal reflect the perspective of the sages, who were opposed to the protocol at the patriarchal court. It seems that there was a civil judicial system throughout the empire that included the most powerful local leaders, including the city council members who took responsibility for the economic welfare of the city and administered public works. As a result of this system, certain families had more power and authority than the rest of the population. Judges were accorded tremendous respect and honor, and judicial positions were often bought. But the sages often had little use for such an arrangement. They wanted judges who would act as representatives of God on earth, and they sought to accord respect to the rule of law rather than to the presiding judge, in keeping with the psalm, "God takes His place in the divine council" (Ps. 82:1).[12]

12. G. Alon, "Those Appointed by Money," *Studies in Jewish History* 2, 15–55.

### ECONOMIC REFORM: TAX COLLECTION

The Talmud relates that in order to raise money to strengthen the walls of Tiberias, Rabbi Yehuda Nesiya collected taxes from all the residents of the city, including the sages. In so doing, he broke with the practice of his grandfather, Rabbi Yehuda HaNasi, who had exempted the sages from taxation. Confronted by an unstable political situation and a deep economic crisis, Rabbi Yehuda Nesiya felt compelled to include the sages in the tax burden. Needless to say, the sages were not pleased with this new reality, as the Babylonian Talmud relates:

> Rabbi Yehuda Nesiya placed the burden of paying for a protective wall upon the rabbis. Reish Lakish said: The rabbis do not require our protection, for it is written, "Were I to count them, they would outnumber the grains of sand" [Ps. 139:18]. Count whom? It is written, "I shall greatly increase your offspring... like the grains of sand on the seashore" [Gen. 22:17], referring to all of Israel. Can the righteous alone outnumber the grains of sand? Rather, this is what it means to say: Were I to count the deeds of the righteous, they would outnumber the grains of sand. And we can reason that if the grains of sand, which are fewer than the deeds of the righteous, protect the shore from the sea, then the good deeds of the righteous, which are numerous, certainly protect them from harm! When he came before Rabbi Yoḥanan he said to him: Why did you not tell him that we derive it from this verse: "I am a wall and my breasts are like towers" [Song. 8:10]? "I am a wall" – this is a reference to the Torah, which protects those who study it as a wall protects the residents of a city. "And my breasts are like towers" – this is a reference to Torah scholars. Reish Lakish held like Rava, who expounded: "I am a wall" – this is the assembly of Israel. "And my breasts are like towers" – these are synagogues and study houses. (Bava Batra 7b)

Rabbi Yoḥanan and Reish Lakish are united in their opposition to the patriarch's decision to impose taxes on the sages as well. But they understand the situation differently. Reish Lakish believes that the righteous are protected by their righteous deeds, just as grains of sand protect the shore from the sea. These righteous deeds may be performed not just by scholars of Torah, but by any Jews who spend time in synagogues and study houses. But Rabbi Yoḥanan is more exclusive. As he sees it, it is the sages and their Torah study that protect the city from harm.

Both Rabbi Yoḥanan and Reish Lakish object to the way in which the sages were gradually stripped of their rights and privileges. We do not know if their protest was effective, but it is echoed in other sources as well. For instance, the story of Rabbi Yose of Maon demonstrates just how vociferously the sages objected to the tax burden:

> Yose of Maon expounded in the synagogue of Maon: "Hear this, O priests, and attend, O house of Israel, and give heed, O house of the king, for unto you pertains the judgment" [Hos. 5:1]. He said: In the future, the Holy One, Blessed Be He, will make the priests stand in judgment, saying to them: Why did you not toil in Torah? Did you not enjoy the twenty-four priestly gifts? They will say: They gave us nothing. "Attend, O house of Israel" – why did you not give the priests twenty-four priestly gifts, as I wrote in My Torah? They will say to Him: Because the members of the patriarchal house took it all. "Give heed, O house of the king, for unto you pertains the judgment" – therefore judgment will be turned against you. (Genesis Rabba 80:1)

Rabbi Yose's sermon follows all the rules of dramatic oratory.[13] Standing in the synagogue in Maon, he begins with a verse from the Book of Hosea. This is a form of exegesis known as the *petiḥta,* which involves starting with a far-flung verse from the book of prophets and closing with the opening verse of the Torah reading for that day. The *petiḥta* was a means of capturing the attention of the audience, keeping them awake until the end, and piquing their interest in the Torah reading.[14]

13. M.D. Herr, "From Synagogues to Theaters and Circuses" [Hebrew], *Knesset Ezra: Literature and Life in the Synagogue – A Collection of Articles Presented to Ezra Fleisher,* eds. S. Elizur et al. (Jerusalem: 5758), 105–120. On the relationship between this story and the version in the Jerusalem Talmud see Y.L. Levine, *The Status of the Sages,* 5.
14. Y. Heinneman, *Public Sermons in the Talmudic Period* [Hebrew] (Jerusalem: 5731), 12–14.

The *petiḥta* offered the audience a wealth of material which they could study all Shabbat long. This is true of Rabbi Yose's sermon as well. He describes a dramatic courtroom scene in which the judge tries to identify who is at fault. First the priests are blamed for failing to teach the people Torah, as they are charged in the Bible in Moses' blessing to Levi: "They shall teach Your laws to Jacob and Your instructions to Israel" (Deut. 33:10). But Hosea's attack on the priests is dismissed because the priests offer a legitimate defense. They contend that since they did not receive the twenty-four priestly gifts promised to them, they had no choice but to work for a living, which left them with no time to teach Torah to Israel. Then Israel is blamed for failing to give the priests their priestly gifts. The people argue that their economic situation did not allow them to fulfill their obligations. The tax burden imposed by the patriarchal house was so enormous that they had to reduce their contributions. Finally, the members of the patriarchal house are summoned to the witness stand: "Give heed, O house of the king, for unto you pertains judgment." The judge turns the engine of justice against them, and they are left with no recourse.

This exegesis compares the sages to the priests, as would have been obvious to Rabbi Yose's audience. In biblical times, the priests received support from the people in exchange for teaching them Torah. So too, in Rabbi Yose's time, the sages responsible for teaching Torah were supposed to receive twenty-four priestly gifts. But the people were negligent about supporting the sages, who then had no choice but to leave their *batei midrash* to make a living.[15] When called to task, the people point fingers at the patriarchal house. They do not care about the wars of the empire, the collapse of Rome, or the larger political situation. They only know that the patriarch is responsible for their welfare, and they blame him for their economic woes. And so Rabbi Yose of Maon succeeds in rousing the masses with his rhetoric, winning their sympathy and turning them against the patriarch.

This is the conclusion of the sermon, but the story does not end here. As the Talmud goes on to relate, Rabbi Yehuda Nesiya hears

15. On the sages' reliance on public donations, see M. Beer, "Yissaḥar and Zevulun: The Economic Support of the *Amora'im* in the Land of Israel" [Hebrew], *The Sages of the Mishna and the Talmud* (Ramat Gan: 5771), 422–435.

about Rabbi Yose of Maon's exegesis, which is essentially an attack on his leadership:

> When Rebbi heard about this, he became enraged. Toward evening Reish Lakish went up to pay his respects to him and to pacify him. He said: Rebbi, we ought to be grateful to the other nations of the world who bring clowns into their theaters and circuses and amuse themselves with them, so that they should not quarrel with each other. Yet Yose of Maon spoke words of Torah and you became angry with him? The patriarch asked: And does he know anything about Torah? He said to him: Yes. He said to him: And is he prepared to learn? He said to him: Yes. He said: And if I ask him a question will he answer? He said to him: Yes. If so, let him come here. He came before Rebbi. (Genesis Rabba 80:1)

Reish Lakish's reasoning is strikingly simple. Everyone has their form of entertainment. The purpose of the public sermon, like the purpose of theater, is to bring people together so that their hands will not be idle and they will not turn against one another. Reish Lakish asks the patriarch not to take Rabbi Yose's theatrical performance so seriously. As he points out, Yose's satirical public sermon offers a controlled outlet for the people's criticism without letting the masses erupt in unrestrained protest against their leadership. The alternative would be far worse. Moreover, the satire found in synagogues is far tamer than the licentious performances in the Roman theaters.[16] The patriarch, relieved by Reish Lakish's words, verifies that Rabbi Yose is not just an actor but also a Torah scholar, and then invites him to speak with him:

> Rebbi said to him: What is meant by the verse, "Behold, everyone that uses proverbs shall use this proverb against you, saying: As the mother, so the daughter" [Ezek. 16:44]? Yose said to him: Like the daughter, so is the mother. Like the generation, so is its patriarch. Like the altar, so are its priests. As people say:

16. M.D. Herr, "From Synagogues to Theaters and Circuses," 111–112.

> The garden goes according to its gardener.[17] Reish Lakish said: You have not completely appeased him for the first offense, and you are already bringing him another? (Genesis Rabba 80:1)

The sage from Maon proves quite relentless. He speaks even more irreverently in the patriarchal house than in the synagogue. Standing face to face with the patriarch, he tells him that all is lost. The daughter resembles the mother, the house resembles the nation (that is, just as the Temple has been destroyed, so too has the nation),[18] and the generation resembles its patriarch. In this exegesis, Rabbi Yose uses a popular folk proverb to convey to the patriarch what everyone is saying behind his back. Society is collapsing. The economic crisis is not just about the Roman Empire, but about the patriarchy as well. And so the sage from Maon manages to incite the patriarch's wrath once again. Not surprisingly, Reish Lakish fumes at Rabbi Yose, who has undermined all his efforts at appeasement by adding insult to injury.

### RABBI YOḤANAN AND REISH LAKISH STRIKE, THE PATRIARCH BUILDS AN EDUCATION SYSTEM

When Rabbi Yehuda Nesiya became angry at Rabbi Yose of Maon, Rabbi Shimon ben Lakish went to appease him. But it was not long before Reish Lakish himself provoked the patriarch. The background to this story is the sages' discussion of the case of an elder who is found to have done something wrong. Is such an elder removed from his public role? When the question is posed in the beit midrash, Rabbi Yoḥanan states that any patriarch who is found to have a blemished record is removed from office. Rabbi Shimon ben Lakish says that such a patriarch is even lashed. Somehow, the patriarch learns of this discussion, which no longer seems to be merely theoretical:

17. This is the version that appears in the printed edition of Genesis Rabba. The most accurate manuscript version, Vatican 30 (Jerusalem: 5731), reads: "Like the house, so is the nation. Like the generation, so is the patriarch. Like the altar, so are its priests."
18. A similar exegesis appears in a liturgical poem by Yannai. See Epstein, *Text of the Mishna*, 141.

> Rabbi Yehuda Nesiya heard this ruling and was outraged. He sent soldiers to arrest Rabbi Shimon ben Lakish. Rabbi Shimon ben Lakish fled to a tower, and some say it was to Kfar Ḥittim. The next day Rabbi Yoḥanan went to the meetinghouse, and Rabbi Yehuda Nesiya went up to the meetinghouse as well. The patriarch said to him: Why do you not teach Torah? Rabbi Yoḥanan showed him how he clapped with one hand and it made no sound. The patriarch said to him: Do people clap with only one hand? He said to him: No, nor is Ben Lakish here [and just as one cannot clap with one hand, so I cannot learn without Ben Lakish]. The patriarch said to him: Where is he hidden? He said to him: In a certain tower. He said to him: You and I shall go out to greet him tomorrow. Rabbi Yoḥanan sent word to Rabbi Shimon ben Lakish: Prepare a teaching of Torah, because the patriarch is coming to see you. Shimon ben Lakish came forth to receive them and said: You set an example comparable to the paradigm of your Creator. For when the Merciful One came forth to redeem Israel from Egypt, He did not send a messenger or an angel, but the Holy One, Blessed Be He, Himself came forth, as it is said, "For I will pass through the Land of Egypt that night" [Ex. 12:12]. And not only so, but He and His entire retinue. The patriarch said to him: Why did you say what you said [i.e., that a ruler who sinned is subject to lashes]? He said to him: Do you really think that because I was afraid of you, I would hold back the Merciful One's teaching from Israel? (Y. Sanhedrin 2:1 [19d])

The patriarch arrests Reish Lakish, and Rabbi Yoḥanan reacts by going on strike. As we learn from a parallel source that appears in *Midrash Shmuel* 7, Rabbi Yoḥanan refused to teach Torah after Reish Lakish's arrest. When the patriarch asked him why he would not unlock the doors of the beit midrash, he demonstrated that he could not teach without Reish Lakish.

As this story suggests, Reish Lakish and Rabbi Yoḥanan were the keys to the entire educational system in Tiberias. If they were not teaching, then no one would bother to unlock the doors of the schools. The patriarch is aware of this situation. He is angered by these sages' harsh criticism of his policies, but he maintains a cordial and open relationship with them. We learn about the patriarch's concern for the educational system from Reish Lakish himself:

> Reish Lakish said in the name of Rabbi Yehuda Nesiya: The world continues to exist only by the merit of the breath that comes from the mouths of the schoolchildren of Beit Rabban.... Reish Lakish said in the name of Rabbi Yehuda Nesiya: We do not distract schoolchildren from their study even for the sake of building the Temple. And Reish Lakish said to Rabbi Yehuda Nesiya: I have received the following teaching from my fathers, and some say Reish Lakish said [it was] from your fathers: Any town in which there are no schoolchildren studying Torah is eventually destroyed. (Shabbat 119b)

Rabbi Yehuda Nesiya knew that the strength of the nation was dependent on the quality of its education, and he practiced what he preached. A midrash relates that he sent students of Rabbi Yoḥanan and Reish Lakish to establish a school system throughout the entire Land of Israel – not just in the major cities.

> Rabbi Yehuda Nesiya sent Rabbi Ḥiya, Rabbi Yose, and Rabbi Ami to travel to the cities of the Land of Israel and appoint scribes and teachers. They went to one place but did not find a single scribe or teacher. They said to them: Bring us the town watchmen. They brought the town ministers. They said to them: These are the town watchmen? These are the men who destroy the city! They asked them: And who are the town watchmen? They said: Scribes and teachers, as it is written: "Unless the Lord watches over the city, the watchmen stand guard in vain" [Ps. 127:1]. (Psalms Rabba 127)

Many authors of historical chronologies of the sages identify the patriarch who figures in this source as the grandson of Rabbi Yehuda Nesiya, based on the fact that the three sages he appoints are students of Rabbi Yoḥanan and Reish Lakish. And indeed this identification has become widely accepted.[19] But I prefer to identify this patriarch as the same Rabbi Yehuda Nesiya who struggled with the sages throughout the entire anarchic period and ultimately came around.

As we have seen, the sages began clashing with the patriarch when he obligated them to bear the tax burden to fund the building of a protective wall around Tiberias. Rabbi Yoḥanan responded by interpreting the verse "I am a wall and my breasts are like towers" as referring to the Torah and sages, respectively. By the end of the patriarch's life, however, he was sending Rabbi Yoḥanan's disciples to teach Torah throughout Israel. This was the victory of Rabbi Yoḥanan, who spent his life working to instill the centrality of Torah in the public and political consciousness.

19. Levine argues that this is a later Rabbi Yehuda Nesiya. But as I stated earlier, I prefer to extend the lifespan of Rabbi Yehuda Nesiya and not divide him into separate figures.

*Chapter Twenty-One*

# The Destruction of Nehardea and Babylonian Migration to Tiberias

## HISTORICAL BACKGROUND: THE RISE OF THE KINGDOM OF PALMYRA

Palmyra, known in the Talmud as Tadmor, was an Arab city in the Syrian Desert, considered part of the Roman province of Syria. It was one of several areas attacked by the Persian King Shapur during the nadir of the Roman Empire. Odaenathus, the leader of Palmyra, who is known in rabbinic sources as Papa ben Netzer, led the city in battle, defeating the Persians in northern Syria and Mesopotamia.[1]

The start of Odaenathus' military campaign against the Persians seems to be directly related to the fall of the Roman emperor Valerian into Persian captivity in 259 CE. Several sources describe Odaenathus' campaign against the army of Shapur, who was drunk with his

1. For the identification of Papa ben Netzer as Odaenathus, see Gafni, *The Jews of Babylonia*, 263, note 104.

victory over Rome. The Persians suffered terrible losses, and among the fallen were Jews from Nehardea who had identified with the local leadership.

In the epistle of Rav Sherira Gaon, Papa ben Netzer is identified as having destroyed Nehardea in the year 570, which corresponds to the year 258–259 of the common era. This source suggests that Odaenathus set forth from his hometown in the Syrian Desert, crossed the Euphrates, and conquered northern Babylonia. Along the way he destroyed Nehardea, a major center of Jewish life from the time of the exile in the days of Jehoiakim.[2] The Babylonian Talmud identifies him as "Ben Netzer: there they called him king, and here they call him a robber" (Ketubot 51b). Rashi explains, "He was a robber who conquered many cities and ruled over them, and became the head of the robbers."

And so Odaenathus went from being the head of a city to being the leader of a vast land. Nearly overnight, Palmyra became the dominant power in the east. In 267 Odaenathus was killed in an imperial struggle. He was succeeded by his widow Zenobia, an enlightened, assertive, and charismatic woman, in what became the golden age of Palmyra's history. Zenobia took over Asia and Egypt, establishing the short-lived Palmyrene empire.

Throughout the 260s, Palmyra dominated the east, instilling fear in the inhabitants of the Land of Israel and Babylonia. Finally, in 272, the Roman emperor Aurelian, who had succeeded in stabilizing the central imperial leadership in Rome, turned his attention to eradicating the eastern threat. After several military victories he conquered the city of Palmyra and captured Zenobia. Aurelian headed back to Rome victorious, leaving behind a garrison in Palmyra. But on his way to Rome, he learned that the people of Palmyra had revolted against and defeated the garrison. Aurelian turned back, conquered the city again, and instructed his soldiers to wipe it out completely. And so just twelve years after it was founded, the Palmyrene empire collapsed.

2. M.D. Yudilovitz, *The Lives of the Jews During Talmudic Times* [Hebrew] (Jerusalem: 5731), 67. For a challenge to this account, see Y. Sorek, "Who Destroyed Nehardea?" [Hebrew], *Zion* 37 (5732): 117–119.

### THE RELATIONSHIP OF THE SAGES OF THE LAND OF ISRAEL TO THE KINGDOM OF PALMYRA

Rabbinic sources preserve several accounts of the sages' encounters with Zenobia. The Jerusalem Talmud cites two stories about Jews who were taken captive and then redeemed by the sages:

> Rabbi Issi was caught in a conspiracy. Rabbi Yonatan said: [There is nothing to be done but to] wrap up the dead in his shroud. Rabbi Shimon ben Lakish said: Until I am killed, I myself can kill. I will go with forces and deliver him to safety. Shimon ben Lakish went and calmed down the men who were threatening Issi, and they turned Issi over to him. He said to them: Come to our elder and he will pray for you. They came before Rabbi Yoḥanan and he said to them: That which you wished to do to him will be done to you. That group of people left his presence, but they had not even arrived in Apipsiros before all of them were gone.
>
> Zeir bar Ḥanina was caught in a conspiracy. Rabbi Imi and Rabbi Shmuel went to calm down the people for his sake. Zenobia the queen said to them: Why have you come to save him? Your Creator performs miracles for you. While they were still speaking, a certain Arab entered carrying a sword. He said: With this sword, Ben Netzer killed his brother and saved Zeir bar Ḥanina. (Y. Terumot 8:4 [46b])

This source has its origins in real historical events. Two sages were caught in what the Talmud calls a "*safsufa*." This term is a variant on the Greek word for "conspiracy," suggesting that they were involved in secret machinations.[3] One of the two sages, Rabbi Issi (known as Rabbi Asi in the Babylonian Talmud), was a close associate of Rabbi Yoḥanan.

3. Lieberman explains that they were involved in a political conspiracy against the government. See Lieberman, "Six Words from Ecclesiastes Rabba" [Hebrew], *Studies in the Torah of the Land of Israel* (Jerusalem: 5751), 500.

The other, Zeir bar Ḥanina (known as Zeira bar Ḥanina in the Babylonian Talmud) was a student of Rabbi Ḥanina bar Ḥama.[4]

In the first story, Rabbi Shimon ben Lakish wishes to liberate his friend Rabbi Issi. At first he thinks to act with force, but then he sobers and realizes that he is better off negotiating with the captors. He persuades them to receive a "blessing" from Rabbi Yoḥanan, who wishes them the same fate that they sought to inflict on their captives.

The second story features Rabbi Ami and Rabbi Shmuel, both students of Rabbi Yoḥanan, who set off to negotiate with Queen Zenobia (or perhaps her representatives) in an effort to release another captive. The story relates that the queen engages the sages in a philosophical discussion about the nature of the Jewish God. While they are speaking, a Palmyran soldier comes on the scene and proudly demonstrates how Ben Netzer killed his brother. Ben Netzer, of course, is Zenobia's husband Odaenathus. It is unclear how this death led to the release of Zeir ben Hinana. Was this a first step in the decline of the Palmyrene kingdom? Or just a changing of the guard?

Both of these stories give voice to a general hostility to the Palmyran leadership, which seems to have been the dominant political sentiment in the Tiberias beit midrash, as we learn explicitly from Rabbi Yoḥanan:

> Rabbi Yoḥanan said: Fortunate is the one who witnesses the fall of Palmyra, for she was involved in the destruction of the First Temple and in the destruction of the Second Temple. In the destruction of the First Temple, she provided eighty thousand bowmen. And in the destruction of the Second Temple, she provided eight thousand bowmen. (Y. Taanit 4:5 [69b])

The Palmyrans are also implicated in the destruction of the Temple in another source that features Rabbi Yoḥanan. This source appears in the

4. Hyman, *Tanna'im and Amora'im*, 404. Also see the entry for "Zeira bar Ḥanina" in Margaliot, *Encyclopedia of the Sages*, 274. Margaliot notes that one of this sage's laws is quoted in the Jerusalem Talmud in Tractate Berakhot as one of the laws that it is permissible to study before praying.

context of a talmudic debate about whether Palmyrans may convert to Judaism. Both Rabbi Yoḥanan and an unnamed elder argue that such converts are not accepted, though they offer different reasons why this should be so:

> What is the reason that converts may not be accepted from Palmyra? This question was the subject of a dispute between Rabbi Yoḥanan and an elder: One said it is because of Solomon's slaves, and one said it is because of the daughters of Jerusalem…. According to the one who says it is because of the daughters of Jerusalem, what is the concern?… When the idolaters entered the sanctuary, everyone turned their attention to the silver and gold, whereas they turned their attention to the daughters of Jerusalem. As it is stated, "They ravaged women in Zion, maidens in the town of Judah" [Lam. 5:11]. (Yevamot 16b)

This source suggests that the Palmyrans will never be forgiven for their treatment of the daughters of Jerusalem at the time of the Temple's destruction. This source also indicates that the sages of the Tiberias beit midrash were not pleased when the Land of Israel fell into Palmyran hands. They had finally learned how to cope with Rome and play by its rules, particularly when it came to shouldering the difficult tax burden of the anarchic period. But the Palmyrans posed a new challenge. Their Syrian culture was entirely foreign, and the sages, it seems, did not have the energy to start all over with a new dominant power.

The following source, too, gives voice to the sages' fear of Palmyran rule:

> "Deliver me, I pray you, from the hand of my brother, from the hand of Esau" [Gen. 32:12]. From the hand of my brother who advances against me with the power of Esau. Thus it is written, "I considered the horns and behold, there came up among them another horn, a little one" [Dan. 7:8]. This alludes to Ben Netzer. "Before which three of the first horns were plucked up by the roots" [Dan. 7:8] – this refers to Macrinus, Carinus, and Kyriades.

> "And behold, in this horn were eyes like the eyes of a man, and a mouth speaking great things" [Dan. 7:8] – this alludes to the evil kingdom which imposes levies on all the nations of the world. (Genesis Rabba, *Vayishlaḥ* 76:6)

This is additional testament to the rabbinic hostility to the Palmyrans, who are referred to as an "evil kingdom" threatening the nations of the world.

*Chapter Twenty-Two*

# Rabbi Elazar ben Pedat

Rabbi Elazar ben Pedat is mentioned hundreds of times in the two Talmuds. He transmitted both the teachings of Rav and Shmuel from Babylonia and the teachings of Rabbi Yoḥanan from the Land of Israel. In the classic talmudic dichotomy between "Sinai" and the "uprooter of mountains" – a repository of knowledge versus a sharp analytic mind – he was the former. Though not known for his original insights, Rabbi Elazar was respected for his command of vast tracts of knowledge.

## RABBI ELAZAR: BETWEEN RAV AND SHMUEL

Rabbi Elazar's formative years were spent in Rav's beit midrash in Babylonia, as several talmudic sources attest. For instance, he figures in Tractate Ḥullin in the context of a debate between Rav and Shmuel about fish cooked in a meat pot:

> Fish that was placed into a hot plate. Rav said: It is forbidden to eat the fish with *kutaḥ* dip [which is dairy]. Shmuel says: It is permitted. (Ḥullin 111b)

The anonymous voice of the Talmud explains that Rav made his statement not as a blanket halakhic prohibition but in the context of a relevant, real-life situation. He was at his grandson's home where they prepared an herbal ointment for Rav's ailing eye, and then cooked food in the same dish. Rav was able to taste the residue of the ointment in the food, and he concluded that the taste lingers in a dish and is transferred to the next item cooked in it.

The Talmud then relates that Rabbi Elazar was once a guest in Shmuel's home, where he was served a dairy dish along with fish cooked in a meat pot. Rabbi Elazar declined his portion and Shmuel reprimanded him for doing so:

> Shmuel said to him: To your teacher Rav, I gave such a dish, and he ate it, and yet you do not eat!
>
> Rabbi Elazar came before Rav. He said to him: Did the master retract his teaching?
>
> Rav said to him: Far be it from the child of Abba bar Abba to serve me something which I hold to be forbidden. (Ḥullin 111b)

Rabbinic stories like this one, which are accounts of specific scenarios that gave rise to particular halakhic conversations, seem more historically plausible than self-contained literary tales.[1] According to this story, Rabbi Elazar was Rav's student, but he was hosted by Shmuel. His host questioned why he did not act in accordance with his teacher, who had accepted his host's practice while in his home. When Rav heard this story he denied it completely.

In another source in Tractate Ketubot we find Rabbi Elazar again standing before Shmuel:

> Rav said: One who says, "I will not feed my wife, and I will not provide for her" must divorce her and pay her *ketuba*. Rabbi Elazar went and stated this ruling before Shmuel. Shmuel responded:

1. On the relationship between "closed" self-contained stories and stories that appear as part of halakhic *sugyot*, see Y. Frankel, "The Halakhic and Aggadic Story" [Hebrew], *The Aggadic Story: Unity of Form and Content* (Tel Aviv: 2001), 220–236.

> Feed barley fodder to Elazar! Instead of forcing him to divorce her, they should force him to provide her with food.
>
> And Rav would answer: A person cannot live with a snake in the same basket.
>
> When Rabbi Zeira went up from Babylonia to the Land of Israel, he found Rabbi Binyamin bar Yefet who was sitting and saying Rav's ruling in the name of Rabbi Yoḥanan. Rabbi Zeira said to Rabbi Binyamin bar Yefet: On account of this ruling they fed Rabbi Elazar barley fodder in Babylonia. (Ketubot 77a)

Rav and Shmuel disagree about the appropriate way of dealing with an abusive husband who refuses to provide for his wife. Rav teaches that the husband should be forced to divorce his wife and pay her *ketuba*. When Rabbi Elazar quotes Rav's ruling to Shmuel, the latter responds harshly that anyone who teaches thus deserves to be fed animal fodder. Shmuel instead holds that the husband should be forced to feed and support his wife within the context of their marriage. The anonymous voice of the Talmud quotes Rav's position that a person cannot be forced to live with a snake. That is, even if the husband is forced to support his wife, she cannot be expected to abide his venom.[2] When Rabbi Zeira, who arrived in the Land of Israel from Babylonia, hears Rav's ruling quoted, he responds just as harshly as Shmuel.

From this sources we can infer that following Rav's death, Rabbi Elazar transferred to Shmuel's beit midrash, and then eventually made his way to the Land of Israel.

### RABBI ELAZAR'S ARRIVAL IN THE LAND OF ISRAEL

Rabbi Elazar left Babylonia following the deaths of Rav and Shmuel. He arrived in the Land of Israel in the midst of an economic crisis. He too was subject to penury:

> Rabbi Elazar ben Pedat was exceedingly poor. Once he had his blood let and had nothing to eat. He took a clove of garlic and

2. On the Talmud's use of this expression, see Y. Brandes, "In One Basket: On Autonomy and Cooperation in the Family Setting" [Hebrew], *Akdamut* 14 (5764).

> put it in his mouth. He grew faint and fell asleep. The rabbis went to inquire about him and they saw that he was crying and laughing in his sleep, and that a ray of light emanated from his forehead. When he awoke, they asked him: Why were you crying and laughing? He said to them: I had a dream in which the Holy One, Blessed Be He, was sitting with me, and I said to Him: How long will I continue to suffer in this world? And He said to me: Elazar, My son, would you like Me to turn the world back to the beginning and create it anew? Perhaps you would then be born at a time of abundant food. I said before Him: You would do all this and still only perhaps my situation would improve? I said to Him: Is what I have lived so far the greater part of my life, or what I am still destined to live? He said to me: What you have already lived is more. I said to Him: If so, I do not want You to turn the world back. He said to me: As a reward for your saying you do not desire that the world be turned back, I will give you thirteen rivers of balsam oil as clear as the Euphrates and the Tigris for you to enjoy in the World to Come. I said before Him: You will give me only this, and nothing more? He said to me: What then will I give your fellow? I said to Him: Do I need the portion of one who has none? He flicked me with His fingers on my forehead and He said to me: Elazar My son, it is My arrows that have struck you, My arrows. (Taanit 25a)

This conversation reflects the richness of Rabbi Elazar's spiritual life. Rabbi Elazar, in a state of wretched poverty, negotiates with the Holy One, Blessed Be He. He is not surprised to hear back from his heavenly interlocutor but merely smiles painfully in response. When he complains about how much he is suffering, God offers to turn the world back to the beginning and create it anew, such that Rabbi Elazar would be born under a new star.[3] But Rabbi Elazar understands that the pain of this

3. Although the sages ruled that the principles of astrology do not apply to Israel, there were those who held that "sons, life, and food are dependent on one's astrological sign" (Mo'ed Katan 28a). See Urbach, *The Sages: Their Beliefs and Opinions*, 246–253.

world is brief and transient, unlike the great reward promised to him in the World to Come. Once he ascertains that he has already lived out more than half his days, he chooses to continue suffering in expectation of the better days that await him.

Other sources suggest that in spite of his poverty, Rabbi Elazar was happy that he merited to study the Torah of the Land of Israel. He speaks of the transition he underwent when he moved from Babylonia:

> When Rabbi Elazar was going up to the Land of Israel, he said: I have been spared from one of the three curses. When they ordained him, he said: I have been spared from two. When he was given a seat on the council responsible for intercalating the year, he said: I have been spared from all three. As it is said: "And My hand will be against the prophets who see worthless visions and divine falsehoods. They will not be in the council of My people" [Ezek. 13:9] – this is the council responsible for intercalating the year. "And they will not be inscribed in the record of the house of Israel" – this refers to ordination. "And they will not enter the Land of Israel" – as it implies. (Ketubot 112a)

The Talmud describes three stages in Rabbi Elazar's rise to a position of leadership in the Land of Israel. His arrival in the land spared him from Ezekiel's first curse. Then, when he was ordained with the authority to rule in halakhic matters (an authority granted only to sages living in the Land of Israel) he was spared the second curse. Finally, when he was included among those responsible for intercalating the year, he was spared the third curse inflicted on Diaspora Jewry.

Rabbi Elazar went on to speak disparagingly of the Jews of Babylonia and their teachings. The greatest concentration of his views on this matter appears in a talmudic passage that focuses on praise for the Land of Israel and the ambivalent attitude of Babylonian Jewry to the Promised Land. Babylonian Jews respected the historical primacy of the Land of Israel but they saw themselves as the current center of Torah learning.

In the middle of this talmudic passage we find several of Rabbi Elazar's statements about Babylonia, his homeland:[4]

> Rabbi Elazar said: Those who die outside of the Land of Israel are not resurrected....
>
> Rabbi Elazar said: Anyone who lives in the Land of Israel lives without sin. (Yoma 9b)

There is no doubt that Rabbi Elazar wished to live in the Land of Israel in spite of the economic hardship involved. It took several years, but ultimately he was fully accepted and respected as a local rabbinic authority.

### INTEGRATION DIFFICULTIES: QUOTING SOMEONE BY NAME

Rabbi Elazar arrived at the beit midrash in Tiberias, but he had a difficult time adapting to its intellectual milieu. The Talmud documents Reish Lakish's anger upon hearing Rabbi Elazar quote a statement without proper attribution. The issue under discussion was the obligation to lean one's hands on the head of the sacrificial animal, which appears in the halakhic midrash:

> "And Aaron shall lean his two hands on the head of the goat" [Lev. 16:21]. This teaches that the leaning of the hands happens with both hands, which is a prototype for all acts of leaning of the hands, which must be performed with two hands. (Sifra, *Aḥarei Mot* 4:4)

Reish Lakish commented on this law:

> For the verse states, "And Aaron shall lean his two hands" [Lev. 16:21]. It is written "his hand" and it is written "two." This verse establishes a prototype: Wherever it is stated "his hand," the Torah implies two hands, unless the Torah specifies one for you. (Menaḥot 93b)

4. For a full analysis of the passage in Ketubot and the Babylonian Talmud's response to praise for the Land of Israel, see J. Rubenstein, "Dealing with Praise for the Land of Israel," in *Center and Diaspora*, ed. Y. Gafni, 159–188.

Reish Lakish offers an incisive teaching. He notes that although the word for "hands" is written in the Torah without the second letter *yud* which would render it plural, it nonetheless refers to the plural form because of the use of "two." Reish Lakish concludes that every time this word appears, it must be understood as a reference to two hands rather than just one. The Talmud relates:

> Rabbi Elazar went and stated his teaching in the beit midrash, but he did not say it in the name of Reish Lakish. Reish Lakish heard about the omission and grew angry. (Menaḥot 93b)

Reish Lakish wishes to teach the new arrival a lesson. He engages in a halakhic discussion about this exegesis:

> Reish Lakish said to Rabbi Elazar: If it enters your mind that wherever it is written "his hand," the implication is that there are really two hands, then why do I ever have to write "his hands" in the Torah? Reish Lakish challenged Rabbi Elazar with the twenty-four appearances of the plural "his hands" in the Bible, including: "With his own hands shall he bring the fire offerings" [Lev. 7:30], "May his hands fight his battle" [Deut. 33:7], [and] "He moved his hands with intelligence" [Gen. 48:14]. Rabbi Elazar was silent. After Reish Lakish calmed down, he said to Rabbi Elazar: What is the reason you did not tell me in reply: I was saying that the prototype of "his hands" applies only to a case of leaning? Rabbi Elazar said: Regarding leaning it is also written, "He leaned his hands on him and commanded him" [Num. 27:23]. Reish Lakish responded: I was saying that the prototype teaching applies only to the leaning of an animal. (Menaḥot 93b)

Reish Lakish's style of learning is aggressive and confrontational, and Rabbi Elazar is not accustomed to being attacked in this manner. He comes from Rav's beit midrash, in which Torah was passed from teacher to student without argument and competition. This way of learning is utterly foreign to him.

**Rabbi Yaakov bar Idi Appeases Rabbi Yoḥanan: The Version of the Land of Israel**

It is still not clear why Rabbi Elazar did not quote Reish Lakish's teaching in his name. The following story, which describes a similar incident involving Rabbi Yoḥanan, will prove instructive:

> Rabbi Yoḥanan was leaning on Rabbi Yaakov bar Idi as they were walking. Rabbi Elazar saw them and hid from them. Rabbi Yoḥanan said: This Babylonian did two things to me. First he did not greet me. Second, he did not attribute a teaching to me. Rabbi Yaakov bar Idi said to him: That is the way they act toward each other in Babylonia. The younger among them do not greet the elders so as not to trouble them to respond. For they hold by the verse, "The young saw me and withdrew" [Job 29:8]. While they were walking, they passed a certain beit midrash. Rabbi Yoḥanan said to him: That is where Rabbi Meir used to sit and expound. Rabbi Meir recited teachings in the name of Rabbi Yishmael. He said to him: But did he not recite teachings in the name of Rabbi Akiva?[5] Rabbi Yoḥanan said to him: Everyone knows that Rabbi Meir was a student of Rabbi Akiva. Rabbi Yaakov said to him: Likewise, everyone knows that Rabbi Elazar is a student of Rabbi Yoḥanan. They came before an imperial statue.[6] He said to him: Should I go around it? Rather I will pass before it and cover my eyes. Rabbi Yaakov bar Idi said to him: Rabbi Elazar acted well. By not passing before you, he treated you with reverence. Rabbi Yoḥanan said to him: Rabbi Yaakov bar Idi, you certainly know how to appease. (Y. Berakhot 2:1 [4b])

Rabbi Yoḥanan leans on his student Rabbi Yaakov bar Idi, the son of the aforementioned Rav Idi who would come to Rabbi Yoḥanan's beit

5. I explained this story according to Louis Ginzberg, *Interpretations and Insights in the Jerusalem Talmud,* 1, 244. It was necessary to add the words "he said to him" after "Rabbi Yishmael." Rabbi Yoḥanan grew up in Tiberias, and it makes no sense that his student would inform him about local history.
6. This was an idolatrous statue, though scholars disagree about what to make of this phrase. See ibid. 244.

midrash as the "one-day student." This story thus takes place during Rabbi Yoḥanan's final years, prior to his death in 279. While the two sages are walking, they catch sight of Rabbi Elazar, who is trying to avoid Rabbi Yoḥanan. But Rabbi Yoḥanan notices what is going on and responds by criticizing Rabbi Elazar ("this Babylonian") for wronging him in two ways: by failing to greet him, and by failing to quote him by name. Rabbi Yaakov bar Idi assuages his teacher's anger by telling him that this behavior is typical of the Babylonians: The younger scholars never greet their esteemed elders. This difference between the Land of Israel and Babylonia is documented both in the Talmud and in the geonic literature that follows it.[7] As Rabbi Yaakov bar Idi assures Rabbi Yoḥanan, the student is not being rude; he is just following his local custom.

They continue walking and pass by a beit midrash, which Rabbi Yoḥanan identifies as the place where Rabbi Meir would teach his students the Torah of Rabbi Yishmael. Since it was widely known that Rabbi Meir was primarily the student of Rabbi Akiva rather than Rabbi Yishmael, Rabbi Yaakov bar Idi asks Rabbi Yoḥanan why Rabbi Meir did not teach the Torah of Rabbi Akiva as well. Rabbi Yoḥanan offers a simple response: All of Rabbi Meir's Torah comes from Rabbi Akiva, and so only when he quotes Rabbi Yishmael does he need to specify that he is doing so. This is just what Rabbi Yaakov was waiting for, and he responds in kind: Everyone knows that Rabbi Elazar is Rabbi Yoḥanan's student; he does not need to quote Rabbi Yoḥanan by name, because everything he says comes from Rabbi Yoḥanan!

Next they pass an imperial statue. Rabbi Yoḥanan teaches Rabbi Idi that he does not need to go out of his way to avoid the statue but can simply close his eyes and ignore it. Here, too, Rabbi Yaakov responds in kind, comparing this behavior to Rabbi Elazar's avoidance of Rabbi Yoḥanan. He tells Rabbi Yoḥanan that in the eyes of Rabbi Elazar, he is like a king. Just like a subject is embarrassed to show his face to the king,

7. As Rabbi Yehoshua ben Levi asks in Shabbat 89a, "Does a servant greet his master?" In his study of the differences in local custom between the Land of Israel and Babylonia, M. Margaliot writes, "Among the people of the East, a student would not greet his master; but in the Land of Israel, a student would say, 'Peace be unto you, Rabbi.'" See Margaliot, *Differences in Custom Between Babylonia and the Land of Israel* [Hebrew] (Jerusalem: 5698), section 33, 151.

Rabbi Elazar cannot bear to greet Rabbi Yoḥanan. It was out of respect for Rabbi Yoḥanan's honor that Rabbi Elazar hid his face. Rabbi Yaakov thus teaches Rabbi Yoḥanan that not every instance of evasion is meant as an insult. Rabbi Yoḥanan accepts Rabbi Yaakov's understanding of the situation and praises him for knowing how to appease another person.

### Rabbi Yaakov bar Idi Appeases Rabbi Yoḥanan: The Babylonian Version

The talmudic account of Rabbi Yaakov bar Idi's appeasement of Rabbi Yoḥanan appears in the Babylonian Talmud with significant variation. The story is preceded by the following halakhic discussion:

> Rav said: They did not treat a nine-year-old's cohabitation like the betrothal of an adult [with regard to prohibiting the co-wife in levirate marriage]. But Shmuel said: Even with regard to prohibiting the co-wife in levirate marriage, they did indeed treat the minor's cohabitation as the betrothal of an adult. And so too did Rabbi Yoḥanan say: They did, they did, and let them do so! (Yevamot 96b)

The debate between Rav and Shmuel deals with a halakhic question relating to levirate marriage, but the dynamics are more relevant than the details. Rabbi Yoḥanan aligns with Shmuel, asserting emphatically that the minor's cohabitation was treated like the betrothal of an adult. It is against this backdrop that the Talmud relates the following tale:

> Rabbi Elazar went and stated this teaching of Rabbi Yoḥanan in the beit midrash, but he did not say it in the name of Rabbi Yoḥanan. Rabbi Yoḥanan heard about this, and he became angry.
>
> Rabbi Ami and Rabbi Assi went up to him. They said to him: Did not the following incident take place in the synagogue in Tiberias, in a discussion concerning the law of a bolt with a knob on its end, regarding which Rabbi Elazar and Rabbi Yose disagreed, until they tore a Torah scroll in their anger? Can it be that they tore a Torah scroll in their anger? Rather, say until a Torah scroll was torn on account of their anger. Rabbi Yose

> ben Kisma was present when the Torah scroll was torn. He said: I will be amazed if this synagogue does not someday become a house of idolatry. And so it was. Rabbi Yoḥanan grew even angrier. He said to them: Do you elevate a disciple to the status of colleague as well?
>
> Rabbi Yaakov bar Idi went up to Rabbi Yoḥanan. He said to him: The Bible states, "As God commanded Moses His servant, so did Moses command Joshua, and so Joshua did; he did not omit a thing of all that God commanded Moses" [Josh. 11:15]. Now, do you imagine that with each teaching that Joshua stated, he would say to them, "So did Moses say to me"? Of course not! Rather, Joshua would sit and expound the law without identifying its source, and all his listeners understood that it was the teaching of Moses. So too here, your disciple Rabbi Elazar sits and expounds the law without identifying its source, but everyone understands that the teachings are yours. Rabbi Yoḥanan said to Rabbi Ami and Rabbi Assi: Why don't you know how to placate me like our colleague, the son of Idi? (Yevamot 96)

Unlike the version of the story in the Jerusalem Talmud, this version features not just Rabbi Yoḥanan and Rabbi Yaakov, but also Rabbi Ami and Rabbi Assi, two of the leading students of the Tiberias beit midrash. They make their own attempt to appease Rabbi Yoḥanan, but instead they only fan the flames of his fury. They relate the story of a Torah scroll that was torn because of a halakhic dispute between Rabbi Elazar and Rabbi Yose, two sages of the Usha generation. According to their account, Rabbi Yose ben Kisma was an eyewitness and prophesied that the synagogue in which the Torah scroll was torn would become an idolatrous temple. And so it came to pass.

It seems that Rabbi Ami and Rabbi Assi are trying to suggest to Rabbi Yoḥanan that his anger at Rabbi Elazar endangers the Tiberias beit midrash, and he should therefore forgive him. But Rabbi Yoḥanan is not appeased. He remains furious at Rabbi Elazar for not quoting his teaching in his name, and he is only further insulted when Rabbi Ami and Rabbi Assi insinuate that Rabbi Elazar is his colleague rather than his disciple.

Rabbi Yaakov bar Idi then offers his own attempt at mollifying Rabbi Yoḥanan. He suggests that everyone knows that Joshua is Moses' student and that everything he says comes from Moses. So too does everyone know that Rabbi Elazar is Rabbi Yoḥanan's student, and all his teachings come from Rabbi Yoḥanan.

Rabbi Yaakov thus appeases Rabbi Yoḥanan and extinguishes his fiery fury, which threatened to consume the Tiberias beit midrash once again.[8]

8. For an analysis of this story, see O. Meir, "I Trust That He Will Go On to Teach Halakha in Israel: The Figure of Rabbi Yoḥanan and His Relationship with His Students" [Hebrew], *Alei Siaḥ* 15-16 (5742), 224–236.

*Chapter Twenty-Three*

# The Death of Rabbi Yoḥanan

At this point we have fully entered into Rabbi Yoḥanan's world. We have familiarized ourselves with the center of Torah learning he founded and led in Tiberias. We have also discussed the two pillars of support who were always at his side, Rabbi Shimon ben Lakish and Rabbi Elazar ben Pedat. Rabbi Shimon ben Lakish competed with his teacher on the battlefield of Torah, while Rabbi Elazar absorbed his teacher's Torah like a sponge and passed it to the next generation of students without challenge or question.

During Rabbi Yoḥanan's lifetime, the city of Tiberias became a center for Torah learning and the Mishna became the halakhic book of the Jewish people. When he died, his disciples would continue to labor over the creation of the Jerusalem Talmud for two generations.

### DATING THE DEATH OF RABBI YOḤANAN: THE EPISTLE OF RAV SHERIRA GAON

> Rabbi Yoḥanan died in the Land of Israel during the lifetime of Rav Huna, and we have said that he reigned in the Land of Israel

> for eighty years after Rabbi Ḥanina, who followed Rabbi Efes, who followed our holy rabbi, as explained in Ketubot 103b. And in the year 590 (279 CE) Rabbi Yoḥanan and Rabbi Elazar both died, and Rabbi Ami took over. (Epistle of Rav Sherira Gaon, Lewin edition, 84)

Scholars have noted that the date given by Rav Sherira Gaon for Rabbi Yoḥanan's death, 590, is the only date in the entire epistle that follows the chronological reckoning used in the Land of Israel. Moreover, he uses an unusual term for "died"; elsewhere in the epistle he generally uses variants on the root *shaḥav* rather than *patar*. This linguistic evidence suggests that Rav Sherira Gaon may have received this information from other sources.[1]

The epistle informs us of the genealogy of rabbinic leadership in the Land of Israel: Rabbi Yehuda HaNasi ("our holy rabbi"), then Rabbi Efes, then Rabbi Ḥanina, and then Rabbi Yoḥanan. But this chronology does not accord with Rav Sherira Gaon's assertion that Rabbi Yoḥanan "reigned" for eighty years and died in 590. Presumably these eighty years refer not to his tenure, but to his lifespan. If so, then we can understand how, as we saw earlier, Rabbi Yoḥanan was a young man when Rebbi died.[2]

## THE DEATH OF RABBI YOḤANAN AS A TURNING POINT IN IMPERIAL HISTORY

The death of Rabbi Yoḥanan coincided with the end of the anarchic period of the Roman Empire. In 284 Diocletian came to power. He reformed the central imperial leadership and fundamentally revolutionized the structure of the Roman imperial government, subordinating the provinces to imperial rule. Diocletian's revolution marked the start of a period of several hundred years in which the Land of Israel would

1. Gafni, *The Jews of Babylonia*, 246 (appendix A).
2. Z. Frankel suggested this solution in his *Introduction to the Jerusalem Talmud*, 97. Also see Kimelman, 5. For other solutions to this chronological quandary, see Gafni, *The Jews of Babylonia*, 257.

transition to Christian leadership.[3] The post-anarchic period in which Jews had to confront Christian leadership will serve as the backdrop to the next volume in this series.

### A CONCLUDING STORY: THE DEATH OF RABBI YOḤANAN ACCORDING TO BABYLONIAN TRADITION[4]

The story of Rabbi Yoḥanan's death became a classic tale taught in every Jewish school and beit midrash for generations. This story is richly embellished in the trappings of *Aggada,* with only a tenuous grounding in social and historical reality. Even so, it is a foundational tale that shaped the image of Rabbi Yoḥanan and Reish Lakish for hundreds of years to follow.[5]

This story involves a dispute between Reish Lakish and Rabbi Yoḥanan which ultimately led to the collapse of the beit midrash and the death of both sages. We considered the first half of this tale in the chapter on Reish Lakish's entry into the world of Torah learning, as depicted in the Babylonian sources. When Reish Lakish jumped into the Jordan, Rabbi Yoḥanan revealed his own strengths, promising to wed Reish Lakish to his sister if only he would dedicate his life to Torah study. Reish Lakish accepted the yoke of Torah and immediately lost his strength. At the point when our story resumes, the weakened hero has fallen into the hands of Rabbi Yoḥanan, who trains him as a Torah scholar in his beit midrash:

> Rabbi Yoḥanan taught him Torah and Mishna and made him into a great man. (Bava Metzia 84a)

The single line encompasses many years in the lives of the two heroes. Rabbi Yoḥanan brings Reish Lakish to his beit midrash and teaches him

3. Alon, *The History of the Jews in the Land of Israel,* 2, 88–91; Y. Tzafrir, "Provincialism in the Land of Israel," *The Land of Israel from the Destruction of the Second Temple Until the Muslim Conquest* [Hebrew], 360–363.
4. For the beginning of this story and for a list of bibliographic references, see my chapter on the Babylonian depiction of Reish Lakish.
5. Ben Shalom, "And I Took Two Staffs," 248–249.

Torah and Mishna. Reish Lakish is receptive to this material, which he absorbs through years of repetition and review.[6] The study of these sources turns Reish Lakish into a "great man," that is, a student who can hold his own in the beit midrash, equipped with the "weapons" required for the high-level halakhic creativity that constitutes talmudic learning.

This is all background for the continuation of the story, which takes place one day in Rabbi Yoḥanan's beit midrash:

> One day they were disputing the following point in the beit midrash. The Mishna states: The sword and the knife and the hunting spear and the military spear and the hand sickle and the harvesting sickle: From what point are they capable of contracting impurity? It is from the time of the completion of their production. And when is the completion of their production? Rabbi Yoḥanan says: From when the metal utensils are tempered in a furnace. Reish Lakish says: From when they are polished with water. Rabbi Yoḥanan said to Reish Lakish: A thief knows the tools of his thievery. Reish Lakish said to him: And how have you benefited me? There they called me rabbi, and here they call me rabbi. Rabbi Yoḥanan said to him: I benefited you in that I brought you under the wings of the Divine Presence. Rabbi Yoḥanan became disheartened because of Reish Lakish's response. Reish Lakish became seriously ill. Rabbi Yoḥanan's sister, who was Reish Lakish's wife, came before Rabbi Yoḥanan. She cried and pleaded with him to pray for Reish Lakish's recovery. She said to him: Act for the sake of my children. He replied to her:

6. In the literature of Jewish philosophy and Hasidut, the study of Torah and Mishna were correlated with wisdom and knowledge, whereas Talmud was associated with understanding, since it involves independent creative thought. A student absorbs verses and laws which he then employs in more advanced study. Along similar lines, the Maharal of Prague (Rabbi Judah Loew ben Betzalel, 1520–1609) wrote, "These are three levels of understanding. Torah involves wisdom without full detailed knowledge, but Mishna is knowledge in all its detail. And Talmud involves understanding on a deeper level than the Mishna. And as we have said, Torah, Mishna, and Talmud correspond to wisdom, knowledge, and understanding" (*Derekh HaḤayim*, chapter 5, 272).

> "Leave your orphans; I will sustain them" [Jer. 49:11]. She said: Act for the sake of my widowhood! He said to her: "And let your widows trust in me" [Jer. 49:11]. (Bava Metzia 84a)

This story begins with the study of the laws of impure metal vessels in the beit midrash. We will try to understand what the talmudic story is hinting at in this halakhic conversation, but first it is important to take note of the human dynamics. Reish Lakish does not merely ask questions about his teacher's position; he also offers his own opinion, which contradicts that of his teacher. Confronted by his student's challenge, Rabbi Yoḥanan responds by attacking his Achilles' heel – his checkered past: "A thief knows the tools of his thievery," he sneers. Rabbi Yoḥanan was known for his scathing criticism, but such a direct, personal attack was unusual even for him.[7]

Reish Lakish responds provocatively: "And how have you benefited me? There they called me rabbi, and here they call me rabbi." He asks what good Rabbi Yoḥanan has done for him. After all, he was already a "great man" when he was the leader of the robbers. If Torah learning does not impact one's relationships with other people, then what is the point? It is an elixir of death rather than of life. Rabbi Yoḥanan offers a surprising response: "I benefited you in that I brought you under the wings of the Divine Presence."

Their exchange unfolds according to the same template we saw earlier during their conversation in the Jordan. Here too, Rabbi Yoḥanan initiates ("A thief knows the tools of his thievery"), Reish Lakish responds with an attack ("How have you benefited me?"), and Rabbi Yoḥanan has the last word ("I benefited you"). This is in fact how every dialogue seems to unfold in Rabbi Yoḥanan's beit midrash.[8] He makes the rules and decides what they will learn, and the role of the students is to master his teachings.

7. Ben Shalom claims that the nature of the Babylonian beit midrash influenced the shaping of stories and dialogues between the sages of the Land of Israel as well. On Rabbi Yoḥanan's relationship with his students, see Meir, "I Trust That He Will Go On to Teach Halakha in Israel," 394, note 419.
8. On the structure of these dialogues, see Y. Frankel, *The Aggadic Story*, 74.

It is worth paying attention to the details of the argument that incited Rabbi Yoḥanan. The topic under discussion is the preparation of a metal utensil for use. A utensil is regarded as complete and therefore susceptible to impurity the moment it becomes a receptacle. But knives, which do not have any sort of receptacle, require another measure to determine when they are regarded as finished products. Rabbi Yoḥanan rules that they are completed when the metal is tempered in the furnace. At this point the metal becomes malleable and can be bent into the desired shape. Reish Lakish disagrees, arguing that they are completed once the metal is polished in water, when it is hardened into its final shape. Rabbi Yoḥanan responds harshly, "A thief knows the tools of his thievery."

When Reish Lakish questions what good Rabbi Yoḥanan did for him and Rabbi Yoḥanan responds that he brought him under the wings of the Divine Presence, he may in fact be referring to his own protective presence. In Rabbi Yoḥanan's words to his sister, too, he takes on the role of God by quoting the prophet: "Leave your orphans; I will sustain them. And let your widows trust in me" (Jer. 49:11). Rabbi Yoḥanan is transparent about the position he assumes for himself in the family hierarchy and in the hierarchy of the beit midrash. This interpretation is supported by a tannaitic midrash:

> "And cleave unto Him" [Deut. 11:22]. Is it possible for man to ascend to fiery heaven and cleave to fire, seeing that the Bible has said, "For the Lord thy God is a devouring fire" [4:24] and "His throne was fiery flames" [7:9]? Rather, the meaning is: Cling to the sages and to their disciples, and I will account it to you as if you had ascended to heaven and had received the Torah there. (Sifrei, Deuteronomy 49)

This midrash suggests that the only way to cleave to Torah is by cleaving to the sages. With this notion in mind, we can better understand the halakhic debate between Rabbi Yoḥanan and Reish Lakish about the final stage of a vessel's production. According to Rabbi Yoḥanan the final stage involves fire; according to Reish Lakish, it involves water. Rabbi Yoḥanan, as a leader among the sages, is like the "devouring fire" in the beit midrash. He seeks to keep Reish Lakish under his wing. The student is encouraged to ask questions which will cause the fire to spread further. But there is no reason for the student ever to leave the fire, that is, to distance himself from the Divine Presence.

Reish Lakish disagrees with his teacher. He posits that the vessel is regarded as fully formed after it is removed from the fire and annealed in water. Their argument about the vessel is a metaphor for the stages of Reish Lakish's spiritual training. Reish Lakish seeks to legitimize the stage at which the student is removed from the devouring fire of his great teacher's all-consuming presence, but Rabbi Yoḥanan refuses to countenance his student's independence.

As the rest of the story shows, Rabbi Yoḥanan cannot accept that confrontation may end in compromise, because every fight is a fight to the death.[9]

> Rabbi Shimon ben Lakish passed away. Rabbi Yoḥanan grieved for him considerably. The rabbis said: Who shall go to bring him comfort? Rabbi Elazar ben Pedat should go, for his learning is sharp. Rabbi Elazar ben Pedat went and sat before him. In response to everything Rabbi Yoḥanan would say, Rabbi Elazar ben Pedat told him: We learned a *baraita* that supports you. Rabbi Yoḥanan said to him: You are supposed to be like Bar Lakisha? With Bar Lakisha, whenever I would say something, he would pose twenty-four difficulties to me, and I would give him twenty-four solutions, and as a result of the give-and-take the subject became clear. However, you say: We learned a *baraita* that supports you. Do I not already know that I have spoken well? Rabbi Yoḥanan would go out and tear his clothes and cry and say: Where are you, Bar Lakisha, where are you, Bar Lakisha? And he would scream until he lost his mind. The rabbis prayed for mercy on him and he passed away. (Bava Metzia 84a)

9. Ari Alon offers a vivid and painful description of rabbinic confrontations in the Babylonian beit midrash, based on this story. See A. Alon, "*Alma Di*" [Hebrew], *Shdemot* 114 (5750): 111–122.

Rabbi Elazar ben Pedat attempts to fill the void left by Reish Lakish's death and alleviate Rabbi Yoḥanan's suffering. His arrival at the beit midrash in Tiberias is mentioned in another source, which is unrelated to our story:

> Rabbi Yoḥanan spent three and a half years without going to the meetinghouse of the sages because of his anguish. Finally Rabbi Elazar saw in his dream: Tomorrow Sinai will come down and teach you something new. He came. (Y. Megilla 1:11 [72b])

According to this source, Rabbi Yoḥanan kept his distance from the beit midrash on account of his anguish. We have no way of knowing if this anguish refers to his broken heart after Reish Lakish's death, or to his lifelong physical afflictions.[10] In any case, the Talmud relates that Rabbi Elazar dreamed about Rabbi Yoḥanan's return to the beit midrash, and that dream came true.

This is how the traditional commentators have understood this source, but there is another possible reading. The line that reads, "Rabbi Elazar saw in his dream" can also be read as "He saw Rabbi Elazar in his dream." And so perhaps it was Rabbi Yoḥanan who saw Rabbi Elazar entering his beit midrash in his absence. According to this reading, Rabbi Elazar is the "Sinai," and his scholarly reputation attracts Rabbi Yoḥanan's attention. Upon hearing that Rabbi Elazar is transforming his own beit midrash, Rabbi Yoḥanan returns immediately.

As a "Sinai," Rabbi Elazar is known for his mastery of vast knowledge, not for his sharp dialectical skills. But Reish Lakish, whom he was supposed to replace, was a master of dialectic. These are not shoes that Rabbi Elazar can fill. He does not challenge his teacher or further develop his teachings. Rabbi Elazar ben Pedat is content merely to echo his master and substantiate his truths. Anytime he is quoted in the Talmud, we know that Rabbi Yoḥanan is the original source for his statement. After all, this was how Rabbi Yaakov bar Idi appeased Rabbi Yoḥanan with regard to Rabbi Elazar, as we saw. A student like Rabbi Elazar can repeat and disseminate Rabbi Yoḥanan's teachings, but he

10. Ben Shalom, "And I Took Two Staffs," 248–249.

cannot expand upon them. The encounter with Rabbi Elazar, who is a far cry from Reish Lakish, only deepens Rabbi Yoḥanan's yearning for his former student.

According to talmudic tradition, Reish Lakish and Rabbi Yoḥanan died in rapid succession. Rav Sherira Gaon adds that Rabbi Elazar ben Pedat died during this period as well, marking the end of an era in the Tiberias beit midrash.

# *About the Author*

Rabbi Dr. Binyamin Lau is an Israeli community leader, educator, and rabbi. He is the rabbi of the Ramban Synagogue in Jerusalem and head of the 929 Bible project. Rabbi Lau also serves as a consultant for a number of leading organizations, is widely published, and is frequently cited in the media. He studied at Yeshivat Har Etzion and Yeshivat HaKibbutz HaDati, and received a PhD in Talmud from Bar-Ilan University.

*The fonts used in this book are from the Arno family*

Other books in *The Sages* series by
Rabbi Dr. Binyamin Lau

*Volume I: The Second Temple Period*

*Volume II: From Yavneh to the Bar Kokhba Revolt*

*Volume III: The Galilean Period*

Other works from Maggid Books by
Rabbi Dr. Binyamin Lau

*Jeremiah: The Fate of a Prophet*

*Isaiah: As Hovering Birds* (forthcoming)

*Maggid Books*
*The best of contemporary Jewish thought from*
*Koren Publishers Jerusalem Ltd.*